PERFECT
HUSBAND

Books by Gary Provost

Across the Border
Finder (with Marilyn Greene)
Perfect Husband
Without Mercy

Published by POCKET BOOKS

PERFECT HUSBAND

The True Story of the Trusting Bride Who Discovered Her Husband Was a Coldblooded Killer

Gary Provost

POCKET BOOKS

New York   London   Toronto   Sydney   Tokyo   Singapore

For making me laugh every day,
For selling me a Mercedes real cheap,
For serving me dinner at Randy's Harbor House,
For quality work at low prices at T-Shirt Heaven,
For picking pretty good horses to show at Rockingham,
For saying "Gail," and for knowing who the real boze is,
And most of all, for being everything that I could have wanted
in a stepson or a son,
This book is dedicated with love and pride,

To Randy Freidus

POCKET BOOKS, a division of Simon & Schuster Inc.
1230 Avenue of the Americas, New York, NY 10020

Provost, Gary, 1944–
    Perfect husband : the true story of the trusting bride who discovered
her husband was a coldblooded killer / Gary Provost.
    p.   cm.
    ISBN: 0-671-72493-2 : $20.00
    1. Murder—Florida—Case studies   2. Fotopoulos, Konstantin.
3. Fotopoulos, Lisa.   4. Hunt, Deidre Michelle, 1969–
I. Title.
HV6533.F6P76   1991
364.1C523C0975921—dc20   91-25331
                                                             CIP

First Pocket Books hardcover printing December 1991

10 9 8 7 6 5 4 3 2 1

Acknowledgments

Thanks go to Cindy Dadonna, David Damore, Frank Goan, Carol Hunt, Deidre Hunt, Kosta Fotopoulos, Kathy Kelly, Bob Knowland, Tim Kostidakis, Jack Levin, Father Nicholas Manousakis, Leon Mindlin, Thelma Mindlin, David Mindlin, Mary Paspalakis, Newman Taylor, Jr., Terry Ramsey, Allison (Ebel) Sylvester, Vinnie Tavernese, John Widdison, Dr. Keith Wilson, the staff of the Daytona Beach Public Library, the staff of the Volusia County Court Clerk's office in Daytona Beach, the staff of the Volusia County Branch Jail, and the staff of the Florida State Prison, and the Daytona Beach Police Department.

Thanks also to those many people who spoke to me but asked that they not be mentioned in the book.

Thanks to Russ Galen of the Scott Meredith literary agency.

Thanks, for the third time, to Claire Zion, my editor at Pocket Books.

And thanks, as usual, to my darling Gail, my editor-in-residence, who reads pages as they are written and catches my mistakes along the way.

And, most of all, thanks to Lisa and Dino Paspalakis, for sharing their lives, their memories, and their pizza with me. This is their story more than it is mine. I only wrote it; they lived it.

Author's Note

This is a true story. The dates, places, and events are all real. The names are real, except when people asked not to be identified. The eight pseudonyms appearing in this book are: Vinnie Speziale, Elena Speziale, Diane Nelson, Mary Mullaley, Thomas Hall, Larry Tarle, Alfred Fuller, and George McGee.

1

A Nice Greek Boy

Lisa first became aware of Konstantin Fotopoulos when one of her aunts slyly informed her one day in May of 1985 that there was a handsome young man available and she wanted Lisa to meet him. Lisa Paspalakis was twenty-five and she had become quite an attractive young woman, a lithe, brown-eyed, brown-haired American with a Greek heritage that leaned into her life from every direction.

"You'll like him," Aunt Poupa said. "His name is Kosta. He's a nice Greek boy."

"Yeah, yeah, we'll see," Lisa said. She had heard this before. "Everybody with pants on looks like a nice Greek boy to you."

This was followed by a series of phone calls from Poupa. "So? When do you want to meet this boy?"

By this time Lisa had met too many nice Greek boys. She was tired. After graduating cum laude from the University of South Florida in Tampa in 1982, she had worked for a year in Tampa at one of the big eight accounting firms, and now, at her father's request, she was living in Daytona Beach, helping to run the family business, Joyland Amusement Center, while her brother, Dino, was at college. Lisa wasn't looking for a man. All she really needed to relax after a long day at Joyland was a pack of cigarettes and a good novel. And on weekends she just wanted to hang out with her friends, most of whom lived in Tampa, on Florida's west coast. Tampa, a three-hour drive across the state, was Lisa's sanctuary. There she had privacy. Her Tampa friends were not plugged into that network of Greek relatives who seemed to know every time she coughed or went to the bathroom.

On one of her Saturdays in Tampa, Lisa's father, Steno, called.

"Lisa, come home now," he said. He sounded excited.

Something must be wrong, Lisa thought. "Dad, what is it?"

"That boy. Kosta. He's going to be at your Aunt Poupa's today."

"So?"

"So, he's a nice Greek boy. Come home now, so you can meet him."

"Dad, I'm not coming home from Tampa just so I can meet some guy."

"But he's Greek," her father said. "He goes to Embry-Riddle. The aeronautical school. Why waste time? Let's get started."

"Started?"

"Well you know what I mean, Lisa. Poupa says he's a—"

"I know. A nice Greek boy. Okay, I'll meet him. But not now. Reschedule it. He's not going anywhere."

Steno, worried that this nice Greek boy might get away before Lisa could snare him, reluctantly agreed.

On the following Monday night Lisa and her father went to Lenny's Barbecue Pit on Atlantic Avenue in Daytona Beach, where Kosta worked as a waiter to help with school expenses. Kosta greeted them at their table, shaking Lisa's hand somewhat shyly. He's as embarrassed by all of this as I am, Lisa thought. Kosta was six foot two, with the straight-backed posture of an army cadet. Dark-haired

2

and handsome, he had a sweet face, with innocent Bambi eyes, and lush lashes that blinked often. When he shrugged his shoulders he looked like a teenager. He would probably have looked even younger, except for his trim dark mustache, which seemed to hide his feelings. He waited on Lisa and Steno graciously, made smiling eyes at Lisa, and was altogether as charming as a televised game show host. At one point he leaned over and, in his thick Greek accent, whispered in Lisa's ear, "I'm the nice Greek boy. Are you the nice Greek girl I've heard so much about?" He made her laugh.

Lisa, who once had vowed never to marry a man from Greece, had to admit that this man from Greece was good looking, as advertised, that he was smart and funny, and that she liked him, even if he was picked out by Aunt Poupa, who knew nothing of Lisa's taste in men. His English was decent, and when he made a mistake in pronunciation, it was adorable.

The morning after the meeting at Lenny's, Poupa called Lisa at the office. "What did you think of Kosta?" she asked.

"He was fine," Lisa said. "What do you think he thought of me?"

"Wait a minute," Poupa said. "I'll ask him."

"You'll ask him?"

"He's right here," Poupa said.

"Oh, for goodness' sake, Poupa. Then you might as well put him on the phone. We don't need an interpreter."

Kosta came to the phone, and the two young people made a date to meet for dinner. Alone.

They ate dinner later that week at Bennigan's, a funky chain establishment, which gave the date the informality that Lisa wanted. Kosta, well mannered as a prince, held Lisa's chair for her and ordered for her. He listened patiently while Lisa talked about her family, the arcade business, her college years in Tampa, and her brother, Dino. Dino, four years younger, was the light of Lisa's life, and she was inclined to go on at length about what a great kid he was.

Then Kosta told her about himself. He was twenty-five years old. He had grown up in Pefki, a suburb of Athens, he said. His grandparents, in the Greek town of Tripoli, raised potatoes. But his father had gotten away from potatoes and now worked for Olympic Airways. In fact, Kosta's family, while not rich like Lisa's, was well off, and they lived in a fine house. Kosta had gone to private school in Greece, but after his junior year had made up his mind to finish high school in the United States.

"I've got four uncles in Chicago," he explained, and he rattled off the names of the uncles and their wives and their children, not that Lisa could keep them straight. They were all named Poulos, a shortened form of Fotopoulos. The uncles, he said, had gone to Australia first, where they had all made money. Then they had all come to the United States and settled in Aurora, outside of Chicago.

"They all own restaurants," Kosta said. He smiled. "Every Greek in Chicago owns a restaurant."

"I know," Lisa said. "Every Greek in Daytona owns a gift shop."

So, just before his senior year, Kosta had come to Chicago and moved in with his uncle Harry. While he went to Aurora high school and then to Lewis University, Kosta worked at his uncle's pancake house. There he washed dishes, cooked, waited on tables. "I did everything," he said proudly.

Though his accent was thick and he sometimes stumbled on the odd English word, or filled in with Greek, Kosta was articulate, and he had a convincing way of telling even the most mundane story. His hands made shapes in the air as he described his hectic schedule for Lisa. He made it sound to her as if he had been getting up at four every morning, working long hours at the pancake house, then going to school, then returning to work until he closed up the pancake house for the night. Kosta certainly seemed like one industrious young man. Lisa was impressed. Steno, her father, had been a hard-working immigrant who had come to America with nothing and forged his own American dream. It was nice to see that a young Greek immigrant of her own generation could have ambition and the same reverence for hard work.

Kosta's real love, he told Lisa, was flying. His shy brown eyes sparkled as he described his lifelong love of airplanes. Flying fascinated him, so he had come to Daytona Beach to enroll at Embry-Riddle Aeronautical School, where he hoped to acquire a master's degree in aeronautical science.

"Of course school and work take up most of my time, so I'm not looking for any serious relationship with a woman," Kosta said.

Lisa squirmed in her chair. She hadn't asked him if he was looking for a serious relationship with a woman.

"The truth is," Kosta said, "I've just broken a girlfriend."

"Broken?" Lisa said, not understanding his strange turn of phrase.

He explained in Greek.

"Oh." Lisa laughed. "You mean broken up. You've broken up with her."

"Yes. Donna," he explained. He told her that Donna and a few other people lived in an old house where he rented a room over by Ridgewood Avenue, a rundown section of Daytona Beach. Even though they were "broken,"—and now he said it, knowing it was funny—Donna would still live at the house.

"In a separate bedroom, of course," he said.

"Of course," Lisa said.

Kosta talked for a while about Donna. Lisa told Kosta that she also was not looking for romance. So it was settled. Neither of them was looking for a long-term relationship.

On that first date Lisa learned little about Kosta's childhood, but one incident that Kosta related that night did stick in her mind. One day in Pefki, when Kosta was twelve, he went exploring in an empty field and found a hand grenade, perhaps a remnant of the German occupation of Greece. Instead of surrendering the grenade to the police or his parents, Kosta took it to his cellar, where he disarmed it.

Lisa was aghast when she heard the story. "You could have been killed," she said. But Kosta smiled proudly. "No problem," he explained. "I know about explosives." Kosta also mentioned owning one pistol, but Lisa took little interest. Guns had never been part of her family. In fact, she had never even held a real gun, and the only shooting she had ever done was against Shootin' Sam, a coin-operated cowboy dummy at her father's beachfront arcade.

"I just keep the gun for protection," Kosta explained that night at Bennigan's.

"Protection?"

"You know, like if somebody jumps me or something."

Lisa laughed. "I don't think anyone is going to jump you in Daytona Beach."

"You never know," Kosta said. "Once in Chicago my girlfriend and I were parking. Lover's lane. Four Mexican men approached us. One of the Mexicans said, 'Hey, why don't you come out of there.' Ha, I pulled out my gun and pointed it at them and said, 'Hey, why don't you come in here.' They left quickly. But if I hadn't had the gun, who knows what might have happened to me, or my girlfriend."

Lisa had to agree that it made sense to have a gun on that particular night. Maybe Kosta was right; maybe it was a good idea for a person to carry a gun for protection.

They talked for a while about people they had dated. Lisa had gone out with a lot of fellows, she said, but had never been involved in a serious romance. Kosta made it sound as if he had squired quite a number of desirable young ladies around Chicago. His most serious relationship had been with a girl named Karen, in Chicago. In fact, at one point he had moved out of his uncle's house and into an apartment with Karen, and all hell had broken loose.

"It's a small community," he explained, meaning the network of Greek-Americans, something Lisa understood very well. "And they were embarrassed because, you know, we weren't married. My sister even flew in from Greece to try to talk me out of it." Kosta laughed. "But I knew I was right."

I knew I was right. Lisa realized it was a phrase he had used a couple of times during dinner. In fact, now that she thought about it, Kosta was certain about everything he said. "I think" or "it is my opinion" were not phrases that he used. He left the impression that he could not be wrong about anything. She liked it. The man was sure of himself.

Over dessert Kosta told Lisa that he liked to fly under bridges. She took that as hollow boasting, a little something to impress a lady. But he promised her he would take her flying.

Though Kosta and Lisa told each other they were not looking for romance, they saw each other every day during the weeks that followed their dinner at Bennigan's. Those weeks could quite nicely be compressed into one of those gauzily filtered "falling in love" sequences that fill the screen about halfway through most romantic movies. With symphonic music swelling in the distance we see Kosta and Lisa on a blanket at the beach. We see Kosta and Lisa strolling in the park. We see Kosta and Lisa holding hands at the movies. We see Kosta and Lisa, their heads almost touching, carrying on intimate conversations in romantic restaurants.

Lisa was falling in love. Like many girls, she had always dreamed of the perfect husband. In her adolescent fantasies this man who would love her so stupendously was always an American like herself, and usually not a Greek-American. But in less dreamy moments she'd felt a subtle pressure on her, an unspoken message from dozens of resolutely Greek relatives, that said if you marry a man who is not

7

Greek, the family will be unhappy. It was her father's dream that Lisa would marry "a nice Greek boy." So by the time she was old enough to wear a wedding dress, Lisa was ready to compromise. She would find a man who was wonderful, for her, but one who was Greek, for Dad and the family. Now, in the spring of 1985, it seemed that such a man had arrived in her life.

Kosta was an incredibly attentive suitor. After a long telephone conversation with Lisa, Kosta would call back immediately to tell her that he missed her. He was affectionate as could be. He was a good-looking, hard-working, ambitious Greek American (that's how she thought of him, though he was not yet a citizen) who was getting a good education. He was, in a word, perfect.

As promised, Kosta took Lisa flying.

"He took me to Daytona Beach airport, next to Embry-Riddle," Lisa says. "He rented a little, single-engine Cherokee there, and he scared the hell out of me. He liked to do crazy things like fly real low to the ground or get up real high and shut off the engine."

Lisa, never a big fan of physical adventure, decided she would live longer if she did not fly with Kosta, and she gave it up. But not before acquiring a story to tell.

"One time, it was hysterical, Kosta was flying along, telling me about how he's got such a great sense of direction. He radios in to tell the air controllers he's ready to come in for a landing, and they say, 'Okay, where are you located?' Kosta tells them, 'I'm two point seven knots, or whatever, from the Daytona Beach airport.' I asked him, 'What does that mean?' He says, 'I'm landing at the Daytona Beach airport.' He points down at the airport. I said, 'Kosta, that's not the Daytona Beach airport.' He said, 'Yes it is.' I said, 'No, it's not, Kosta. I was born in Daytona, I've come into that airport a lot and that's not it.' Well, he insisted he was right. And then the air traffic controller comes on and says, 'We don't see you, you must be over the Ormond Beach airport.' It was a riot. Kosta was over the wrong airport. Mr. Always Right was wrong. 'See,' I said, 'I told you.' "

Though Kosta was almost obsessive about being right, he did not get angry or blow his stack when proven wrong. In fact, Lisa noticed right from the beginning that Kosta showed very little emotion of any type. Since she was the type to cry easily, or scream and yell, she liked this in Kosta. He would always be the calm and stable one in an emergency, she thought.

There was, however, one disturbing chapter in this storybook romance. By the time Memorial Day rolled around Lisa and Kosta had become a pretty serious item, and Donna, the ex-girlfriend, still had not moved out of Kosta's house.

Lisa, who still had not met Donna, was getting peeved. "I don't like it one bit," she told one of her cousins, "but what can I do?"

Kosta explained that Donna was a poor girl from a poor family. "Have a heart," he said when Lisa lobbied for Donna's eviction. "I can't just throw her out in the street."

Though Lisa didn't care for the arrangement, she never doubted Kosta. If he said that he and Donna had separate bedrooms, then they had separate bedrooms.

In July Lisa and Kosta became engaged. Lisa's mother, Mary Paspalakis, threw a party for her daughter and invited a hundred people. On the day of the party Kosta had lent his car to Donna, who also worked at Lenny's Barbecue Pit, so Lisa had to drop Kosta off at the restaurant so he could pick up his keys. When Kosta came out of Lenny's, his collar was smeared with lipstick.

"What's that?" Lisa said.

"Oh," Kosta said. He dabbed at the collar with a tissue, trying to make the pink stain go away. "Donna's," he said sheepishly.

Lisa felt her body go rigid. Her temples began throbbing. "Donna's?" she said.

"Now calm down, it's nothing," Kosta said. "She just

gave me a little kiss and said, 'I hope you'll be happy with your new wife.' "

"I'm sure she's thrilled that you're marrying me," Lisa said.

It didn't occur to Lisa that Kosta was lying or that he had encouraged the kiss. But she was sure that Donna was being a bitch, putting her mark on Kosta for all the world, or at least all the employees at Lenny's, to see.

"I can't believe it," Lisa said. "Here I am being Miss Nice Guy and she has the nerve to kiss you. Well, I'm not going to be nice anymore. I want her out of there."

A few weeks later Donna was gone.

But not forgotten. In late July, shortly after Kosta and Lisa returned from Aurora, where they had visited with Kosta's relatives, Lisa drove her burgundy Porsche to Kosta's house one night. It was an old and shabby house on the other side of the Halifax River in a neighborhood of strip bars and all-night hamburger joints, where hookers and dopers sold their wares. It was the kind of area that was completely foreign to Lisa, who had always walked on the safe streets east of the Halifax. She looked forward to the day when Kosta would move out of this wretched place.

"I've got something I got to tell you," Kosta said. They stood alone in the poor yellow light of the kitchen, where the plumbing barely worked.

"What is it?" she asked.

Kosta stared down at his hands. "Donna's pregnant."

Lisa said nothing. She waited for the other shoe to drop. God, she hated this house.

"She claims the baby is mine," Kosta said.

"Is it?"

"No, of course not, Lisa. She's due in February. That would be ten months after, you know, the last time."

"I see," Lisa said.

Lisa's trust in Kosta was firm and she didn't require much convincing. A few days later she told a friend, "The baby's not Kosta's. I talked to people at Lenny's and they've seen her with this guy and that guy. So she gets pregnant, and who does she want the father to be? Kosta, of course. That's the only way she can get him back."

As Lisa complained more and more about the dump Kosta was living in, Kosta hinted more and more that he would have to renew his lease in October unless other arrangements could be made. Finally, it was decided that Lisa and Kosta would go ahead with the big wedding, scheduled for January, but that they would actually marry before a justice of the peace in October, so that Kosta could move out of his rented house and into the Paspalakis mansion on the river.

As the wedding date approached, Lisa heard doubts about Kosta from more and more of her Tampa friends. Lisa, they said, are you sure you really know this man? Lisa, they said, you've only known this man a few months, it's not like you to do something this rash.

This was true. It was very unlike Lisa to make a major move without first analyzing it to death. She was known to everybody as a detail lady. People often said to her, "Lisa, you look so carefully at the details that you might miss the big picture." But in the matter of Kosta Fotopoulos, there were many details that Lisa didn't know. What she did know was that Kosta loved her, that he told her he had never said that to any other woman, that the family was thrilled about Kosta, and that she loved him deeply. That was enough.

Certainly Lisa had her doubts, but they emerged in indirect and playful ways. With each new commitment for the wedding she would ask Kosta if he was sure that he wanted to marry her.

"Now I'm calling the photographer," she would tease. "Are you still sure you want to get married?" Kosta would say yes.

"Now my girlfriends are ordering their bridesmaids gowns. Are you sure you want to get married?"

"Yes."

In October of 1985 Lisa Paspalakis and Kosta Fotopoulos were married in a small civil ceremony. The bona fide Greek wedding took place the following January 4 at St. Demetrios Greek Orthodox Church on Halifax Avenue in Daytona Beach with Father Nicholas "Nick" Manousakis celebrating the traditional ceremony.

The reception at the Hilton Hotel was a magnificent and opulent affair. There were enough Greek guests to stage an invasion of Turkey. They ate filet mignon, they kissed the bride, they danced the Greek dances. By the time the dust settled, Augustine "Steno" Paspalakis, the beaming father of the bride, had spent about two hundred thousand of the quarters that had been dropped into video games at Joyland, and for him it was money well spent. The family loved Kosta and Kosta loved the family. In the videotapes of the wedding you can see Kosta, the attentive groom, glowing in the presence of his lovely bride, and as the camera pans from cousin to uncle to mother to brother, you can see that the family was thrilled by it all. The nice Greek boy had married the nice Greek girl.

As the newlyweds danced to Greek music, Kosta held Lisa close. He felt strong and masculine against her. Yes, she had had her doubts, she thought, but now there was something reassuring about being married, about having a man to share her life with. Certainly she was an independent American female, a woman with a career. But it was also imprinted in her culture that it was good to have a man to protect you, to take care of you. And Lisa liked that idea of being protected. She would keep her career, but she would also cook supper for her husband. And by the time she and Kosta were ready to have babies, Dino would be back from college to help Dad with the business.

Kosta kissed her softly on the cheek and pressed his mouth close to her ear. "You know," he said somewhat devilishly, "You're only sixty percent of the reason I married you."

"Oh," Lisa said. "And what's the other forty percent?"

"Your family," Kosta said.

Lisa squeezed him close. "That's nice," she said. "I think."

2

The "Most Good Boy" in the World

What Lisa Fotopoulos didn't know, and had no way of knowing, was that the man she had married was a psychopath, capable of bloody murder. Or, to put it in more currently acceptable language, Kosta Fotopoulos was a sociopath.

Dr. Jack Levin, a criminologist, professor of sociology at Northeastern University in Boston, and the co-author (with James Alan Fox) of *Mass Murder: America's Growing Menace,* (Plenum, 1985) explains.

"A sociopath is what we used to call a psychopath. 'Psychopath' has fallen out of use because it sounds like psychosis. Psychosis is an extreme mental illness, which can take the form of schizophrenia and include hallucinations, delusions and profound thought disorder. Psychopathy, or sociopathy, is quite different. Sociopathy is not a profound mental illness or disorder. It is a character or personality disorder. What we are talking about is the lack of a conscience. A sociopath is a person who just simply does not have the capacity to feel guilty and feels no remorse if he does the wrong thing. He might feel regret, he might wish he hadn't done something if he gets caught, but he doesn't feel any pangs of guilt. The sociopath can do the wrong

14

things with moral impunity. The lack of a conscience, of course, is a continuum. Some people have weaker consciences than others, but at some point we draw the line and say this conscience is so weak that it is virtually nonexistent. This is a sociopath."

Levin is quick to point out that the vast majority of sociopaths are not killers, or even criminals. They function in normal jobs, though they may be more successful in jobs where the lack of conscience is an asset. Sociopaths, generally, are not people who *need* to kill. They are simply people who are *able* to kill without remorse if killing becomes expedient.

"Killing is not a big deal for the sociopath," Levin says. "For him it could be like mutilating a puppet or a doll."

If you gathered Levin and all the rest of the world's experts on sociopathy in a hotel ballroom and forced them to tell you what they know, you still would not have the definitive answer to the question: why was Kosta Fotopoulos a sociopath? In the matter of understanding sociopathy we are, says Levin, "still in the dark ages."

Kosta Fotopoulos's childhood, according to his parents, Despina and Charalampos, was happy and normal. They say that only Kosta's love of guns gave them any concern (an obsession which is considerably rarer in Greece than in the United States), but even that comment barely rises above the level of small complaint. Despina, who speaks little English, says, "My son is the most good boy in the world."

In turn, the members of the Paspalakis family have only praise for the Fotopouloses and say that the odor of evil was never present when the families gathered.

"I loved Kosta's family like my own," Lisa says. "They are wonderful people. They were always very kind to me."

It would be comforting to think that the Paspalakises are foolishly naïve and that the Fotopouloses are lying, that Despina and her husband protect some hideous secret, that Kosta endured some sort of haunted childhood, was tor-

mented, abused, perhaps tortured in the cellar of his home
in Pefki. Such a belief would suggest a way to prevent
sociopaths: don't abuse children. But the truth almost certainly is that the Fotopouloses, just as much as Lisa, were
unaware that a heart of stone beat within their family.
Kosta probably did have a normal childhood. Normal child-
hoods quite often produce sociopaths, just as loveless and
violent ones can produce kind and compassionate people.

Levin says:

"It is a matter of controversy as to why some people
are sociopaths. There is a growing body of evidence that
sociopathy is a result of a profound disruption, especially
during early childhood, so that the child fails to bond. That
lack of bonding between parent and child may be at the
root of sociopathy. That could explain why so many serial
killers, all of whom are sociopaths, are adopted. Of course,
most adopted people grow up to be normal, successful people. But the ones who are sociopaths might have been
abused or abandoned. Whatever it is, the conjecture is that
it starts early, probably in the first years.

"On the other hand, many psychiatrists believe that
some people are born without a conscience, that it is simply
a matter of wiring. Biology. Nobody really knows for sure."

Levin notes that there are millions of sociopaths who do
no harm, just as there are probably millions of sadists who
satisfy their needs with voluntary partners in sadomasoch-
istic sex. The truly frightening combination, as Levin sees
it, is the sociopath who is also a sadist.

"When a sociopath has a sadistic need he is able to exer-
cise it with moral impunity," Levin says. "He doesn't have
guilt to stop him."

Unfortunately for Lisa Fotopoulos, the man she had
fallen in love with and married was also a sadist.

But none of that would come out for a while. For now,
still basking in the glow of a wedding for which four thousand dollars had been spent on flowers alone, Lisa and
Kosta were happy.

Kosta Fotopoulos had married rich. Always a good dresser, he was now a better dresser. He liked to strut along the boardwalk in his fine new clothes. At Razzles nightclub on Seabreeze Boulevard, where he and his pretty new wife often went to dance and meet friends, he liked to flash the Rolex watch that his new father-in-law had given him. Kosta held dearly the image of himself as a big success and a savvy businessman, though it was baseless. Except that in many ways marriage to Lisa helped lift Kosta closer to that image.

Lisa, herself, became for Kosta a measure of his success and proof of his importance in the world. When someone would compliment his wife, tell her she was pretty or smart, Kosta would puff up like a proud papa. Later, recalling the kind comment in private with Lisa, Kosta would shower her with kisses. A compliment to Lisa was a compliment to him. One day a Daytona Beach city commissioner who had done committee work with Lisa on zoning issues told Kosta that Lisa Fotopoulos was one smart cookie. Kosta was so pleased with the compliment that he drove all the way home to crow about it to Lisa. It made him so proud of his wife that he couldn't stop kissing her and hugging her. Lisa felt doubly blessed. Not only did she have a nice compliment, but she had a husband who appreciated her.

Though Lisa realized even on her wedding day that she didn't know her groom quite as well as a bride ought to, it was clear in the early months of the marriage that she had made a wise choice. Kosta was a perfect husband. He often arrived at the door of their three-bedroom rented town house in Ormond Beach with flowers in his hand. Kosta remembered the birthdays of all her family members. Steno and Dino and Mary all got presents. Kosta played gin rummy with her father, and video games with her brother.

Kosta even developed a special relationship with Lisa's mother. Mary Paspalakis is a quiet and trusting woman who grew up in Greece on the island of Symi. Devoted to

17

home and family she is, says her priest, "an old-type Greek." Mary, who minimized her education in English so that her American children would learn to speak two languages, is, says Father Nick, "perhaps a bit simplistic in her outlook and her perceptions of people. That is because she is such an honest person and the honest person tends to see honesty in other people."

Simplistic or not, Mary did not take immediately to Kosta.

"At first I said to my husband, 'I don't really like him,' " she says. "But Steno said he seems like a good boy, it's a good family, and he will have his master's degree. We can help him if we need to. He can marry our daughter and we will have a nice family.

"I didn't like him because I preferred someone who had a profession, an office. But after I met his family I started to love him like my own child. He always treated me very nice."

Kosta teased Mary Paspalakis with good humor, pretending not to recognize her voice on the phone, hiding surprises for her behind his back when he saw her. He was quick with a quip in two languages. He made her smile. And if Mary so much as hinted that she was low on milk or sugar, Kosta would be off like a shot to the 7-Eleven. "You want milk?" he would say, usually speaking to her in Greek. "You'll have milk."

Mary, in turn, looked after Kosta. When she learned that Kosta loved *tsoureky*, a Greek bread, she learned how to make it so that she could put it on the table whenever her handsome new son-in-law came for dinner.

If Mary had one secret wish for her daughter's husband, it was that he would go to church. St. Demetrios had long been the center of the Paspalakises' social, as well as spiritual, life. Steno had for years been a stalwart of the church. Lisa and Dino had been in all the youth groups. Lisa, an accomplished pianist, had been the church organist from the age of twelve to the age of sixteen. Of the approximately 500 Greek-American families in Daytona Beach, 485 had membership in the Greek Orthodox Church. The fact that Kosta was not a churchgoer felt wrong to Mary. Perhaps when they have children Kosta will go, she told herself.

Lisa, whose own church attendance had dropped off dramatically with her marriage and with the demands of a seven-day-a-week business, was thrilled about the way Kosta was fitting in with her family. Kosta was fun to have around. He made jokes with everybody; he was a very funny guy. And, unlike many husbands she could name, Kosta was not embarrassed to show affection in public. On the beach in front of the boardwalk he kissed Lisa. At parties he held her hand. Several of the aunts and female cousins told Lisa they envied her for having such an attentive and affectionate mate. "Has he got a brother?" the single ones joked. But Kosta had no brother, only one sister.

Lisa and Kosta, like most newly married couples, talked baby talk, cooing in each other's ears in bed at night where they sketched out plans for their careers, the big house they would someday build, and the children they would bring into the world. They engaged in mock arguments about who loved who first. They snuggled, they gabbed about their friends, and they made love.

Though the first year of marriage was occasionally punctuated with spats over silly issues, such as who was entitled to which side of the closet, Lisa and Kosta got along fine. Kosta liked to tease, but he could take teasing, too. Lisa, for example, often teased Kosta about his mispronunciation of certain English words. And he would tease her about how emotional she got over small things. The air conditioner would break down and Lisa would be frantically searching through the Yellow Pages for repairmen while Kosta would pour himself a lemonade, put his feet up, and say, "Just calm down and think that it is cool." In fact, once, to make a point about the mind's power to screen out discomfort, he took a lighted cigarette from Lisa, put it on his forearm, and left it there to show her that he could ignore the pain.

"It's not the end of the world," Kosta would say, when things went wrong. "It will get taken care of. Remain calm at all times." He would smile and she would see how silly she was being. Kosta never got emotional about small problems and she loved that about him. And she knew that he loved her. He hated the fact that she smoked, and though she didn't care for the nagging, she appreciated his concern. She couldn't give up cigarettes, but she wanted his approval, and for a while she smoked only in secret.

And they teased each other about cheating.

"Now you better not be cheating on me," Lisa would say. "Because if I find out you're cheating on me, I'll leave you." For Lisa this was not completely funny. Her fear of being rejected for another woman was real and even pretty waitresses flirting with Kosta could cause her pain. Cheating sexually was about the worst thing Lisa could imagine a husband doing. Still, she smiled when she said these things, and Kosta smiled back.

"You won't leave me," he would joke.

"No? Why not? Because you're so adorable?"

"Because I'll get my gun and shoot you," Kosta would say, his Bambi eyes shining. He liked to say such things with a straight face.

"You won't shoot me," Lisa would say, shaking a finger at him. "I'll be gone too fast for you."

They would laugh over this, and hug, and sometimes fall into bed and make love.

If there was anything that made the marriage bed less comfortable during those early months it was the fact that Kosta was unhappy about having a woman support him.

"It's not right for a man to depend on a woman," he told Lisa. "I want to provide for you. I want to make something of myself."

Lisa found this admirable. He wants to take care of his

family, she thought. Though she had always seen herself as a career woman, and she knew that the family business could certainly include Kosta, she also knew that it was important to her husband that he have something of his own.

In June of 1986, when Kosta graduated from Embry-Riddle with a master's degree in aeronautical science, he wanted to go to work for Olympic Airways, his father's employer, in Greece. Lisa had been to Greece many times and thought it was a great place to visit. But she wanted no part of living there. And Kosta, for all his Greek chauvinism, was comfortable in America, too. So Greece was scratched. Kosta began sending resumes around to General Electric, Pratt & Whitney, and other big aviation companies. There were a few nibbles, but none from cities to which the couple wished to move. Besides, Lisa didn't really want to leave Daytona Beach. Steno needed her to help run the business.

In time Kosta just stopped applying for work in aviation. It was decided that Kosta would work, at least for a while, at Joyland, along with Steno, Lisa, and Dino.

Kosta was an early riser, and Lisa a late sleeper. So Kosta would come into Joyland early each morning while Lisa stayed in bed. Kosta made change, he repaired broken video games, he puttered around, did a little of this and a little of that. He became friendly with other boardwalk businessmen and they all thought the world of him.

Frank Goan, who operates Mill/Go, a boardwalk arcade with video games and dodg'em cars, says, "Honest to Pete, Kosta was just the nicest guy, quiet and polite. You'd see him all the time on the boardwalk carrying his briefcase. Sometimes he'd come by and we'd talk."

Tim Kostidakis, who is Dino Paspalakis's closest friend, owns a gift shop a block from the boardwalk.

"Kosta joked a lot," Kostidakis remembers. "I would tease him about the fact that he read comic books and he would say, 'You better watch out or I'll take out my gun and shoot you,' but he'd be smiling and kidding while he said it. Kosta was a good talker. When he wanted to make a point he was very convincing."

Kosta became known as a fellow you could always shoot the breeze with and he was usually good for a joke or two. "Did you hear the one about the two Turks walking down the street? One of them says, 'If you can tell me how many apples I've got in this bag, I'll give you both of them.' The other says, 'Three.' 'Wrong,' the first Turk says, 'you missed it by two.' "

Kosta was a popular figure on the boardwalk. Thomas O'Neil, a police officer who included the boardwalk on his beat, says Kosta was "an outgoing, charismatic individual." Others found him "charming," "delightful," "smart," and "funny."

Kosta was all of these, and he was also a man who saw himself as a chief, not an Indian, so he took little joy in his duties at the arcade. Most mornings Lisa would arrive in the office around eleven and by twelve-thirty Kosta would be off to the bank to make the daily Joyland deposit, which he carried in a briefcase. Almost invariably, he would be gone for hours.

Lisa was never quite sure where Kosta went on these afternoon excursions, but she thought it better to have Kosta happily roaming around town than miserably sweeping floors or handing out quarters at Joyland. Besides, she felt more than a little guilty about the fact that Kosta was stuck in Daytona Beach because of her devotion to her father. Still, her husband's mysterious excursions caused her some anxiety.

"Kosta," she said, when her husband showed up at four in the afternoon, "you went to the bank four hours ago. What happened?"

"Oh, I ran into Peter Kouracos," or this one or that one, "and we got to chatting," or "we had some lunch." It was always something.

In time Kosta developed the habit of calling Lisa in the

22

afternoon and announcing "I'm at Peter's," or "I'm at Angelo's" and the male friend in question would shout into the phone, "Hi, Lisa, how are you?" Lisa was never quite sure whether Kosta had been with his friend all along, or had swung by on his way back from some secret assignation to create an alibi. Sometimes she worried that Kosta really might be fooling around with women. But it seemed unlikely. Lisa had a million friends in Volusia County, many of them nosey as beagles, and not one ever hinted that Kosta had been seen with another woman.

When Kosta did work at Joyland, he was something less than the prudent businessman he imagined himself to be.

Dino Paspalakis, who had graduated with honors from the University of South Florida and returned to work at Joyland around the time that Kosta was leaving Embry-Riddle, recalls, "Whenever Lisa and I went to lunch, we would give a few hundred dollars in quarters to one of our employees for making change, and of course, we would write down the amount. But when Kosta would give out the quarters he would never write it down. He could be careless like that. One morning Lisa was talking to the snack bar manager. He asked her if she wanted the five hundred dollars in quarters that was in his freezer. What five hundred? she asked. 'The five hundred dollars Kosta gave me to hold for him in the freezer. He forgot to ask for them back.' When Lisa asked Kosta about it Kosta said, 'Oh yeah.' "

Though Kosta kept his own hours, he couldn't shake the feeling that he was a Joyland employee, not an owner. He was getting a paycheck, three hundred dollars a week, but he had no legal claim on the business. It was Kosta's dream that his father-in-law, Steno, would see that a man shouldn't be working for his own wife and make the proper arrangements. Steno, as Kosta saw it, should regard Kosta as a second son and make him an equal inheritor of all that Steno had acquired. But Steno, fond as he was of his son in-law, and despite the fact that he and Kosta spent long and raucous hours together playing gin rummy, was not so inclined. The papers he had signed, which made Lisa and Dino the inheritors of his business, were not changed just because Lisa had gotten married, even if it was to a nice Greek boy.

So Kosta Fotopoulos was frustrated. He was a man who needed to do well. From the very beginning Kosta was intent on achieving success by having a business of his own. He could not hear about a business being for sale without thinking he might want to buy it. "If General Motors were for sale," Lisa once quipped, "Kosta would want to buy it." His plans were legion and they were grandiose. There was the plan for Kosta and his friend Peter Kouracos to manufacture and market their own bullets. Lisa thought this was hysterical. "Let me see now," she said, "I need some bullets. Now, do I want some Winchester or Remington, or . . . no, how about some 'Kosta and Peter' bullets, do you have some of those?" Equally amusing to Lisa was Kosta's plan to market automatic cracker dispensers for the home, and his plan for an automatic fertilizer.

If some of Kosta's plans were unorthodox, others were viable, or at least would have been in the hands of a capable businessman. There were restaurants he could buy, stores he could open, services he could operate. And with each new plan Kosta would be as enthusiastic and as innocent as Mickey Rooney saying to Judy Garland, "Hey, I got an idea, we could put on a show." Unfortunately, Kosta had no money of his own, and his great business ventures always called for financing from Steno, or Dino, or Lisa. The money was not forthcoming, because as much as the family admired Kosta's zeal, it was clear that Kosta was no businessman. Though he was quick to count the imagined profits, Kosta gave little thought to details like acquiring licenses, witholding taxes, establishing employee benefits, incorporating or filling out the myriad forms that land in the mailbox of anybody who tries to set up shop on a public street. To Lisa, the accountant, "Little Miss Detail," attention to these things was at the heart of good business sense, and she was always shocked to realize Kosta thought that the rules and regulations that governed small businesses did not apply to him.

"There was one business," Lisa recalls, "that was obviously losing money. They gave us financial statements, but the guy says don't go by them, I've been skimming money off the top. Kosta falls for that, and I tried to tell him, Kosta, anybody who's selling a losing business is going to tell you that. The guy had checks bouncing all over the state and he had an outrageous amount in bank service charges, and he was saying to Kosta, 'Oh, but you should see how much I really make.' So I said to Kosta, people who are making money don't have checks bouncing. You want me to help you evaluate the business? He says, ah, what do you know? I said, well, I'm a CPA, people pay me money for this sort of thing. I tried to tell him, and he would just say, 'Oh, you don't know what you're talking about.' He always had to be right."

One of Kosta's money-making schemes involved the purchasing of stock options. For several months Kosta and Peter Kouracos carried on like Donald Trump and Ted Turner. They read *The Wall Street Journal* religiously. They exchanged financial information the way other guys might fill in each other on football scores. In their separate homes, they would sit for hours in front of the television watching the financial news, and they would call each other up, always greeting one another with "Hey, bro." (Though this greeting began as a diminutive for "brother," it eventually turned to "Brosky," for Ivan Boesky, the Wall Street crook who was something of a hero to the men. Boesky, incidentally, is a name that Jack Levin mentions when he wants to make the point that sociopaths do well in jobs wherein their lack of conscience is an asset.) On the phone Kosta and Peter would tell each other what they had learned. At the end of the year, when Lisa sat down to evaluate all the stock option transactions that the two men had made, she discovered that all their efforts had earned them about two thousand bucks, which they would have had to pay to their certified public accountant if she were not married to one of them.

Though Kosta had not achieved the success he expected for himself, he did what he could to project an image of success to his friends and boardwalk associates. Even the Rolex from Steno was not enough, and soon after he received it he traded it in for a Presidential, a Rolex of higher rank.

Kosta bought a brand-new black BMW during the first year of their marriage. He preened over the BMW as if he had made it by hand, and when he drove past people he knew, he would honk the horn so that they could see him tooling along. When friends came to visit from Chicago, Kosta would ask them to gather around his car to have their picture taken. When he drove the BMW north with Lisa on a trip to Chicago and rammed it into a guardrail on a slippery exit ramp he was uncharacteristically irate.

"What are you screaming and yelling about?" Lisa asked him on that snowy exit ramp. "Nobody was hurt. It's only a car." It was one of the few times Kosta had shown emotion.

"You don't understand," Kosta said. "I wanted to show it off to my uncles."

Lisa, who had been disheartened as a teenager to discover she became more popular after her father bought her a Pontiac Trans Am, despised the idea of trying to impress people with wealth. She always wore simple jewelry and clothes that were chosen for comfort, not because they looked expensive. So she was never at ease with Kosta's need to be showy.

"I was brought up not to be a show-off," Lisa says. "In fact, when I was a kid I didn't even realize we had anything more than anybody else. We had a house on the river, my cousin had a house on the river. I didn't know a house on the river was more expensive than a house that was not on the river. When we went to Greece to visit family, people would say, 'Lisa, you're lucky, you get to go to Greece.' But to me it was the same as when they went up north to visit their family. So I wasn't brought up to brag about anything. All of a sudden I see my husband bragging about owning a BMW. It was kind of embarrassing."

Lisa was sure the bragging would not last. He's just insecure, she told herself. He'll get over this when he has a business of his own.

Jack Levin would have disagreed. "This need to impress other people with status symbols is typical of the sociopath," Levin says. "Sociopaths are masters at making an impression on other people and status symbols and conspicuous consumption are the way they do it."

The business of his own that Kosta wanted most was the Denny's project that obsessed him in the summer of 1987.

In June of that year Lisa's parents flew to Greece for an extended visit. Kosta and Lisa moved out of their Ormond Beach town house and into the Paspalakis house at 2505 North Halifax Avenue. It was a big white house with a long horseshoe-shaped driveway and four Greek columns surrounding the wide front double door. It was a spacious home, expensively furnished in the Mediterranean style, lots of red velvet cushions and gilded frames and color everywhere. Kosta had always liked the house. Certainly to live in such a place, situated as it was on the Halifax River with a wide front lawn and a swimming pool in the back, reflected well on him. Lisa's brother, Dino, still lived there, but there was plenty of room. It seemed only sensible that Kosta and Lisa might as well get the use of the place and save some of that rent money, which they could put toward their own house, the one they planned to build in Ormond Beach.

For many years there had been a restaurant called Bali's, on Broadway, two blocks from the boardwalk area. When

Lisa was growing up, Bali's had been the place to eat and dance on the beach side. Bali's had gone out of business, and it seemed that no matter what kind of restaurant moved into the location, the crowds never came. Now, in the summer of 1987, when Kosta heard that the building was for sale, he carried on as if someone had died and left him a fortune. This, he said, was his big opportunity. He would buy the place, refurbish it, and turn it into a Denny's franchise restaurant. It would be a twenty-four-hour restaurant. With tourists roaming the streets until all hours of the night, the place would make a fortune.

"Kosta was more excited about this than any of his other projects," says Dino Paspalakis. "He was always talking about it, discussing the menu, the decor, how much money it would make. But Kosta didn't have any money and the whole thing was going to cost over nine hundred thousand dollars. He wanted us to finance it, but my family was not going to jeopardize almost a million bucks. I figured that if the restaurant grossed a million, two hundred thousand, even with a conservative figure for expenses, it would clear about sixty thousand dollars. That was not a smart business move in my opinion, not with a twenty-four-hour operation, which is a constant hassle. Not only that, but this particular location, for some reason, had never been real successful after Bali's. A lot of other places had gone under."

Lisa, as usual, was torn. Though Kosta's business visions sometimes exasperated her, they also made her proud. She found it admirable that Kosta wanted to build his own fortune so he could support his wife, and if ever she suspected that Kosta had married her as a meal ticket, those fears were vanquished by the zeal with which he unveiled each new project, especially this one. She felt sorry for Kosta. He so desperately wanted to be a businessman, but he was all image and enthusiasm and had little understanding of the day-to-day financial realities. In the end she had to agree with Dino. This was not a good deal.

Kosta, however, was determined. He was not to be dissuaded by his brother-in-law and his wife, both of whom were accountants and business operators. He was desperate to have this restaurant and he was hopeful that his father-in-law would help. He called Steno in Greece to ask him to cosign for several hundred thousand dollars in loans.

"I've got a great location on Broadway," Kosta said.

"I hope it's not the old Bali's restaurant," Steno said from Greece. "That place is a loser."

Kosta was crushed. But he made his pitch for the money. He told Steno how much he wanted it, how he would work hard, how he would set it up. But Steno agreed with Lisa and Dino. It was a bad investment. He turned Kosta down. Shortly after that, Steno and Mary returned from Greece. Steno, feeling bad that he had rejected Kosta, lent Kosta ten thousand dollars and told him to try to make something of his own with it. But Kosta was still depressed.

"I've never seen Kosta so devastated as when my father turned him down on the Denny's deal," Dino says. "He took it very hard."

Five weeks after refusing to finance Kosta, Steno Paspalakis suddenly died.

3

Steno

Her father's name was Augustine, but everybody called him Steno. They spelled it with an *e* even though it sounded just like Dino, her brother's name. He was a big man, big like a bear, and his voice when he got excited sounded like summer thunder. When Lisa was a little girl, Steno took her to the beach. He lifted her in his strong hands and hoisted her high above his head. "The Atlantic Ocean," he announced. Even then she sensed the awe in his voice. She thought she could see all the way to Greece.

Then Steno spun her around until she had looked in every direction.

"Elevator coming down," he said, and he lowered her to the hard sand. He pointed both ways.

"This, Lisa," he said, "is the world's most famous beach."

Lisa knew it was true, because whenever she twirled the postcard carousel at the sundry store on the boardwalk, many of the colorful pictures of Daytona Beach said The World's Most Famous Beach.

"They used to race cars," Steno told her. "Right here." He stooped down and poked a finger in the sand. "See. It is hard. So they could race. All the way from Granada Avenue in Ormond," he told her. "For a dozen miles they would race. *Vroom, vroom."* He made racing noises. "Then they would turn around and drive the other way. *Vroom. Vroom."*

Back then, Lisa thought her daddy had seen it all, that he had stood out on the sand waving at the drivers as their cars roared by. Sometimes she imagined him behind the wheel, his car in the lead, spitting up sand all the way to Daytona Beach and all the way back to Ormond. But later, when he told her about his coming to America, she understood that when Mr. Oldsmobile and the others were racing cars, her father was just a boy growing up in Greece.

"I grew up on Khalki," he said one night, holding Lisa on his knees. Actually, he said it many nights, but for Lisa it all compressed into a single memory of her dad. "It is a small island in Greece," he told her. "No water, no electricity. And worst of all," he said, raising a hand dramatically in the air, "no Beatles."

This was the mid-sixties and little Lisa thought that was funny.

He told her that when he was a young man he left his village and hooked passage on a westbound ship that took him across the Atlantic. He came first to Venezuela, then to Texas, where he had relatives who had come over a few years earlier. In 1955 he went back to Greece to marry Mary Manousakis.

"Your mama," he said. "This was a wedding that had been planned since we were both your age."

But Steno didn't bring Mama to America, not right away. "I wanted to be able to say first, 'I have made something of myself.' "

Steno came back to America alone. He worked in Charleston. "In South Carolina," he explained. There some other Paspalakises had settled. By 1957, three years before Lisa was born, Steno owned a bar in Charleston and had become a U.S. citizen. He sent for Mary.

"But we got tired of Charleston," he told his daughter. "So we came here like the others. The sunshine. The ocean. The fine fishing waters. It reminded us of home. We were going to build houses, my cousins and me. But after we built the first house, this one you live in, your mother and I wanted to live in it."

He paused then, gazed off into space. "I fell in love with my own creation," he said to Lisa. "Just like Pygmalion."

"Pig who?" Lisa asked.

Steno smiled. "It's a myth," he said. He laughed. "Not even Greek."

So Steno and his cousins built no more houses. The year before Lisa was born, Steno rented a snack bar on the boardwalk. Then, after the baby was born, he rented the Satelite game arcade on the boardwalk and renamed it Funorama.

"And that," Steno explained, with a big laugh and a final bounce of his knees, "is how I got my start in America running my arcades and snack bar."

Lisa heard the stories many times about how Steno and the uncles and the aunts and the cousins came over from Greece. "Did I ever tell you about how your uncle Demitrius came to America?" Steno would say. "Nope," Lisa would say. Up on the knees she would go and Steno would wrap his wide arms around her and lean down and tell her one more story about a Greek immigrant making good in America.

So, for Lisa Paspalakis, childhood was safe and it was secure. Daddy worked on the boardwalk and that was a wonderful place. People came from all over the country just to drive on the beach or play games at the arcades, or throw baseballs at fake milk bottles at the other end down by the bandshell, and, of course, to eat hot dogs at her father's snack bar.

In the silvery hours of each early morning Lisa listened for the sounds of her father leaving his bed, talking in Greek to Ma at the breakfast table, and then leaving the house to open the boardwalk snack bar. Her father worked hard and she knew what that meant. "Lisa," he often told her, "if you work hard, the rewards will come." Little Lisa burrowed down in her bed and thought about those rewards.

At three each afternoon Dad came home. "What a morning," he would say in his rich baritone voice, a voice that was frightening to some, but music to Lisa. "What a morning." Lisa's mother would cook *pastitsio* or moussaka for lunch and then Steno, not one to forsake a fine Greek tradition like *to mesimergino ipno* ("the afternoon sleep") snoozed for three hours. By seven o'clock, he was off again to work at the snack bar until one in the morning.

By 1969, when he was also operating the Mardi Gras Fun Center, Steno at one time or another had opened the gate on just about every snack bar on the boardwalk. He prospered, and when people asked him what it was all for, he smiled broadly. "Send my kids to college," he would say. "Send my kids to college."

By the time Lisa was in the fourth grade her father had made enough money to buy a few blocks of local property. But when he got the chance to buy the Joyland Amusement Center he sold everything so he could make a down payment.

This was before the advent of the computer chip and Joyland was mostly pinball machines, Skee-Ball, pokerino, and "21." Lisa was nine and her favorite attraction was a mechanical fast-draw cowboy dummy by the name of Shootin' Sam, who would ridicule her every time he beat her to the draw, which was every time she went up against him. "Better luck next time, pardner, and don't forget to wear your glasses," Sam would say. Little Lisa thought this was the biggest riot and she would giggle hysterically long after Shootin' Sam had put down his six-shooter and gone dark.

If Lisa wasn't much of a cowpoke, there were signs in early childhood that she did have the makings of a savvy businesswoman. Though her father would gladly have spoiled her with any number of toys, what young Lisa loved most was playing with an adding machine. Steno would come home at night, clutching his stack of business bills. "Here, honey," he would say, "you think you could add these up for me?" And Lisa would joyously add the figures up over and over, taking great delight in the fact that the total was always the same. By the time Lisa entered high school she knew she wanted to be in business, and after her first accounting course her heart was set on being an accountant. In accounting, as in life, she loved the idea of things being balanced, organized.

Though Steno had been in the arcade business for years before he bought Joyland, he seemed to stand a little taller after that purchase. Now he was entrenched. No longer a renter, he was an owner. As time passed, the Joyland became for him a symbol of all that he had accomplished in America. It was not simply an investment. And operating it was certainly not just a job. It was his legacy. Joyland was something he could never sell. Just as some people passed down a watch or a ring to their children, Steno would pass the Joyland Amusement Center down to his, and in that he took great pride.

Steno, who always spoke Greek at home, was prosperous and content. Most of the other businessmen on the boardwalk were Greek, and with those who weren't, Steno often joked that if they wanted to stick around they had to learn the Greek dances. He had a good business, a wife he loved, and children he adored. Moreover, he had the extended Greek community of brothers, cousins, nephews and nieces with their husbands and wives, and *their* cousins and nephews and nieces. He was a Greek and he was an American and he rarely longed for the homeland. But, no less clannish than other immigrants, Steno did look forward to the day when his daughter would marry a nice Greek boy, and his son a nice Greek girl.

Steno Paspalakis was not a man to throw curveballs. If he

didn't like you, you knew it. And if he did like you . . . well, you weren't always so sure. He was gruff and he was direct. Those who knew him well never took his grumbling too seriously, but to the timid he was a daunting figure. Some of the salesmen who called on boardwalk businessmen were scared to death of him. He was not a man to stand on ceremony. If a salesman arrived when Steno preferred solitude, he would shout, "Go away, I'm busy." In time, however, the salesmen learned how to win Steno's attention and his affection. They would speak to Lisa, who, along with her brother, spent many hours as a teenager working at Joyland.

"You want my dad to look at your sample books, you want him to like you?" Lisa would say. "You've got to say nice things about his daughter."

The salesmen would go in proclaiming, "Boy that's one smart daughter you got there Mr. Paspalakis. And pretty! Just as pretty as a picture. You are one lucky man."

"You like my Lisa?" Steno would say. The eyes would light up, the chest would puff out with pride. "You think she's pretty and smart? You're all right! Come on in, show me what you got."

By 1977 Steno and two of his cousins had bought an old hotel on Atlantic Avenue, razed it, and built the Circus Gift Shop. Pleased with the business, Steno decided to build another gift shop on his boardwalk property. He yanked out a few pinball machines and partitioned off a narrow section at the south end of Joyland. There he installed a gift shop where tourists could buy T-shirts with alligators and racing cars on them, painted seashells, postcards of The World's Most Famous Beach, and bikinis. He named the new store Lisa's Gift Shop, after his pride and joy.

While the gift shops were enterprises that earned money, they were not as dear to Steno's heart as the arcades, and he looked at the need for additional management as a burden. Steno, who was never entirely comfortable turning over authority to outsiders, asked his smart and pretty daughter to manage the shop. "After all," he argued, "it is named after you." She was sixteen.

Still in high school, Lisa took over the gift shop business. She placed the orders, counted the inventory, hired and fired the help, and banked the receipts. Though the work was ten times more exhausting and demanding than she had imagined it would be when she signed on, Lisa took to the business like a porpoise to the sea.

Augustine Paspalakis, unfortunately, did not share Lisa's affinity for the finer points of bookkeeping. He once told his daughter, "What I know about money is I take some in and I put in the safe. In the morning I take the money out of the safe and I put it in the bank."

Steno was a man who could add up any column of figures in his head, but start talking debits and ledgers with him and his eyes would glaze over. To him accounting meant you had to turn over all your receipts and various scraps of paper to someone who had gone to college to learn about such things, and then you trusted him.

By the early seventies Steno's business tax records were a horror. His own bad habits, combined with incompetent accounting help, resulted in his being miles behind on his income taxes. In 1975 he was taken to court for tax evasion. The prosecution, acknowledging that Steno was an honest, if unsophisticated, businessman, did not ask for jail time. The judge, however, was less forgiving. Perhaps as a warning to other well-meaning businessmen, the judge told Steno he would have to spend three months in jail at Eglin Air Force base, on the Florida panhandle, beginning in September, after the busy season.

The sentence was not a harsh one. Eglin was a country club kind of jail, with no guns, no bars, and no searching of visitors. In fact, it was at Eglin during this same period that Howard Hunt did his penance in connection with the Watergate scandal.

Nonetheless, the tax evasion incident had enormous impact on the family, most keenly on Lisa, who was then a teenager trying to find her identity among her peers. For starters, her father was sentenced on a slow news day, so the story of a small-time Daytona Beach boardwalk businessman given a slight sentence for minor tax evasion made the newspapers and the local TV. Steno had just built for his family the gorgeous new house on the Halifax River, and before the furniture was even in place reporters were crowding the doorstep and cameramen were peeking in windows. It was not the kind of attention a teenage girl likes brought to herself.

A week before Steno was to enter the jail, Mary Paspalakis took her son and her daughter to Pensacola, where they rented a small apartment near the jail so they could visit Steno on Saturdays and Sundays. On those weekend days Mary and the kids would go off to the jail, carting baskets that contained enough food to feed an army, and the family would stay together from eight in the morning until five in the afternoon. When the time came for his wife and children to leave, Steno would put his arms out for one last bearish hug and, holding back the tears, would say, "Don't leave until I have a chance to get to the fence, so I can wave good-bye."

Out to the fence the family would go, and there would be father once again separated from them by steel. As the family moved away, Lisa would glance back at her dad after every step. Steno would stand all alone, waving until his wife and children were out of sight. It broke Lisa's heart every time. In her life there had been no more touching sight than that of her father being left behind, waving good-bye. It was an image that became so deeply imbedded in Lisa's mind that even years later when she was grown up, the memory of it would always bring tears to her eyes. Though her dad ate well and was treated decently, it was profoundly sad to Lisa that she had a father who she could not go to whenever she wanted to, and that experience set in her an abiding fear of anything illegal. You break the law and this is what happens, she thought. She vowed that she would never do anything unlawful and she would never associate with anybody who did.

Steno Paspalakis lived most of his adult life as a solid citizen of two worlds, Daytona Beach and the Greek community of Daytona Beach.

Daytona Beach, a hundred miles south of Jacksonville on Florida's east coast, is a city of moderation. It doesn't have Miami's crime rate. It doesn't have Orlando's Disney World. Its winters, mild and short, make it a lot warmer than New York in February. And its summers, with breezes shifting from the Atlantic Ocean on one side and the Halifax River on the other, make it a lot cooler than Fort Lauderdale in July. Which is why Daytona Beach draws tourists all year-round and, in fact, has more visitors in summer than in winter. Thousands of people from all over the world come to Daytona Beach to fish, boat, surf, jet-ski, and bake on the beach.

Daytona Beach (also referred to simply as "Daytona") is best known for two things: its beach, and the auto races that began on the beach years ago and are now run at the famous Daytona International Speedway. It's the chamber of commerce that first declared it The World's Most Famous Beach, and that ubiquitous phrase cannot be avoided even by the most passive of tourists. It is proclaimed on postcards, towels, brochures, billboards, and souvenirs of every type. The beach, hard white sand firmly packed by the tides, slopes at a small angle into the Atlantic Ocean and runs for twenty-three continuous miles. As wide as five hundred feet in places, the sand is an oceanside boulevard where tourists walk, or ride on rented bicycles known as beach cruisers, or zip along on mopeds, or, for a small beach access fee, drive their own cars. The speed limit on the beach is ten miles per hour.

Along the World's Most Famous Beach, above the seawall, is the strip known as the boardwalk. The boardwalk, which began in the Forties with a couple of bowling alleys, is not really a boardwalk at all, just a cement walkway about as wide as a two-lane blacktop, and about twice the length of a city block. The boardwalk is lined with old, riotously colored stores, all fairly weathered by the wind that skates off the Atlantic. The strip is a life-sized cartoon of video game arcades, souvenir shops, miniature golf courses, and narrow eateries where you have to squeeze in sideways to take a stool at the counter. There is Walkin Charlie's (Games-Prizes-Snack Bar), The Pit Stop (Beer-Pool-Games), Mardi Gras Fun Center, Fun and Fascination, Midway Fun Fair, Pizza King, and, of course, Lisa's Gift Shop and Joyland Amusement Center.

Though they don't face the ocean, Main Street on the north and Ocean Avenue parallel to the boardwalk on the west are also loosely referred to as the boardwalk. These streets are filled with more gift shops, casual clothing stores, and a few more bars, including one with "exotic dancers," where college boys go to watch sad-eyed girls dance naked (well, almost naked) for tips that are shoved into their garters.

For decades the boardwalk has been a popular vacation spot. If the Miami Beach crowd is borscht belt and New York deli, this one is more grits and motor oil, at least when the cars are racing. Daytona Beach does a brisk family vacation business, and school holidays help to fill hotel rooms along Atlantic Avenue. But Daytona Beach tourism to a large extent revolves around three events: the auto races at the Daytona International Speedway, the motorcyle races at the speedway, and spring break. And with few exceptions, beach businesspeople will tell you that the best behaved people are the motorcycle crowd and the worst are the college students.

While Daytona Beach is a sunny haven for people of all ages, most of the people who eat hush puppies on the boardwalk and plug quarters into the video games are young. There are the locustlike swarms of college students who in recent years, for better or worse, have anointed Daytona Beach as spring break headquarters. There are the local kids who head for the beach every chance they get. And despite the best efforts of local businesspeople to keep them out there are the lowlifes . . . teenaged runaways and drifters. When kids on the East Coast run away they go to Florida and Daytona Beach gets its share. Like Forty-second Street in New York and the Sunset Strip in Los Angeles, the boardwalk at Daytona Beach has become a stopping place for America's lost youths, many of whom are quite dangerous.

So this was the working world of Steno Paspalakis, a world where shoptalk meant sitting at the counter of the snack bar in Joyland with one of the other boardwalk business owners and discussing the upcoming Speed Week, or the arrival of the college students, or the new machine that could roll quarters faster than the old one.

Steno's other world was the Greek community, which is more or less synonymous with the Greek Orthodox Church. Ninety-eight percent of Greeks are Greek Orthodox, and almost all of Daytona's Greeks are members of St. Demetrios.

Though many of the area's Greeks are descended from the 1,200 Greeks who settled in New Smyrna Beach south of Daytona two hundred years ago, most are not.

"There is not a line of continuity that extends back to those Greeks," says Father Nick Manousakis. "The Greeks in Daytona today came on their own in recent generations, or were brought over by relatives. They were drawn here by the tourism. Many Greeks are involved with the tourist industry, especially gift shops. And probably the biggest draw for Greeks to this area is the climate and the ocean."

(Father Nick is no doubt correct that a climate similar to that of Greece was the magnet that attracted Greek immigrants to Daytona, which also explains the large Greek communities in St. Augustine, Florida, and Santa Barbara, California. But he notes with interest the fact that the largest Greek community west of the Mississippi is in, of all places, Salt Lake City, Utah.)

Augustine Paspalakis was typical of these people. He was, says Father Nick, everything a Greek should be.

"I took a very personal liking to this man," Father Nick says. "He was very industrious and he had a strong kinship to his ethnic roots, although he resided in America. He was a man of great pride and high values, which is characteristic of the Greek mentality. He was part of a very close family, and that is typically Greek. Among Greeks there is a lot of respect for the family, and a high regard for the church. The families are extended families, with the uncles and the aunts and cousins all in close touch with each other. The Paspalakises have many relatives here, to be sure."

Steno liked to eat Greek food, dance Greek dances, and celebrate Greek holy days. Perhaps his favorite time of the year was November, when the Greek Festival was held.

The Greek Festival is a cultural festival, not a religious one, and it is the largest ethnic festival of the year in Volusia County. It is the main fund-raiser of the year for St. Demetrios, and people come from miles around to buy Greek food and crafts at the church and activities center, which is on Halifax less than a mile from the Paspalakis house. The festival has always been a major yearly event in the life of the Paspalakises, and the family always donated its time to work there.

In 1987 the festival was held during the third week of November, the weekend of another major event for the family: Kosta's becoming a citizen. It would turn out to be a weekend of great tragedy. Lisa recalls:

"The day that Kosta was to become a U.S. citizen Dad woke up all excited. This was a very big day to him. But he wasn't feeling well. He had a pain in his lower back. We drove over to the courthouse in Deland, where Kosta would take the oath of citizenship, Dad, me, and my mother and Kosta. Dino had to stay and take care of the store. At the courthouse there was a ceremony, with women taking pictures and handing out little flags. Dad

41

was so proud that Kosta was becoming a citizen. To him this was a major accomplishment. Before the ceremony we had to sit separate from Kosta because he was with all the other people who were becoming citizens. Dad was having trouble sitting because of the pain, but there was a baby in front of us and Dad was having a blast playing with the baby.

"After the ceremony Dad said, 'Let's go to lunch, we'll celebrate.' We went to a restaurant in Deland, but when we got there Dad said, 'I don't feel well,' and you could see that he didn't look well. Kosta had gone off to make a phone call. To check on the store, he said. Dad looked like he was in pain. I said, 'Dad, if you don't feel well, let's go home, we're leaving now.' My dad was always the type to say, No, no, it's okay, I'll be all right. But now he looked at me and he said, 'Okay.' So I knew that he was really hurting. I ran up to the lady at the reception area and asked her to call an ambulance, but Dad said, 'No.' He said, 'I don't want to ruin this special day.' I could tell from the expression on his face that there was something really wrong. Dad wasn't the kind of person to complain. So we didn't get an ambulance, but the woman gave me directions to the hospital in Deland. So we got out to the car. And there's Kosta across the street. I said, 'What are you doing?' He goes, 'Oh, the phone over there wasn't working,' or something. I said, 'Come on, my Dad's sick and we're going to the hospital.' When we got to the hospital Dad said he was feeling a little better and he wanted to go to Daytona, to Halifax Memorial Hospital, where his doctor was.

"When we got to Halifax Dad's doctor was out to lunch, so we made an appointment for two o'clock and we ended up at Morrison's cafeteria. I was getting nervous, I guess, and I didn't want to wait until two. So I drove Dad up to the hospital in Ormond Beach. When we finally did see a doctor he said that Dad probably just bumped himself in the middle of the night and it was probably nothing. But he told Dad to rest and he suggested that Dad not go to the Greek Festival that night. Dad was disappointed, but he was the kind who would do what the doctor said.

"At six o'clock Mom and I were scheduled for work at the festival, Mom in the food line and me at the T-shirt booth. Kosta had already gone to work at Joyland. Dad says, 'Don't worry about me, I'll be all right, I feel much better.' He says, 'You guys go.'

"When we got to the festival they didn't need me to work yet. They said just wait a while, so I said, 'Do I have time to have dinner?' By that time Dino had gotten to the festival. I was sitting with my cousin Kally having dinner, and this lady walks up to me and says, 'There's a telephone call, it's your husband and he says it's an emergency.' Now, as far as I knew, Kosta was working at Joyland. So I got up and I walked back to the telephone in the office. When I got on the phone there was no answer. I kept saying, 'Hello, hello.' Then I heard a moan. It sounded like my father. I said to the lady, 'It sounds like my father.' She said, 'No, it's not your father, it's your husband.' Then I heard another moan, louder, and I knew it was Dad. So I took off. I went running through the festival, but not running past the food line, because my mother was there and I didn't want to panic her, I didn't want Mom having a heart attack because something had happened to Dad. I went and got Dino and I said, 'Something's wrong, let's go.'

"I put in a quick call to Kosta at Joyland and said, 'Meet me at the house.' Then Dino and I just took off running. When we got to the house Dad was lying on the floor in between the family room and the kitchen area. He said, 'I'm hot.' We called an ambulance. Dad was sweating. I got down on my knees and held him and kept fanning him. My heart was racing. I just went into a speech, 'I love you, Dad, hang on, we're here, don't worry, you're going to be all right.' And the whole time all Dad said was, *'Elenitsa mou,'* my Lisa. The ambulance came. When Kosta got there I told him, 'Go get Mom, bring her to Halifax Hospital.'

43

"They rushed Dad to the hospital. In no time the whole waiting room was filled with first cousins and second cousins and friends. There were probably thirty-five people in the hospital waiting room because everybody was at the Greek Festival.

"Then the doctor walked in and said, 'I'm sorry, Mrs. Paspalakis.'

"That was the most dramatic moment of my life. There was screaming and yelling and crying and wailing, it was awful.

"Then the doctor took me aside and he said he thought it was an aneurism that killed my father, but he wasn't sure, it could have been a heart attack or something else. It looked strange and he wanted to do an autopsy, to enhance medical knowledge or something. He said something wasn't quite right and he couldn't understand why they had lost him. I didn't really ask him much, because I was anxious to get back to the family. I just said, 'No, you can't do an autopsy because it is against our religion and it didn't make any difference what Dad died of.' I mean at the time there was certainly no reason to suspect foul play."

A few days later, Dino recalls being told by the undertaker that Augustine Paspalakis had not died of an aneurism. "He said that they didn't find any blood when they drained the body fluids and that with an aneurism there would be blood in the fluid."

The significance of the phone call that Lisa received at the Greek Festival is difficult to assess. As she sees it, if it was Kosta on the phone, he did have time to leave the house and get back to Joyland in time for her call to him.

"The woman who answered the phone had to leave the office, go through the festival, and find me first," she says.

While it seems a bit far-fetched to imagine Kosta making the phone call, then putting the phone next to Steno and dashing out the door, especially when there is no clear motive for all of this, there is another detail about the call

44

that is intriguing. The person who made the call asked for Lisa Fotopoulos.

"The woman who answered the phone seemed certain that it was my husband, though he didn't identify himself," Lisa says. "The strange thing is that I can't imagine my dad calling and saying, 'Could I speak to Lisa Fotopoulos, please?' Dad would say, 'This is Steno, I want my daughter.' Whoever answers the phone in the church office is somebody who knows us well."

Though later events would show that Kosta was certainly capable of acting in bizarre ways, the scenarios that put Kosta in the house and on the phone when Steno collapsed are all speculative. It's just as likely that he was at Joyland the whole time and that the woman who answered the phone just made an incorrect assumption.

However, it is fact, not speculation, that Kosta had in the house a small bottle of mercury, which he had bought from a dentist when he and Lisa had gone to Greece. By this time Kosta had become a full-fledged gun aficionado and he told Lisa that mercury would make bullets go faster. It is also fact, not speculation, that Steno's death was consistent with mercury poisoning.

Dr. Keith Wilson, author of *Cause of Death* (Writer's Digest Books), says that a small amount of mercury added to a person's food could, within thirty minutes, bring on symptoms such as those that Steno had: abdominal pain, shortness of breath, staggering, and confused thinking. Mercury poisoning, he says, could also lead to death within hours. "There would be no way to detect mercury poisoning without a blood test or an autopsy," Wilson says, "and death by mercury poisoning could certainly appear to be caused by an aneurism."

And it is fact, not speculation, that months later Kosta bragged to some of his unsavory friends that he had murdered Steno Paspalakis, his father-in-law.

4

Rambo

"I put in a deck of cards," Kosta said to Lisa as they were leaving the cemetery.

"Huh?"

"In the casket," he said. "I put in a deck of cards. You know. Because of how we used to always play cards, me and Dad."

"Oh, Kosta." She took his arm. Through it all he hadn't shown any emotion, but now she knew Kosta was hurting, too. Kosta had loved Steno, and if he hadn't been able to cry about it, then this gesture with the playing cards was his way of showing his love and his grief.

After Steno was buried the family began to put its life back in order. Lisa, along with Dino and Kosta, went back to work at Joyland and the gift shops. Mary, still deeply in mourning, sought the company of old friends, looking forward to lunchtimes and the evenings when she could cook for her family. It had been decided that Lisa and Kosta would stay with her and Dino in the house on Halifax, at least until they built a house of their own.

But healing would take a long time. Lisa's worst moment came several days after the funeral.

"When my father died I decided I was going to be strong," Lisa says. "I was going to pick out the coffin and it was going to be the best. I was going to make the arrangements. I was going to take care of my dad. And I did. I did everything that had to be done and I held up. But a few nights after the funeral I was in my bedroom with Kosta, and I just lost it. I totally fell apart. I was hysterical. I screamed. I cried. I was out of control. My whole body was heaving with grief. I went from the bed to the sofa to the floor. I lay on the floor wailing like a baby. And my husband, Kosta, stayed with me through every moment of that. He held me. He comforted me. He told me everything would be okay. Never was a man more kind and loving than Kosta was that night. I don't know how I would have gotten through it without him."

Kosta's sensitivity that night, and the feelings he had revealed by placing the deck of cards in Steno's coffin, went a long way toward making Lisa more hopeful about her marriage.

By November of 1987, when Steno died, the blush had left the rose. The marriage was not in crisis, but neither was it blissful. After two years of cohabitation, the inevitable personality differences had emerged. Kosta, who had been an enthusiastic partygoer when he was engaged, now balked at going out to socialize. Still dedicated to the family, he attended all family-related parties, weddings, and graduations. But if Lisa's friends—and she had many— wanted the couple to come over, have a few drinks, play some games, Kosta usually declined.

When he did attend a party, Kosta, who never drank, usually pooped out early. At most gatherings Kosta was horizontal by ten o'clock. Sacked out on the host's couch, he slept like the proverbial man with a clear conscience. He slept through gossip. He slept through laughter. He slept through arguments. In fact, Kosta became so notorious for his naps that when friends gathered to celebrate his birthday they gave him a big napping pillow as a gag present.

At other gatherings Kosta headed for the door early, leaving Lisa to fend for herself. While this habit annoyed Lisa, it was hardly grounds for divorce. Her marriage, as she saw it, was good, but not the romantic perfection she had hoped for. In other words, it was a typical marriage.

Kosta and Lisa went to movies. And occasionally they went out to dinner, though even that had its fractious moments.

"My idea of going out for dinner," Lisa says, "is you sit down, maybe have a drink, then you get an appetizer, smoke a cigarette, relax, talk for a while, then order dinner. Kosta thought of eating out as something you did because you were hungry. So we would get to the restaurant. I would order an appetizer and Kosta would make a face. 'An appetizer,' he would say. 'Well, sure,' I'd say. 'Let's just order,' Kosta would say, 'I came here to eat.' "

At home Lisa and Kosta watched TV together, mostly rented videos that they would play on the VCR. Kosta loved adventure movies, which was an interest that Lisa shared with him.

"But Kosta had terrible taste in movies," says his friend Peter Kouracos, who often watched films with Kosta and Lisa, and then stayed up late talking with Lisa long after Kosta had nodded off. "If you let Kosta pick out a film you'd end up with some awful B Kung Fu movie."

They watched comedies and police stories, but their favorites were the big adventure films. Lisa loved the Sylvester Stallone and Arnold Schwarzenegger flicks where everything got blown to hell and half the cast got scorched into oblivion. All that high-tech carnage was a vicarious thrill for a woman who couldn't stand to have a decimal point out of place. Often she wished she were the kind of person who could leave her office looking as if Sly and Arnold had just been through on a search-and-destroy mission.

Lisa was thankful that at least she didn't have shortstops and quarterbacks as rivals. Kosta was not much of a sports fan, though he did like football and would now and then watch a few quarters of a Buccaneers or Dolphins game with Dino on a Sunday afternoon.

By the beginning of 1987 Kosta had become less affectionate, less attentive. Gone were the kisses on the beach, the rush to pull out her chair for her. Gone was the jealousy of cousins who used to say, "Gee, you two are kissing all the time." The fire had cooled, and for that Lisa accepted half the blame. I could be a little more attentive, myself, she thought.

What energy Lisa withdrew from the marriage, she deposited in political action. It had become clear that the city's plan to "redevelop" the boardwalk was a poorly veiled threat to boardwalk businesspeople. The city was saying, "clean it up or we'll tear it down." And it was also obvious to boardwalk businesspeople that if they didn't get involved in the redevelopment they would get shafted by the city. So the Boardwalk Property Owners' Association had been formed, with Frank Goan as president, and Lisa as secretary and treasurer.

The secretary's job occupied much of Lisa's spare time, of which there was little to begin with. Hours that could have been spent curled up in front of the television with her husband, she spent going to meetings, sitting on committees, discussing redevelopment plans, and just generally lobbying for the interests of the boardwalk businesspeople. She became a well-known figure about town and there was talk of her maybe running for the city commission.

So by the time Steno died, Lisa had become "Miss Boardwalk," a protector of what Steno had left behind. Kosta, during this same time, had become "Rambo." And therein lay the acres of difference between them.

"Rambo" is what Lisa called Kosta, not to his face, but in her mind. "Rambo" was an affectionate way of looking at Kosta, a code word for what Lisa had learned to think

GARY PROVOST

of as the little boy in Kosta, the macho, adventurous, naïve, but nonetheless harmless, part of Kosta. Though Rambo got on her nerves sometimes, he was, on the whole, adorable.

Kosta was Rambo because he was infatuated with men's adventure, with survival techniques, with camping in the woods. He loved to read adventure comic books and survivalist magazines like *Soldier of Fortune* as well as gun magazines like *Guns and Ammo*. Kosta's idea of quiet time alone was decimating targets with a .44 Magnum pistol at the Strickland Shooting Range on Williamson Boulevard, west of Daytona, or shooting his Uzi submachine gun in the woods on the other side of the highway.

Though Lisa shared Kosta's love of adventure movies, that was as close as she was likely to come to being Mrs. Rambo. For one thing, Lisa had no use for the great outdoors.

"Kosta would ask me to go camping with him. 'What, are you, kidding,' I'd say. 'If there's no place for me to plug in a hair dryer I'm not interested.' 'Come on, you'll love it,' he'd say. 'Kosta, I'm afraid of bugs, I'm afraid of cats, and I'm afraid of dogs. And you want me to go out where there's bears? Forget it.' Kosta didn't press it, so I never knew if he really wanted me to go camping with him, or if he just knew I'd turn him down. He used to go out of town on gun shows, and I went with him to a few of those. But when he went camping or hunting I let him go alone. I didn't want to do those things but I couldn't ask him not to go just because I didn't want to. That wouldn't be right."

If Lisa wasn't going to march into the woods behind Kosta, she was at least going to make sure that he came back from them alive. Kosta, who always acted as if he were bulletproof, often wore a camouflage outfit to go camping. Lisa explained to him that he was nuts, but Kosta would always wave her off, "Ah, nobody is going to shoot me." When Lisa found out there was a law requiring a

50

hunter to wear a red vest, she bought the redest one she could find and presented it to her husband without a smile on her face.

"Wear this," she said.

When he left for subsequent hunting trips Kosta would slip into his vest, all the time grumbling like a little boy who was being forced to wear a hat and mittens to school. He complained about what worriers women were, but he wore the vest, at least until he was out of Lisa's sight.

Kosta's greatest passion was guns, something Lisa never understood. When she'd met him, he had owned one pistol, but after two years of marriage (and the acquisition of several credit cards) it seemed that Kosta owned enough lethal weapons to start an insurrection. Lisa had less interest in firearms than she did in sports, and when Kosta would start talking about Magnums and dumdums and impact velocity her eyes would glaze over.

Lisa could never keep an accurate count of just how many guns Kosta owned, because he was always buying, selling, trading, and borrowing guns. All she knew was that guns seemed to be everywhere. Kosta had a gun in the car. Kosta had a gun in the office. Kosta had guns under the bed.

"One time he was driving along," Lisa says, "and he had a gun on his lap, with his finger playing with the trigger. I said, 'Kosta, you want to have guns, okay, have guns. But not like that.' The gun was on his lap in his right hand and he was driving with his left hand. I said, 'Do you realize what could happen? What if you hit a car and the gun went off and shot the other driver. How would you explain in court that you were carrying a gun on your lap?' But Kosta just laughed. He acted like he was always in control, like he was invincible. A bullet wouldn't go through him, that's for sure; it would probably go around him it would be so scared. That's the impression you got. I think he did some of these things just to make me mad. He wouldn't argue with me. He'd just sit there. And he would never say 'I'm sorry.' I never heard him say, I'm sorry."

These oddities occurred within the context of a normal marriage, in which there was, says Lisa, "a lot of love." Kosta was a well-dressed, articulate man with a master's degree. He was still a man who brought flowers occasionally, who remembered small things, who took Lisa jet-skiing and for romantic walks on the beach. In his own way, he was thoughtful.

Lisa was a devout Rolling Stones fan, and once at a party somebody mentioned that the Stones were coming to Miami, but that all the tickets had been sold. Lisa was disappointed in a way that only a Stones fan who's been denied tickets can be. Mick Jagger's going to be *here*, and I'm not going to see him? Kosta, on his own, learned that the Stones also were playing Jacksonville on their tour. He came home, smiling devilishly, his hands behind his back. "I've got something for you, sweetheart." He presented Lisa with a ticket for the Stones concert in Jacksonville. Lisa was quite touched, though it did seem odd that Kosta had bought just one ticket. "Aren't you going?" she asked. "Nah, I don't like the Rolling Stones," Kosta said, as if it were the most common thing on earth for an attractive young woman to drive a hundred miles to go to a rock concert alone at night.

By the middle of 1987 Kosta was wearing a gun more often than most men wear a necktie. "For protection," he explained. Most people accepted easily the fact that Kosta packed a pistol. After all, he carried cash bank deposits in that briefcase.

When Florida passed a gun law that made having a concealed weapon illegal but an unconcealed one just fine, Kosta took to wearing a gun in a belt holster.

Lisa went through the roof.

"It's legal," he calmly explained.

Lisa, less calmly, explained that she was running a business and that customers could get a sudden desire to take

52

their quarters elsewhere if they saw some guy walking around Joyland with a gun strapped to his waist like Billy the Kid.

The notorious Florida gun law was soon rewritten anyhow, and Kosta went back to carrying his concealed gun in a shoulder holster under a sports jacket.

"He liked to let his sport jacket slip back so that people could see that he was carrying a gun," Dino says.

Though Lisa didn't care for guns, the fact that Kosta loved them was not a big deal. Certainly she didn't want one strapped to his hip or sitting on his lap while he drove, but except for those incidents she could live with firearms. Like many women, Lisa suspected that the only difference between men and boys was the price of their toys. Guns were Kosta's toys, and as long as he didn't own any illegally, as he assured her was the case, Lisa saw guns as a minor annoyance, not a major problem.

"My father hated the guns, though," she says. "He used to say to Kosta, 'What do you need a gun for,' and Kosta would say, 'For protection.' 'Protection from what?' 'What if someone jumped me,' Kosta would say. 'You yell at them, they'll go away,' Dad would tell him. It always worked for Dad. He was on the boardwalk all those years and he had never needed a gun for anything."

Kosta, reminding Lisa about his lover's lane incident with the Mexicans, convinced her she should have a gun. He took her to the shooting range on Strickland a few times, then he gave her a pistol.

"He told me I needed a gun to protect myself and he told me guns don't kill people, people kill people and all that. So I talked to other people who owned guns, people I respected, and I thought, okay, maybe Kosta's right. What if something were to happen in my office or in my car? So he gave me this thirty-eight and it had a safety on it and he says, 'Here let me show you how it works.' And he's explaining, 'Here's how the safety works, when this thing is red you can shoot it, and first you pull this little whatchamacallit.' So I said, 'Kosta, I don't want a gun where I have to remember all this. It's too complicated. If somebody tries to rob me he's not going to stand there and wait while I try to remember how to get this thing to work. Don't they make a gun anymore where you just shoot it?' And he says, 'Okay, I can get you a revolver.' So he got me two revolvers. One I kept in the office and one in the car."

While Lisa worried that she might be robbed, Kosta worried that he would not be robbed. When Lisa asked Kosta if he was afraid to carry money to the bank every day he said, "I'm not worried. I would love somebody to attack me," and he patted the gun that sat in the shoulder holster under his sports jacket. Kosta often made similar comments about the house. "I wish somebody would break in so I could shoot him," he said. Dino recalls another time, when Lisa was talking about the city's concern that the boardwalk was becoming a haven for lowlifes. Kosta said, "I know how to clean up the boardwalk. You take a few of those bums out in the woods and shoot them."

These comments were typical of Kosta and nobody took them seriously. Certainly not Lisa and Dino. Kosta had a dry sense of humor. He could make any number of absurd comments with a straight face. One local Daytona Beach bank teller recalls telling Kosta that she had just gotten a counterfeit hundred dollar bill. Kosta asked to see what it looked like. She handed it to him. He held it up for a moment, then smiled. "It must be one of mine," he joked, and they both had a good laugh over that.

Kosta's flirtations with danger sometimes hit close to home. One afternoon Lisa found a hand grenade on her dresser. She upbraided Kosta about it. "Kosta, are you crazy. A child could wander up here and play with this thing." But Kosta assured Lisa that it was not a live grenade, he knew about explosives, and there was nothing to worry about. In fact, he had several hand grenades.

Lisa preferred not to have an arsenal under her own roof,

so she was not troubled when she learned that Kosta was burying guns in the woods. Though it seemed an odd thing for him to do, she was relieved. Every weapon that Kosta buried in the woods was one less weapon in the basement, or under the bed, one less gun that could fall into the hands of a visiting child.

"I knew he was going into the woods and burying guns. I didn't know what else he was burying. You know how a little boy has a tree house and goes and sits there for hours on end? That's how I saw Kosta and his woods. He read comic books, he liked to be secretive. I just figured it was part of his antics. It was boyishness. He was just playing."

This business of burying things in the woods was a survivalist game with Kosta. He buried weapons one day, then came back another day to see if he could find them before an imagined enemy could get him. If Kosta had been alone in all of this advanced Boy Scout activity, perhaps it would have seemed more bizarre to his friends and relatives. But he was not. His cohort in the woods was Peter Kouracos.

Lisa had known Peter Kouracos almost all of her life. Peter, thirty-four, was a member at St. Demetrios. Kouracos was not the type of person you would expect to find crawling on his haunches through the woods with an assault rifle cradled in his arms. A bachelor, and sometimes a law student, Peter had been vice president of the Daytona Beach Young Republicans and had sat on several city boards, including the Daytona Beach Drug Related Nuisances Abatement Board. A Jaycee, Kouracos had been active in many political campaigns and had served as local administrator for Congressman Lou Frey. For many he was the model of the clean-cut, enthusiastic young public servant.

Peter was strongly attached to Kosta, and to Lisa. There were times when Peter would say, "Kosta, I'm stealing your wife," and he would take Lisa out for an evening.

Today he says that he and Lisa were "like brother and sister." For Lisa, that's putting too fine a point on it, but she does recall a good many late-night bull sessions with Peter.

If Peter Kouracos's connection to Lisa was less strong than he remembers it, his attachment to Kosta was perhaps stronger than he would now care to acknowledge.

"Peter used to call up all the time," Dino says, "and he'd ask for Kosta. I'd tell him Kosta isn't here. 'Well where is he?' Peter would say. 'I don't know, Peter.' 'Well, where was he last time you did know?' 'Peter, I don't know where he is,' I'd tell him. It got annoying sometimes."

Today Kouracos, who describes himself as "a survivalist," and "a populist, despite being a conservative Republican," says there was a good deal that Kosta kept from him. He says, for example, that he went with Kosta to bury things at least three times. But he has no idea of what those things were.

It was Kouracos that Lisa went to when the guns started to get to her.

"I asked Peter, I said, 'All these guns you and Kosta trade, that's all legal, right? I mean you're not doing anything that's going to get my husband thrown in jail.' 'Don't worry, Lisa,' he said, 'don't worry, I have a federal firearms license to buy and sell guns. Everything is legal.' "

While Lisa might have worried that Kosta's love affair with weapons was going to bring the police to her door, there were only two occasions when he really did have contact with the law. They were both minor, and only one involved a gun.

One occurred on a trip to Chicago.

"This was early in our relationship," Lisa says. "I had never even seen a gun, except on police officers. We drove from Florida to Chicago, and Kosta had a gun in the car, which seemed reasonable. I mean you're driving all alone that distance, something could happen. In Chicago we went to a restaurant and they had valet parking, so after dinner the guy got our car. He was going to be deputized or something the following Monday. Anyhow, I don't know if he searched the car or just saw the gun or what, but soon after we left the restaurant we were chased by a police car, with the siren and the lights flashing and everything. They ordered us out of the car and made us put our hands up. We were a well-dressed young couple driving a Porsche with Florida license plates, so I guess that meant drug smugglers to them. I was scared out of my mind. I almost lost it. I mean here they are handcuffing my poor husband and arresting him. He was charged with having a concealed weapon. Kosta had to go back six months later for the trial. It was his first offense, so they gave him probation."

The other incident occurred one night when Lisa, Kosta, and Peter Kouracos went to the Daytona Jai Alai arena.

"The three of us went to Jai Alai. We all went up to make bets. Peter and I went back to our seats. We were sitting there through the whole game and Kosta didn't come back. Where could he be? After the game we walked out to look for him. He's coming toward us from the parking lot. 'Where did you go?' I said. 'I had a counterfeit hundred-dollar bill,' he said, 'and I had to give it to the police.' I said, 'Where did you get that?' 'Probably from the store,' he said. That's not unusual, in a place like Joyland you're bound to get some phonys. So that was the end of it. Kosta had to give up his hundred-dollar bill, but the cop told him he could deduct it from his income tax."

Though all of the things Kosta did in the woods, and in the workshop, which he had built in the basement, were legal, as far as Lisa knew, some of the things he proposed to do were not. One night, for example, Kosta let it slip that he had a plan that would make them a million dollars.

"A million dollars huh?" Lisa teased. "If you've got a plan that will make us a million dollars, it's got to be illegal."

Kosta smiled. He loved it when she was wrong and he was right. "It's not illegal."

"Then what is it?"

"I can't tell you."

"You can't tell me. You've got a plan that will make us a million dollars but you can't tell me."

"I can't tell you right now," Kosta explained. "I can't tell you until you have a need to know."

"A need to know? Like in the CIA?" Lisa asked.

"Yes," Kosta said.

Lisa sighed. Kosta was such a little boy. She loved him for it, but sometimes it was exasperating because he took himself so seriously.

A few weeks passed before Lisa heard the whole story.

As Kosta explained it, he knew a guy who was a big wheel in the Nigerian government and this guy was receiving kickbacks in gold and diamonds.

"So he needs to get the gold out of there," Kosta said. "You can't just take ten million dollars in gold and ship it out, you know. The place is under military control. My friend confided all this to me and he wants me to smuggle the gold out for him."

Lisa tried not to howl with laughter. She knew Kosta could take a ribbing, but outright ridicule might hurt his feelings. "You're going to smuggle it out?" Lisa said. "Kosta, what do you know about smuggling?"

Kosta smiled slyly. "More than you think," he said. "More than you think. I'm going to rent a sailboat in Europe and sail it to Africa, I'll get the gold and sell it and come back to America. I get ten percent. That's a million bucks."

"Are you nuts?" Lisa said. There was always a part of her that was afraid that Kosta really had gotten into something and would act out one of these fantasies. "When you get the gold in the sailboat they are going to shoot you and dump you in the Pacific Ocean."

"Nigeria is on the Atlantic Ocean," Kosta said, as if that

proved that he was entirely right and Lisa was entirely wrong.

"Well, whichever ocean it's on, they'll dump you in it. And if they don't, you better not come back to me. I told you a long time ago I won't have a husband who cheats on me and I won't have one who does anything illegal."

"It's not illegal," Kosta said.

"Right," Lisa said. "Well it's one thing to have you going into the woods and possibly getting shot by a hunter, but if you think I'm going to sit and have you go to Nigeria while I hope and pray that you get back in one piece you're crazy."

Lisa and Kosta had many conversations like this and they were, for the most part, good-natured. Kosta would explain some scheme, Lisa would tell him he was nuts, then she would worry that her husband was serious this time. Kosta would smile, as if he had secret knowledge that Lisa would never understand, and that would be the end of it. Lisa would end up shouting sometimes, but Kosta was always unruffled.

Though Kosta never did go to Nigeria, there was one mysterious European trip that Lisa did allow him.

One night in June of 1987, five months before Steno's death, Kosta told Lisa that he was going to Italy in two days.

"What are you talking about, you're going to Italy?" Lisa said. "You just walk in and announce you're going to Italy. Why are you going to Italy?"

"My grandfather's money," Kosta said. "He's got four hundred thousand dollars in a Swiss bank. And he's going to let me have it so I can start my own business."

Lisa was skeptical. Kosta explained that under Greek law citizens were only allowed to carry out a small amount of money. "Doesn't matter how long you're going away for. You could come to America for a year, and they would still only let you take about two hundred and fifty dollars," he said.

"So?"

"So everybody in Greece sneaks money out of the country. They put it in foreign banks. Swiss, mostly."

"And your grandfather has done that?"

"Yes," Kosta said.

"Four hundred thousand dollars?"

"Yes."

"And he's going to give it to you?"

"Yes. He's an old man, he doesn't need that money."

Lisa was uncertain. The part about people sneaking money out of the country was believable. She had heard that before. But she had been to Greece and had met Kosta's people. Most of them were potato farmers. They owned many potato fields, and they would sell the potatoes at various markets around Athens. It seemed unlikely to Lisa that someone could squirrel away four hundred thousand dollars from selling potatoes. On the other hand, she had been to their home, a handsome two-storied house in Tripoli outside of Athens, and though it was modest by American standards, she had to admit it was quite fancy for Greece. Still. Four hundred thousand dollars.

"Kosta, for God's sake," she said, "your people are potato farmers. They don't have that kind of money."

Kosta smiled. "Yes, they do." Then he patted her face, took her by the hand and led her to the couch, where he explained carefully. "Lisa, you know how people walk by a business, maybe on the boardwalk, and they think this guy is making maybe a hundred dollars a day, but because we know the business we can see that he might be making five thousand. Well, it's the same thing. Potato farmers in Greece make a lot of money when they own a lot of fields, like my grandfather does. If you're not in the business you wouldn't know that. Also, he has bought and sold land and made money at that."

Kosta's logic seemed reasonable. After all, Lisa thought, what do I know about potato farming? Maybe there is big money in it.

Lisa still doubted Kosta's story, not because it wasn't plausible, but because she was sure Kosta was really sneaking off someplace to cheat on her. He wasn't going to Europe at all, he was going someplace to be with a woman. So she hounded him, kept asking questions, thinking she would trip him up.

"Where are you going exactly?"

"Zurich."

"Well, why are you going to Italy first?"

"I've got to meet my sister Merca there and your cousin Sotirios, we'll drive up from Italy."

Kosta told Lisa that he had to meet his sister Merca, who lived in Greece, because there were two keys to the safe-deposit box containing the grandfather's money. He had one key, Merca had the other. The story sounded a little dramatic, but not impossible. And the idea of Merca being with Kosta was comforting. Certainly Kosta wouldn't be cheating on Lisa if his sister were around.

However, the presence of Lisa's cousin Sotirios was not so reassuring. Lisa didn't know why her husband was meeting her cousin in Italy, but she knew that her cousin was not a good influence on her husband. Her cousin Sotirios, to her mind, was a bum. He was supposed to be attending school but seemed always to be traveling all over the world. There was something a bit shady about him. He had money with no apparent source. Once Lisa had heard her cousin tell another male relative, "If you want to cheat on your wife, make sure you wear a rubber," and she knew this was not the sort of man she wanted to be paling around with her husband. When Sotirios had come to Florida to visit, it seemed that he and Kosta spent all their time gambling. They had gone to Jai Alai every day in Daytona Beach, and when the Daytona fronton was closed they drove to Jai Alai in Melbourne on Florida's famous Space Coast. Lisa's cousin was the kind of guy who could play poker from morning to night, and he wasn't shy about asking Kosta to join him. Sotirios was, she had often said, a man without scruples.

Still, the more Lisa thought about it, the more absurd it seemed, to think that Kosta would go all the way to Europe and meet with his sister and Lisa's cousin just so he could screw around with another woman. Furthermore, he would have to come home with four hundred thousand dollars. She realized she was just being paranoid. So when the day came, she drove Kosta to the airport in Orlando, kissed him good-bye, said, "You'd better come home with money," and then drove home so she could start worrying.

Lisa did not tell her friends what was up. She told everybody that Kosta had gone to Chicago for a graduation. She would wait to see this miraculous four hundred thousand bucks before she started crowing about it.

Kosta, who was only gone for three days, called every day. He put Merca on the phone, so Lisa knew that her sister-in-law really was with him.

While Kosta was gone, Lisa and Dino went to a lawyer. Lisa was fairly certain that you couldn't just dump four hundred thousand dollars into a suitcase and send it through airport baggage. Kosta would need to convert the money into a bank check or money order or something. The lawyer told her what needed to be done, and she dutifully passed on the information to Kosta when he called.

When Kosta came back from Europe he was, apparently, empty-handed. "It didn't work out," he explained tersely. "They said my grandfather was supposed to be there, too."

Kosta seemed reluctant to donate more details, so Lisa let the matter drop. Because of the phone calls she was fairly sure that Kosta had not been shacking up with another female, and that's what really mattered. Still, she thought, that's the last time he goes off without me.

5

Funny Money

The details concerning Kosta Fotopoulos's involvement with counterfeit currency are not as accessible as those concerning his other crimes. Dealing in counterfeit money is a federal offense and it comes under the purview of the Secret Service, an organization not known for its loquacity.

However, documents on file at the federal court in Orlando, Florida, along with the statements of witnesses, provide a fairly vivid picture of the counterfeit money operation, one aspect of Kosta's secret life.

In June of 1987 when Kosta told Lisa that he was flying to Milan, Italy, to meet his sister Merca and pull four hundred thousand dollars of his grandfather's money out of a Swiss bank, Lisa need not have worried that her husband was going to meet a girlfriend. Kosta did go to Milan. There he purchased a thousand counterfeit U.S. hundred-dollar bills, for twenty cents on the dollar. The seller, allegedly, was none other than Sotirios, Lisa's cousin. Where Kosta got the twenty thousand dollars to pay for the funny money can only be imagined.

According to the Secret Service, Kosta actually had some counterfeit bills before he went to Milan. This was money he had gotten from Lisa's cousin Sotirios. Perhaps it was a sample, of sorts, so that Kosta could experiment with passing it. On April 23, when he passed a fake bill at Chess King, a men's clothing store in North Daytona Beach, the bill was discovered but Kosta was not detained. Presumably, during this time he was passing a lot of other bills that were not detected.

Kosta's friend Peter Kouracos also saw Kosta with counterfeit bills before the Milan trip.

"Kosta and Sotirios came to me all excited about the counterfeit the cousin had brought from Europe," Kouracos says. Kouracos describes Sotirios as "the serpent who first came into the garden and tempted Kosta to eat the apple."

"But what could I do?" Kouracos says. "Call the police and tell them my friend is passing counterfeit money?"

When Kosta got back from Milan in June and explained to his wife that he was empty-handed, he had in fact acquired the hundred thousand dollars in counterfeit money, which he would eventually bury in the woods off John Anderson Drive.

The role of Peter Kouracos in all of this is difficult to discuss. The federal jury that heard charges against Kouracos acquitted him.

Kouracos does, however, admit to a rather strange scenario in which he went along while Kosta buried things in the woods at night and Kouracos never asked Kosta what he was burying.

As Kouracos tells the story he drove Kosta three times to a deserted area along John Anderson Drive on the west side of Daytona Beach. On one occasion Kosta had a big vinyl bag. On the others, a metal cannister.

"We would drive along in the dark and at some point Kosta would tell me to stop. He didn't seem to be watching for any marker or counting telephone poles or anything like that. Kosta would get out of the car and tell me to come back in a half hour or forty-five minutes. I would drive around for a while, and when I came back he would be there waiting for me on the road."

While Kouracos's story does not go down easily, it is no less credible than a good many other stories that would be told after the world learned that Kosta Fotopoulos was a murderous sociopath.

Less mysterious than Kouracos's role in the counterfeiting scam is the role played by Vasilios and Barbara Markantonakis, a couple that worked for Lisa at Joyland.

Vasilios, who is known as "Bill," and Barbara Markantonakis, were hired by Steno to work at Joyland in 1987. Steno met the two at a restaurant where Kosta once worked, but Lisa and Dino aren't sure who knew who first. In any case, Steno liked to help out fellow countrymen who were down on their luck, so Barbara was put to work giving out prizes and making change in the back of the arcade.

Bill, who did free-lance house renovations when he could, started out doing carpentry and painting at Joyland, and when there was no such work left, he was given an apron and a job making change.

"Barbara was one of the best workers I ever had," Lisa says, "but Bill drove me nuts sometimes. He'd come down and tell me exactly how he was going to fix something. I'm going to take off *all* this paint and I'm going to put down a *thin* layer of this, and then I'm going to *put down tar* and I'm going to take off this and put on that. And he would go on and on, telling me every detail of what he was going to do. But he wouldn't always do it. He was not the most reliable guy."

Bill was eventually relieved of his apron, but he still hung around Joyland, where he did odd jobs. He also spent a lot of time going to gun shows with Kosta. Bill, who was in his fifties and the father of a small boy, thought Kosta was the greatest guy in the world. He used to call him the Golden Child.

"Kosta and Bill went to a lot of gun shows," Lisa says. "Tampa, Miami, Fort Lauderdale. They would buy and sell and trade guns at these shows. He and Bill would usually stay overnight. When I asked Kosta why he was going to so many gun shows he would say, 'I'm doing it for Bill. The guns are Bill's. He needs the money, but he doesn't know a lot about guns.' "

Lisa asked many times if everything was on the up and up, and was assured just as often that everything was legal with the guns. However, she had her doubts when Bill Markantonakis came to her one day and said, "Don't you worry, Lisa, I have a floorboard," and he told her about a secret compartment under the floor of his car, where he could carry twenty or thirty guns.

She went to Kosta.

"Kosta, I thought you told me everything was legal with these guns you trade."

"It is," Kosta said.

"It is? Well then how come this guy has a floorboard?"

"Oh, Lisa," Kosta said.

" 'Oh, Lisa?' Never mind 'oh, Lisa.' If everything you're doing is legal, then why do you have to hide guns under the floor?"

"Honey," Kosta said. He patted her cheek. "Think about it. You've gone to gun shows with me, you know what I do there. But this guy, Bill, he's trying to make a few extra bucks, you know, selling guns. It's not against the law, but if you were a police officer and you stopped someone for a traffic ticket and you saw thirty guns, what would you think?"

Kosta's explanation, as usual, made sense. Lisa pushed the incident from her mind, and had no further reason to suspect Bill, and certainly not Barbara, of being a criminal.

But Kosta knew otherwise. In the autumn of 1987 Kosta sent Bill and Barbara to Georgia, South Carolina, Alabama, all over the South to pass the funny money in convenience stores, race tracks, supermarkets, and restaurants. According to the Secret Service, Bill and Barbara were allowed to keep half the profits on the money they passed.

The Secret Service also says that Peter Kouracos was brought into the scheme and was paid a thousand dollars to help pass the counterfeit bills.

During this time Kosta hid his counterfeit money, or at least part of it, in a military ammunition can at the North Peninsula State Recreation area in North Daytona Beach. Whether he buried this on one of his nocturnal trips with Kouracos, or by himself, is open to speculation.

On March 18, 1988, the counterfeit scheme began to unravel when Barbara Markantonakis was caught passing a fake hundred-dollar bill at the Gateway Supermarket in Gray, Georgia. Bill and Barbara were picked up. Bill, who speaks little English, took a lie detector test, and the couple was released, pending indictment. Bill and Barbara went back to Daytona Beach.

Kosta was not at ease with the idea of Bill and Barbara going to trial. He decided to do something about it. According to the feds, Kosta and Peter Kouracos took Bill for a ride one night in January, 1989.

As Michael Pritchard, a special agent with the Secret Service's Jacksonville office, tells it, both Peter Kouracos and Kosta were armed. This is not surprising. Kosta and Peter were the kind of guys who strap on a gun to go buy a loaf of bread at the Winn-Dixie. They took Bill for a drive out near the Volusia Mall. They asked him about his lie detector test and his conversations with the Secret Service.

Bill swore that he had told the feds nothing about Kosta.

"We know everything that went on during the polygraph test," Kosta told Bill. "The Greek interpreter was a friend of ours."

"Nothing," Bill said. "I told them nothing about you."

"Do you know what would happen if you had squealed?" Kosta asked him.

"Nothing," Bill said. "I said nothing about you."

"You would be dead," Kosta said.

According to the Secret Service, once Kosta and Peter were convinced that Bill had kept his mouth shut, they shook hands with him and told him that he was an okay guy.

Bill and Barbara were indicted in the Middle District Court of Georgia, and on January 25, 1989, they were arrested by the Secret Service. They went before a magistrate and were released on bond.

Bill called Kosta and told him that he was worried because too many people knew about Kosta's connection with counterfeit. (Though Kosta's involvement with counterfeit was still unknown to the police and his friends and family, by this time he had begun to acquire a good many lowly acquaintances and many of them knew what he was up to.) Bill assured Kosta that he would not talk, but said he was worried that others would, and wanted to know what he should do.

Kosta, according to the Secret Service, gave Bill a hundred bucks and told him to buy a suitcase. "This is never going to court," he said. "You're taking a trip."

"To where?" Bill asked.

"Home," Kosta said. "Greece."

Kosta told Bill to pack, bring his wife and son, Angelone, and meet Kosta that night in the parking lot of the Circus Gift Shop, a business owned by Lisa on A1A. "I'll give you five thousand dollars," he told Bill. "You'll fly to Greece."

Bill and the family pulled up in their van that night. Kosta was waiting in the empty parking lot. Kosta carried a two-way radio with him, and he checked with his cohort on the other end to make sure that the Markantonakises had not been followed and that the Secret Service had not set a trap. The voice on the other end told him that everything was okay. The voice, according to Bill, was that of Peter Kouracos. Bill says that when Kouracos called Kosta back to see if everything was okay, Kosta said, "Everything is okay, Pete."

Once Kosta felt safe, he gave Bill an envelope containing $4,800 and told him to drive to New York and fly out of JFK.

"Once you get to Greece there will be more money," Kosta said. He told Bill the money would be channeled through Mercina.

"Oh, one other thing," Kosta said.

"What is that?"

"If you do not stay in Greece your son will be killed. And your wife's parents, they might have an accident."

The Markantonakises understandably were afraid that they might not even make it to New York. Bill certainly knew Kosta to be a dangerous man. In fact, Bill says that Kosta once offered him money to murder Mary Paspalakis, an offer that Bill turned down. After the meeting at the Circus parking lot, Bill, Barbara, and Angelone went to Barbara's parents' house. According to the couple, when they got to the house they saw a car, which they believed to be Peter Kouracos's. They knew they were being followed.

Barbara's father agreed to drive the family to New York the next day.

Around the time they were crossing the Florida-Georgia line, they say, a car with Kosta and another person passed them. Kosta beeped his horn several times, then exited in front of them. Kosta, apparently, had followed them out of town to make sure they were obeying his orders.

In Greece there were at least three transactions that the Secret Service knows of, in which Kosta got money to the Markantonakises through his sister. But when the money stopped coming, Bill and Barbara were reduced to poverty.

During this period Dino Paspalakis received a call from Bill in Greece, which seemed absurd at the time.

"Bill is not a guy you can depend on for the truth," Dino says. "He called up and said that Kosta was planning to kill me and my sister and my mother. It was such a ridiculous thing to say. I was at Joyland and I told Lisa and Kosta and we all had a good laugh about that."

Bill and Barbara yearned to return to America. They drummed up enough money for air fare, probably from relatives, and they flew from Athens to Montreal. From Canada they came across the border into Syracuse, New York, and there they moved in with Barbara's sister.

Bill called Kosta from Syracuse. He told Kosta that he and Barbara were back in the country. Kosta was not pleased, but he sent Bill some fake ID and a phony Social Security card in the name of James Stanley Dill. He told Bill that more documents would be coming so that Bill could take on a new identity. He also sent five hundred bucks.

On September 12, 1989, Secret Service agents caught up with Bill and Barbara and arrested them. In time this arrest would lead the feds to Kosta and he would be charged with dealing in counterfeit money. But by that time, a charge of counterfeiting would be the least of his problems.

6

Top Shots

Atlantic Avenue, a section of route A1A that runs the length of Daytona Beach, is the easternmost thoroughfare in the city. If you are a tourist coming into town by air, bus, train, or highway, you will drive through the more urban sections of Daytona Beach, past the shopping malls and auto repair shops and Kentucky Fried Chicken franchises, across the Halifax River, and continue to Atlantic Avenue, because that's probably where your hotel room is. When you reach Atlantic you've reached the beach.

Atlantic is like the main drag of any heavily populated beach resort in the south: an infinity of hotels and motels, all of them done up in cupcake colors, mostly pink or mint or white. They have names like Tropical Seas and Tropical Winds, Ocean Breeze and Ocean View, Surf this, Palm that, Coral something, and Sandy whatever.

As you drive up Atlantic toward Ormond Beach, or down Atlantic toward Daytona Beach Shores, the signs flash by: Color Cable TV, Heated Pool, Efficiencies Available, Unique Family Resort, Jacuzzis, Family Restaurant, Large Balconies, Bikers Welcome, Vacancy. Restaurants, lounges, and gift shops fill in the gaps between hotels, and

71

here and there you'll find a little mall with a supermarket or hardware store, proof that the area does have permanent residents who eat in and sometimes need nails.

One thing Atlantic Avenue and Daytona Beach did not have until recently was a convention center. In the early eighties the city of Daytona Beach, feeling the need for such a facility, seized a parcel of land on Atlantic Avenue across the street from the north end of the boardwalk. A meeting and exhibition complex called Ocean Center was built there. To go along with Ocean Center the city wanted a fine new hotel that was suitable for conventions. Daytona Beach hotels were, for the most part, old and small. The city wanted something big and classy, the kind of place that could charge $140 a night and still draw a crowd.

Daytona Beach laws allowed the city to grab land under eminent domain and turn it over to private developers, such as mall builders or hotel chains, if the land was "blighted," a catchall term that, one might imagine, could be deciphered to suit the needs of politicians and developers.

The coquina area, which is the carnival booth section between Joyland and the bandshell, was declared blighted. It was torn down and in its place construction was begun on the Marriott resort complex—seventeen stories, two pools, health club, restaurants, meeting rooms, the works.

To Lisa and other boardwalk businessmen, the writing was on the wall. As they saw it, the city had ruthless disregard for the fact that people had put their lives into the boardwalk. Big hotels meant conventions. Conventions meant money. On the scale of things a thousand Shriners counted for a lot more than a few second-generation Greeks. The coquina area had been an appetizer. The boardwalk, if the developers had their way, would be dinner.

"They've got it worked out very nicely," Lisa told Kosta one night in the office. "Let's say you're a hotel builder and you want to build a hotel in a certain area and you come to the city and you say, I want to build a hotel, but I don't want to deal with every one of those little people in their houses. So the city says okay, we understand, we are the city and we have the right of eminent domain and under our redevelopment provisions this is a blighted area, it's a public nuisance, so we'll get rid of it, then we'll turn it over to you so you can build a hotel."

Things were perhaps not that simple, but they sometimes felt that way to Lisa and the other businesspeople on the boardwalk. By the time the Marriott was up and running, it was clear that the city had its eye on the rest of the boardwalk. The police had cleaned up the area that now was the Marriott, but many of the bums they had rushed had taken up residence on the boardwalk. Late at night there were teenagers dealing drugs outside of Krystal's hamburgers, and by one A.M. finding a hooker on the boardwalk was easier than finding a taxicab on Atlantic Avenue. Clearly, the city fathers were watching all this with an eye to the future. Like children waiting for Christmas they were counting the days until the boardwalk decayed into something that could reasonably be labeled "blight." The boardwalk, after all, was oceanfront property, and nothing fills a resort hotel faster than the sound of waves out back.

The Boardwalk Property Owners' Association had been formed to prevent that day from ever coming. And that is why Lisa, in her role of secretary, had become a highly visible spokeswoman for the campaign to save the boardwalk. After long hours in Joyland she drove to city meetings, or to meetings with developers. She raised her voice. She circulated petitions throughout the area, where there was a good deal of sentimental attachment to the boardwalk among people who had gone there as children. Her picture often appeared in the newspaper.

"My father was the last person to buy boardwalk property, in 1969," she told the papers. "And he didn't buy it as an investment. He bought Joyland because he saw a vision of something he could pass on to his children. Joyland was his life. And there are many others just like him. These boardwalk businesses represent people's lives. Some family businesses have been here for fifty years. You can't just come in and cut them down like a bunch of trees."

The Property Owners' Association decided it could win over its detractors not with the vinegar of resistance, but with the honey of cooperation. They made more of an effort to keep riffraff out of their establishments. They got the police to redouble their efforts at night. Before long the area got too hot for the dope dealers. The hookers headed across the river to Ridgewood Avenue. The bums found shelters away from the beach. The boardwalk was again relatively free of lowlifes. Blight, it seemed, had been cut off at the pass.

Still, with powerful forces like Hyatt, Omni, Marriott, and Sheraton all salivating for the boardwalk property, Lisa and the others knew they would have to come up with something more. They devised a plan whereby a hotel would be built behind the boardwalk. Since the new hotel would tower over the one-storied arcades and snack bars it would still be an oceanfront hotel. Furthermore the association would hire an architect and redevelop the boardwalk with an overall theme that was consistent with the architecture and theme of whatever hotel was built there.

By winter of 1989 it looked as though the flies had been caught with honey, and that the danger to the boardwalk had passed. Lisa got excited just thinking about the boardwalk's revitalization, its return to old glories. The new plan, if it passed, would be good for everybody's business. There would be no further erosion in the number of families and small children who ate hot dogs and played games on the boardwalk.

And then something happened to threaten the recovery. A man wanted to open a business that could give the boardwalk one more nudge toward "blight" and extinction. And what's worse, the man was Lisa's husband.

At the south end of the boardwalk there had been a Sound Trax recording studio, where visitors to Daytona Beach could swivel their hips and sing like Elvis or shout out their impression of Whitney Houston, and cut a record of their own. In early 1989 the studio moved out and the location became available for rent. Kosta decided that he wanted to open a pool hall with a bar at that location.

"A pool hall?" Lisa said when he told her. She couldn't believe it. Kosta had about as much investment sense as a loan officer at a Texas savings and loan, and would probably get eaten for lunch in any business. But a pool hall. It was the single worst idea she could imagine. She was, after all, Miss Save-the-Boardwalk, and a pool hall—with a bar, no less—pretty much symbolized everything that had put the boardwalk in jeopardy.

This pool hall, which he wanted to call Top Shots, would be Kosta's second venture into business. In October of 1988 he and Dominick, a machine mechanic at Joyland, had formed ABC Vending Company, to place video games in bars and restaurants around Daytona Beach. (Kosta had gone first to Dino with that idea, but Dino, with similar plans for his own future, chose not to go into business with Kosta.) One of the locations where Kosta placed video games was a pub in south Daytona owned by a man named Vincent Speziale.

Kosta and Vinnie, a tall, manly Italian with dark wavy hair and a lot of jewelry, became quite friendly. Kosta would come by every week to split up the money from the machines, and he stopped in almost every day for lunch, sometimes bringing Lisa with him. The Speziales and the Fotopouloses became friends. Though it was clear to Vinnie right from the beginning that Kosta was a bullshit artist, he found Kosta kind of likeable, and Kosta's tales, which were always toned down when Lisa was around, were entertaining.

"He said he was a commando assassin and he had been trained by the army in Greece," Speziale says. "He was constantly carrying a weapon and he wanted people to see it. He would purposely cock his jacket back so people could see it."

Kosta, who neither smoked nor drank, would stay at Vinnie's place shooting the breeze until all hours of the night. ABC Vending failed after a few months, but when Kosta got this idea about a pool hall he approached Speziale, who agreed to go in on it with him as a one-third partner, along with Dominick.

Lisa was torn. She knew how badly Kosta wanted a business of his own, how it diminished his pride to have a wife earning most of the money. "Greek men are not macho, but they are chauvinistic," says Father Nick. And Lisa did want Kosta to find a business that was right for him. She knew that pool had become the favorite trendy sport of yuppies lately, but they were interested in real full-size pool tables in classy surroundings. What Kosta proposed was really a cramped little bar that would have four or five small coin-operated pool tables. It would attract all the wrong people. It was unthinkable. It was almost as if Kosta had gone out and said, "Let me see, what kind of business would really piss Lisa off?"

Long before it was a reality, Top Shots became for Kosta and Lisa a presence in the marriage, more powerful than any pregnant ex-girlfriend.

Lisa insisted he not open the business. "You can start another business," she said. "You can open a pool hall over on Ridgewood, near where you used to live, that's where all the bums are anyway."

But Kosta dug in his heels. "You just don't understand," he told her. "I know what I'm doing. You'll see."

The tension between Lisa and Kosta about the pool hall came to a head one night when Lisa and Kosta were having dinner at the Speziale house in South Daytona with Vinnie and his wife, Elena.

Over eggplant parmigiana and red wine (none for Kosta) Kosta went on at great length about his love of pool halls and his plans for the business. It would be the kind of place where friends could meet, shoot a little pool, talk about sports, have a beer. And with him around most of the time—he patted the pistol—nobody would get out of line. He would let no bums, no dope pushers, no whores hang around. The boardwalk would be just like Lisa wanted. Respectable.

"And I'll be nearby for Lisa, if she needs me," he explained.

"I've tried to convince Kosta that pool halls attract the worst kind of people. Lowlifes," Lisa said after dinner. She knew she was swimming against the tide. After all, Vinnie was a partner in the pool hall. "I mean I know there are family pool halls, with tangerine felt on the tables and all that. But they're in bowling alleys in the suburbs, not bars."

She waited for some agreement, but none was forthcoming. "It's not right," she said lamely. She didn't know what to do with her hands. It was one of those moments when she desperately wanted a cigarette, but didn't need to deal with Kosta's disapproval on top of everything else.

"This is for families," Kosta insisted. "People on vacation with their kids."

"Is that why you've got a liquor license?" Lisa said. She was trying to remain cool, but this thing was really bugging her. It was such a slap in the face, after all her work for the Association. "Is that what the bar is for, the kids?"

"*You* serve beer and wine," Kosta said in his own defense.

"Yes. I also serve hot dogs and hamburgers and French fries. You can't compare the two."

"Don't worry, don't worry."

"Well, I am worried." Ah, the hell with it, she thought. She pulled a pack of cigarettes out of her pocketbook and lit one. "This," she said, "is not a good investment. It will attract the wrong element."

"Says who? You?"

"Yes, me. I've been working for four years to make the boardwalk a place we can be proud of again. Now there's a pool hall coming in so the bums will have a place to hang out. And who's bringing it? My own husband."

The Top Shots issue led to a big fight that night at the Speziales, though Lisa and Kosta had such different styles of arguing that it is deceptive to say they fought. When it came to strong disagreements Lisa was fire and Kosta was ice. Lisa would raise her voice, wave her arms. Her heart would race, her hands would shake, and she would try most of all to be heard, to communicate. Kosta, on the other hand, would fight not with words, but with the silences between the words. He would be at first stubborn, paternalistic, righteous. He made it clear that he knew better than anybody else. He was smarter, braver, more clever. Facts were beside the point. Opinions he didn't agree with were held by idiots. Regulations, rules, and even laws were made for others, not for him. And if none of this led to persuasion he would not raise his voice or stamp his feet. He would simply clam up. And when it was over, he would never, ever say "I'm sorry."

Kosta certainly was not to be swayed on this pool hall thing. He needed about eighteen thousand dollars to get Top Shots going. He put up six thousand dollars, and so did Vinnie and Dominick. Long before the first rack of billiard balls was ever broken, the partnership was troubled.

"They were supposed to remodel it and do this and that to it," Vinnie Speziale says. "And they were supposed to open up May the first. Then they half did everything. They tried to do stuff without getting licenses. Kosta, not Dominick. Dominick would try to do it, and Kosta would say, 'I'll take over all this deal.' And he was going to do this without getting a license and he knew this person, trying to circumnavigate the whole system, which wound up getting fines and all this kind of stuff."

Once Lisa saw that the opening of Top Shots on the boardwalk was a certainty on the horizon she made the best of it. If she couldn't talk Kosta out of this lunatic idea, she would at least encourage him to create the classy operation that he said he wanted. She suggested colors, floor plans, music. She gave him as much accounting advice as he would accept, and urged him to acquire the proper licenses, fill out the proper forms, send in the proper fees.

Even if Lisa didn't care for Kosta's plan, it was nice to see him happy. He would have his own place. He could strut around, be a big shot, the way he'd always wanted.

To celebrate this truce the couple went to Montreal for a short vacation. It was May of 1989, but Top Shots was not yet ready to be opened. In Montreal Lisa and Kosta visited the Basilica of Queen Mary of the World, Mount Royal, and the Château de Ramezay. They rode in a carriage, they ate in fine restaurants. More and more the irritant of Top Shots was receding from Lisa's mind. When they got back to Daytona something happened to push the pool hall even further from her thoughts.

She found out she was pregnant.

"I was ecstatic," she says. "We were both so happy. Kosta would be a daddy, everything would be great. He was excited. I was excited. I loved Kosta more than ever. We both wanted to have this baby."

Though the prospect of having a child filled Lisa with joy, the joy was not untainted. Kosta was hard to read. He hugged her often during the first weeks of the pregnancy, and told her how happy he was about the baby. But she was never certain that he *felt* the happiness. So often, when it came to feelings, Kosta seemed like an actor who was only reading his lines. He never showed emotion in a way that was convincing. Once, when Kosta's father was ill in Greece, Lisa and her family had called Athens every day. How's he doing? Does he need anything? Our prayers are with you. But Kosta never called to see how his dad was. Kosta, aren't you worried about your father? Nah, he'll be okay, if anything happens they'll call me.

To Lisa, this detachment seemed all the more strange in

a Greek man. Her father had been able to gush emotion without inhibition. Her brother could cry easily. Her male cousins and the uncles could all express love and fear and anger and sadness. But not Kosta. Kosta was a machine.

With a baby on the way, these thoughts were particularly unwelcome, so Lisa pushed them from her mind, as she always had. Kosta's just a very calm, stable person, she thought, the strong silent type, like Clint Eastwood. She reminded herself of those mournful moments when Kosta had so nobly comforted her. If he couldn't show emotion, at least he understood it in others, she thought. When she wasn't at Joyland she busied herself with baby magazines and plans for a nursery.

Opening day for Top Shots was to be June 25, 1989, and Lisa dreaded it. As hard as she tried, it was difficult to imagine young well-dressed yuppie businessmen driving over to Top Shots to talk about the baseball scores after a day in the office on the other side of the Halifax River. It was equally hard to see mom and dad from Charleston bringing the kids into Top Shots to shoot pool while the parents threw back a few brews at the bar. No matter how many times she envisioned the Top Shots picture in her mind it always faded into a scene where thugs, hustlers, hookers, and scam artists hung out, swilling beer out of the bottle and eyeing the tourists for an easy mark. Because of this, and because she was pregnant and didn't feel well, Lisa delayed her first look inside the pool hall.

But Dino and his cousin went to Top Shots the first night, and what they found was Lisa's nightmare.

"We went there to play a game of pool," Dino says. "It was a bad crowd, a bunch of drifters and bums. I felt very uncomfortable. We left, went over to McDonald's. I kept saying to my cousin, I can't believe what was there, and he kept teasing me about all the bums. When I told Lisa, she pitched a fit over it. And I couldn't sleep that night, it bothered me so much. The next day I went to the Owners' Association and I complained about the pool hall. Actually,

I guess it was more of an apology than a complaint. After all, it was owned by my own brother-in-law."

When Lisa did take a stroll over to Top Shots, on June 29, a Thursday, what she saw was not much different from what she had imagined. The customers crowded into the small, boxy pool hall, were not all felons, of course. There were vacationers stopping in for a beer, nicely dressed college kids shooting pool, even people she knew, like Peter Kouracos. She sat at the bar for a while talking to Peter and keeping one eye on the clientele. A couple of rough-looking kids with tattoos came in, and when they said "fuck this" and "screw that" nobody rushed to tell them they couldn't talk that way in here. Later there was a girl named Dixie whose skirt was not only short, but it was also purple and leather. She asked Lisa if she'd seen a guy name Stanley—she didn't know his last name—who was supposed to meet her here.

What was worse, Kosta, the big shot businessman preening and schmoozing, seemed to like his customers, and they liked him. In thirty-five years of working on the boardwalk, Lisa's father had never gotten to know any of the boardwalk people, except business owners. But four days after opening the pool hall, it seemed Kosta knew every hooker, every crack addict, and every loser who blew into town.

The next day Lisa started to miscarry.

"I had gone down to see the place. I went home and started to miscarry," she says. "I had to stay in bed for a week. And Kosta was never there. He was at Top Shots all day and all night long. Here I was going to have his first baby. I wanted this baby. And no Kosta. Dino was around and calling me all the time, and Mom of course was always with me. But I wanted my husband. I told him, 'You don't care.' I said, 'I know there's nothing you could do, but at least you could come here and hold my hand.' I called him up at Top Shots. 'It's twelve o'clock at night,' I said. 'Can't you come home?' He said, 'I need to stay here and take care of the business.' 'I might lose our baby,' I said. I was scared.

"Then I lost the baby.

"Kosta's attitude was, 'Well, we'll have another.' He was upset about it, but not to the point where you'd think it really affected him."

After the miscarriage, Kosta spent almost all of his time at Top Shots, or so it seemed to Lisa. He would go to Joyland in the morning. Lisa would arrive at ten-thirty. Kosta would leave to make the bank deposit and that, usually, was all she saw of him until after midnight.

While it seemed to Lisa that Kosta was spending too much time at Top Shots, it seemed to Vinnie that Kosta was not around enough.

Speziale recalls, "After we opened the business and I saw the way that things were going, I wasn't very happy with Kosta's selection of people that he had in there. I wasn't very happy with this and that, his bookkeeping methods, his not keeping receipts, and always, you know, saying, I need more money, I need more money. I said, 'Hey, you know, this thing's getting a little bit old for me.' I have to leave and close my business and then go down to that business and close it down."

By the end of July, Kosta's friend Angelo had bought out Vinnie's and Dominick's interest in Top Shots for the same six thousand dollars each they had invested. Vinnie later was reinstated as partner, in return for managing the place when Kosta was not around.

When Lisa recovered from the miscarriage she went back to work at Joyland. Often during the day she would walk down to Top Shots to see how Kosta was doing. Kosta tried to appease her. He promised her he would keep a closer eye on things. He even threw out a couple of troublemakers and told them if they came back they would be killed. Such threats were typical of Kosta. Honest people never took them seriously. (Though by this time there were

Top Shots regulars who knew that Kosta was a dangerous man.)

Despite all that had happened, Lisa was very much in love with her husband. Sometimes she would go to the bar and tug on his arm, asking him to take a break for a walk on the beach with her. They would walk to the end of the boardwalk and down the ramp that led cars onto the beach. To the shore they would go, where the sand was softer and cars were not allowed. Lisa would walk barefoot, holding her sandals in her hand. Kosta would point to the hotels, talk about how he might like to buy one someday. The love of the ocean was something they had always shared, and as they walked along the edge of it, Kosta would take her hand. Would he do that if he didn't love me, she wondered. Would he come home to me every night if he didn't love me? It was a question that had always been there, but lately it rose more often to the surface of her thoughts. Does Kosta really love me? She was never quite sure. On the beach she and Kosta would talk about the baby they would someday have, never the one they had lost, and the house of their own in Ormond Beach, which Lisa's uncle began building for them in July. These were hopeful moments for Lisa, and with Kosta's arm around her, she told herself that Top Shots would not be such a problem after all. But the mood was often shattered when she and Kosta would head back, and as they walked along the boardwalk, young women wearing too much makeup would drive by and shout, "Hi, Kosta, how ya doing, Kosta?"

During this period Lisa was partly guilty of Kosta's great sin: she didn't show what she was feeling. In the summer of 1986, when she and Kosta had visited Greece, she had lost her beloved grandmother. Then in November of 1987, her father had died. And now it was 1989 and she had lost her baby. Though Lisa was quick to scream and shout in an argument and could get almost hysterical in situations like the arrest in Chicago, she was also the type to hold in her deepest, most painful feelings. The sadness she was feeling in the summer and autumn of 1989 was something that she shared only with her younger brother Dino, her closest confidant. Dino was something beyond a brother and a friend. He was like her second self. But no one else really knew that Lisa was hurting. Certainly she had bawled and bawled when she lost her baby, but wnen she got back to work at Joyland that was the end of the sobbing. She stood straight, she worked hard. She was, for all the world to see, a woman in control of her life.

As bad as things were, they were about to get worse.

On October 18, Lisa was driving along Seabreeze Boulevard when she noticed that a pickup truck behind her seemed to be out of control. She swerved off the road and avoided being hit by the truck. The truck screeched to a halt and ended up on the side of the road in front of her.

"I remember the boy driving the truck looked real shook up and I thought I ought to get out of my car and see how he is," she says. "After I started driving I thought again maybe I ought to turn around and see how he is. But there were lots of other cars around, so I figured he'd be okay. At this time I had a brake light that was broken on my car and I'd been asking Kosta to fix it. That was unusual, for me to have to nag him about it, because usually Kosta was good about changing my oil and doing things on the car. Anything that was a man's job he would take care of."

Lisa didn't know that it is an old private detective's trick to break one rear light on the back of a target's car because it's so much easier to follow a car at night when it's the only one with a single rear light.

On the afternoon of October 25 Lisa was in another auto accident. "I was sitting at a light," she says. "It took forever to change. When it finally did change, I just went. I didn't look both ways. I just went. This guy in a pickup truck ran into me. He was towing a sailboat and he had another guy with him. I stopped the car to get out and look at the damage. There wasn't much. But I thought,

Gee, this is weird, two incidents with pickup trucks in seven days. The guy from the pickup truck was a young guy, kind of hefty, but not fat. He said, 'Come here let's talk about it.' He motioned me to get on the main street. I got in my car and made a U-turn to get it out of the road, and when I got out of my car again the guy was gone. I thought that was awfully strange. I went to the boardwalk and told a couple of the cops I knew there. I was shaking and crying. They told me to calm down and go to Joyland. I told Kosta what had happened and he held me in his arms and told me everything was okay."

The two accidents were frightening, so Kosta and Lisa turned it into a running gag. They had seen a movie in which all the villains were in Volkswagens. Now the joke became that all pickup trucks were out to get Lisa. "Lookout, Lisa, it's a pickup truck," Kosta said when they went out to eat later that afternoon. Lisa made a face and ducked, and the two of them had a good laugh.

The laughter stopped, however, that night at about seven o'clock when Lisa Fotopoulos got the phone call that every wife dreads.

7

Deidre

Only Kosta Fotopoulos knows for sure when he decided to kill his wife. Maybe it was the day he met Lisa and realized that she was the heir to about three million dollars in assets. Maybe it was the day he concluded incorrectly that her death would bring him half of seven hundred thousand dollars in insurance money. Maybe it was much later. In any case, before the summer of 1989 it appears that Kosta had achieved a delicate balance between his sociopathic *willingness* to murder his wife, on the one hand, and the fact that he didn't particularly *need* to kill her, on the other. But in the summer of 1989 something came into his life to throw that balance out of whack. Her name was Deidre Hunt.

Deidre Michelle Hunt, the twenty-year-old woman who would become Kosta Fotopoulos's primary agent for murder, was born in 1969 in South Weymouth, Massachusetts, south of Boston. Her mother, Carol Hunt, was then twenty-two, and it might have been best if she hadn't had a baby. For one thing, Carol was not married to Deidre's father, a man who had less interest in his daughter than he did in the art of Japanese finger painting. For another,

Carol was a mental case, and she was unable to get through even the first day at home without punishing her baby for crying.

"Deidre wouldn't stop crying, so I slammed her down in the crib," Carol says. "She was only a few days old."

Carol Hunt prayed day and night for the strength to nurture her baby with tenderness. But strength did not come. She brutalized the baby often.

"I knew in the back of my mind that I always resented Deidre. I would say Deidre suffered a terribly rejected childhood. That's an understatement."

If Carol Hunt had deliberately tried to create a sociopath she could not have done a better job than she did. Certainly Levin's "profound disruption" and "lack of bonding" are descriptions of Deidre's infancy.

The guilt Carol felt over this abusiveness led her several times to the brink of suicide. There was at least one bona fide suicide attempt. In particularly dark and desperate moments, Carol hatched bizarre plans to do away with herself, her daughter, and her son, Carl, who was born two years after Deidre.

Carol, who is now forty-three years old and stable, after decades of therapy, says, "It seemed to me we'd be better off not in this world."

Deidre must have felt the same way. She reports that she was using drugs and alcohol by the time she was in the second grade.

Deidre Hunt's father lived in nearby towns when Deidre was growing up. But, according to Deidre, who is also known as "Dee," he steadfastly refused to spend time with his daughter. In fact, by Deidre's own reckoning, much of the chaos of her life has resulted from inappropriate attempts to capture the father's love that she never had.

"Not having my father love me was the worst thing I could imagine," Deidre says now. "I became obsessed with getting my father's love."

As a kid, Deidre resented the men her mother dated.

"If I couldn't have my father's love, I wanted to choose the man who would love me as his little girl," she says. "I didn't want my mother choosing that person for me."

As a small child Deidre wore braces on her feet to correct a leg problem, and for many years after that she wore braces on her teeth. She felt homely and unloved. When the braces were removed she was delighted, surprised, and confused to realize that suddenly boys wanted to be with her. Whether the boys really felt differently about a girl without braces, or whether Deidre suddenly allowed herself to be attractive is hard to say, but no doubt she learned that when it comes to attracting men, being pretty is better than not being pretty.

Deidre was precocious and she was flirtatious. When she was nine she came home wearing a boy's ring. Her mother made her take it off. But boys were not the problem. Men were. Even at an early age Deidre attracted the attention of grown men. It was not the sort of attention she craved. When she was eleven she was raped by a neighbor. But her mother never reported it. "I just couldn't deal with it," Carol Hunt says now. When Deidre was twelve she was almost raped again, and she was stabbed in the attempt. But fearing that her mother would again do nothing, Deidre kept her secret to herself.

"And when I was fourteen a guy who lived nearby left his wife and kids because he was in love with me," Deidre says. "I mean I hardly even knew this guy. He was obsessed with me and it came as a complete surprise."

By the time she was a young woman Deidre was quite pretty. She was the kind of girl every boy gets a crush on, with big brown eyes and long brown hair and a lithe young body that could dance up a frenzy. But when she sent out her strong sexual signals she sent them in every direction. She was the kind of girl who could make a man feel like God one day and shit the next. Not just a pretty face, she was also bright, and quite talented with a pencil and sketch pad. She had a great facility for working numbers in her head. She was a reader, too, mostly of romance and adventure novels. She liked the outdoors, fishing, camping. Her dream: to open her own bar.

The obsession with her father's love did not dissipate as Deidre grew. Once, in the seventh grade, another girl told Deidre about her mother's "wonderful new boyfriend." The boyfriend turned out to be Deidre's father, and Deidre was crushed.

"That," she says now, "is when I really just hated him."

Deidre says that once in a bar she tossed a beer can in her father's face, and another time she got several of her friends to beat him up.

Deidre passed through this crucible for the most part without professional help. When she'd been in the second grade, Deidre, Carol, and Carl went into family therapy, but when Deidre attacked her brother while acting out her anger toward her father, the therapy was brought to an end. Over the years there were other attempts at therapy, but no program that was long enough or successful enough to pull her off the self-destructive path she was on.

"One psychiatrist told me I was a sociopath," she says. "But that doesn't make sense to me. I cry a lot. I have feelings."

Not surprisingly, Deidre came in conflict with the law at an early age. When she was twelve she was arrested for breaking into a house with another girl and several older boys.

By the time Deidre was in the ninth grade Carol had taken the children and moved to Goffstown, New Hampshire, where Deidre, deeply depressed, dropped out of school.

Soon Deidre was on her own. She started hanging around the streets of Boston. She worked a short stint as a hooker, then she worked the phones for a drug dealer. She lived on the streets, camped out at friends' houses. Still just a kid, she was headed, it seemed, for an early demise.

One brush with the law came when Deidre told the

police that two men with knives had kidnapped her and another girl, taken them to New York, and sexually abused them. Deidre flunked a lie detector test and police concluded that she had gone willingly with her alleged kidnappers. For filing a false police report she was fined a hundred bucks.

When Deidre's dope pusher boss got in trouble with the mob, Deidre headed north, back to New Hampshire, and for a while it looked as if she might emerge from the darkness into a somewhat sunnier existence. She hooked up with a new boyfriend, Kenny Adams. It was a unique relationship, inasmuch as Kenny was the only fellow she'd ever had who didn't beat her. Carol Hunt started dating Kenny's father, and before long the two couples set off for Florida to begin life fresh. It was a time, says Carol Hunt, "when everything was going to be roses."

But the roses were not to bloom. Kenny's father and Carol couldn't say no to booze and cocaine. Deidre, who also had a problem with 'no's, got pregnant and had a miscarriage. Then Kenny's father was killed in a truck accident. Carol retreated into a pit of depression. Kenny joined the air force. And Deidre and Carol went back to New Hampshire, this time to Manchester.

Deidre, already toughened by a life of disappointment, hardened. Apparently filled with self-loathing, she sought out relationships with men who would mistreat her. By this time she was quite promiscuous. She knew what to give men and they knew what to take.

"A lot of times I slept with a guy just to avoid the hassle of him trying to talk me into it," she says.

She was preoccupied with her looks, her makeup, her clothes. Hungry for a love that she could never seem to get, she became a sexual adventurer, and she did not confine her sexual adventures to the opposite sex. Deidre became a bit of a cult figure for the other street kids along Elm Street in Manchester's "combat zone." The kids would scream her name in the night when she cruised by with one of her boyfriends. "That," Deidre says now, "was fun."

Carol Hunt, living in a housing project where Deidre stayed with her off and on, and dwelling in her own world of booze and despair, was oblivious to the fact that Deidre was free-falling into a sordid life of drugs, booze, bisexuality, and crime.

In 1987 Deidre became friends with Bridget Riccio, another street girl, who was a year younger than she was. It was, says Riccio, "a sick friendship." Riccio remembers that Deidre enjoyed playing with guns, that she made vague boasts about having committed murders. Riccio recalls Deidre Hunt saying to her, "After the first shot it gets easier."

"Once when I was thinking of committing suicide," Riccio says, "Deidre offered to shoot me."

Deidre and Riccio were part of a group of kids that Catherine Divine, an assistant county attorney in New Hampshire, calls "amoral." "That group," Divine says, "had no values, no idea at all about the consequences of their actions."

On July 5, 1987, Deidre and Bridget Riccio walked up to Veronica Rudzinski, a twenty-nine-year-old woman who was waiting in her car for a friend in Manchester's Derryfield Park. One of the girls shot Rudzinski four times with a .25 caliber pistol. (Deidre and Bridget each claim the other pulled the trigger.) The victim did not die, and Deidre did only six months in jail because she made a deal to testify against her friend. (Ironically, Bridget didn't do any time at all, because Rudzinski did not identify her at the trial.) In jail Deidre went through drug and alcohol rehabilitation programs, and when she got out in June of 1988, she proudly greeted her family wearing a pink satin dress. After that Deidre tried again to save her own life. She did some waitressing. She enrolled in a school of cosmetology in Manchester. But before long Deidre, who was easily dominated, had taken another imperfect man into her life.

91

His name was Anthony Pfaff, and she met him on Elm Street on her twentieth birthday, February 9, 1989. Pfaff brought Deidre two cases of beer and some marijuana to celebrate. When she asked him where he got the money he said that it came from a tax refund. But the real source of the money, according to Manchester police, was far more significant, at least in the light of later events.

The police say that Pfaff's money was part of a five-thousand-dollar payoff from a man named Kenneth Johnson, who allegedly hired Pfaff to murder his wife. Pfaff, Johnson, and another man have been charged with the murder. Specifically, police allege that Johnson's two hired assassins killed Johnson's pregnant wife at a construction site while Johnson watched and taunted his wife as she died. Deidre is not suspected of being involved in that murder.

The next brute in Deidre's life, after Pfaff, was a young man named Larry Tarle. It was a typical Deidre Hunt romance. She loved him. He beat her.

Deidre got pregnant by Larry Tarle and, according to her, Tarle beat her until she miscarried. This, however, was no reason to stop loving him, and when Tarle split for Daytona Beach in the summer of 1989, Deidre went running after him.

In Daytona Beach Deidre took up with Tarle again. But before long they drifted into the old patterns, and Deidre broke off with him. She left him, she says, "with no hard feelings."

Soon Deidre was dating Newman Taylor, Jr., known around the Daytona boardwalk as "J. R." J. R., a good-looking young man with a strong body and big tattoos on his forearms, was a street kid like herself. He had come down from West Virginia "for spring break," he says, and "to party," and had stayed.

"At first Deidre didn't like me," J. R. says, "because I beat up some guy right in front of her. But then we got to know each other and we liked each other and before long I was fucking her."

J. R., who fancies himself a ladies' man, didn't let his relationship with Deidre stop him from seeing other ladies. Nor did Deidre shy away from other men. She got a job as a barmaid at Top Shots. It was there that she lobbied for tips in her bikini, blatantly rattling her tip jar in the faces of customers who forgot her. It was there that her magnetic personality drew all sorts of characters to the boardwalk establishment and Deidre became, in the words of one Daytona Beach cop, "some strange type of role model, sleazy but alluring." And it was there that Vinnie Speziale, who hired Deidre, introduced her to Kosta Fotopoulos.

The Kosta that Deidre Hunt met at Top Shots was quite a different character from the sometimes daffy and adorable Rambo that Lisa Fotopoulos slept with every night.

"I met Kosta around the end of July, beginning of August," Deidre says. "It wasn't a heavy relationship at first, we were just friends. We went wave running and we went a few places and he bought me some clothes, then we ended up sleeping together."

In a matter of weeks after her arrival in Florida Deidre learned more about Kosta Fotopoulos than Lisa had learned in four years. Deidre learned that Kosta was a pimp, a counterfeiter, a sadist, a car thief, an arms smuggler, and a murderer. Most of all, she learned that Kosta, the funny guy who fell asleep on couches when he went to parties with his wife, was an extremely dangerous person. These, apparently, were the qualities she looked for in a fellow, because she quickly fell in love with him. She was smitten with Kosta, and she was thrilled when he told her he loved her also. To her Kosta was a classy guy. He was handsome, he was a sharp dresser, and he drove a BMW. Before long Kosta was in and J. R. was out. But, typical of Deidre, she and J. R. remained friends.

In Deidre Hunt, Kosta had found a young woman who

was beautiful, a good lay, and, perhaps most important, one who thought that he was a big wheel. Around the boardwalk Kosta had cultivated the idea that he was the one who had money and owned property, not his wife, and this fabrication went down quite easily with Deidre, as it did with the boardwalk bums. They were people who believed in money. If a guy wore a nice suit and drove a fancy car, then he was somebody. It was that simple.

In Deidre, Kosta had found an adoring young woman who would listen to his heroic tales, who would bat her beautiful brown eyes in admiration and never express a doubt. He showed her his guns and she cooed. He told her about an armored car robbery he was planning, and she marveled. He asked her if she might be interested in laundering counterfeit money, and she said, "Sure."

It's not surprising that Kosta would fall for Deidre. She was not just pretty and sexual and naïve. She was also someone who didn't mind getting whipped now and then. She was someone with whom he could express a dark side of himself, a side that Lisa and Dino and all of their friends, and all of the Greek aunts and cousins and nephews, had never seen. Deidre Hunt was someone that Kosta could torture.

Kosta Fotopoulos had what Jack Levin, the criminologist at Northeastern, would call "a sadistic need." And, being a sociopath, he lacked the inhibiting influence of conscience. After the romance had faded from their relationship, Deidre would tell the world that Kosta had tortured her in a variety of ways. He beat her, she said: he burned cigarettes on her breasts, he shot knives at her feet, he put a gun to her head, and he threatened to kill her and have her stuffed. "This," she says, "is a very sick person."

If Kosta is the kettle, then Deidre is the pot calling him black. Teja James, one of their boardwalk acquaintances, recalls, "Deidre wanted me to kill six kittens that were in her yard. She wanted me to put them in a sack and shoot them. She said they were getting all over everything in the house." James also reports that Deidre once wanted to get a gun and stalk a man who had stolen a pair of sunglasses from her, and another man who had insulted her on the boardwalk.

So this Kosta-Deidre thing was not a healthy relationship, but if Deidre had any complaints about her new honey back in July and August, she kept them to herself. By all accounts she was in awe of Kosta.

"He used to tell me, 'You have to know about all this survival stuff,' " Deidre says. "He said it was good to know about guns. He took me shooting a couple of times. He shot an AK47 in front of my face one day. He shot it right out the window of the beamer with a silencer on it one day, shot it into the trees. Another time he took me shooting at night out by the state park where he and Peter Kouracos used to go shooting."

Kosta also told Deidre that he had been trained by an Israeli terrorist group.

"Six months of training," he said. "Severe training. Once I had to sit underground, under camouflage for four days without moving, me and another assassin. That's the kind of training we did."

He told Deidre he would teach her how to swallow her tongue to kill herself if she were ever captured and tortured and couldn't take any more pain. Another time he lit a cigarette and placed it on his forearm and left it there for five minutes while he talked to her. "This is not hard," he explained. "This is easy."

Kosta also told Deidre that he was connected to the CIA.

One day in the BMW Deidre noticed an envelope from the CIA. It was addressed to Kosta. (Most likely the envelope from Washington contained a form letter rejecting him for a job. In June of 1988 Kosta had applied for a job with the CIA, like thousands of other crackpots, and had been rejected.) Deidre was impressed. To her the CIA envelope was just further proof that Kosta was quite a guy.

"Are you in the CIA?" Deidre asked him.

"No," he said. "But I do jobs for them."

"What kind of jobs?"

"Personnel elimination," he said. "Contracts. Hits."

He explained to Deidre that a CIA contact would call him on the phone. "I might not even know who is calling," he said. "They'll ask me if I want to do a job for a certain amount of money, but they won't tell me anything about the job until I accept it. They might say if it's hard or easy. I can usually tell from the price range, anyhow. If I say no, it goes no further."

"And what if you tell them yes?" Deidre asked.

"Then they send me a package that tells me everything I need to know. Once they send me a package I have to do it. There's no backing out."

Kosta also showed Deidre a number of checks, allegedly CIA payments for assassinations, though it is hard to imagine the CIA issuing a payroll check "to Kosta Fotopoulos for murdering John Doe."

Kosta also told Deidre that he treated his wife wonderfully. He told Deidre about the flowers, the presents. "I am," he said, "the perfect husband."

In August of 1989, Kosta set up Deidre in a room at the Casa Del Mar hotel for a week. For the first few days at the hotel Deidre was available for sex with both Kosta and a male friend of his. However, as Kosta became more possessive of Deidre, the friend was edged out.

Deidre's first assignment, according to her boardwalk acquaintances, was to recruit teenage hookers, who Kosta could set up as "dates" with men at Top Shots.

After the Casa Del Mar, Kosta put Deidre up in a house owned by a friend of his on South A1A. Then he moved her to an apartment on Schulte Avenue, then to a house on Lenox.

The reason for the frequent moves was that no sooner would Deidre move in than she would have a group of friends over for dope and sex parties. Kosta, who did not smoke, drink, or do drugs, did not like having all these people around Deidre, and whenever he moved her he warned her not to give out the address.

While Kosta said the drugs were okay, he told Deidre that having sex with another man was not. Soon it was well established among the boardwalk lowlifes that if you got in bed with Deidre Hunt you risked getting a bullet in the head.

J. R., who continued to see Deidre and occasionally sleep with her after they broke up, recalls one incident when Deidre was staying in the apartment on Schulte Avenue in Daytona Beach Shores.

"Me and this guy named Rich was at Dee's. My girl-friend, Gail, was in the bedroom asleep. We had been up all night partying. Early in the morning Kosta pulled up and we didn't have time to run out the side door to the garage so we went and headed into the bedroom and hid in a closet.

"Well I thought I locked the door but I didn't, and this time Kosta wanted to search the house. So he came into the bedroom and he opened the closet door. He whipped out a gun and stuck it to Rich's head and he said, 'Have you been fucking Dee?' And Rich said no. And Kosta said, 'What are you doing here then, boy?' Rich said, 'We was partying.' When he said 'we' Kosta seen me where I was ducked down underneath these clothes, and he took a shot at me. He missed, and the bullet went into the floor, but I don't think he meant to miss. Then he put the gun to my throat and he said, 'J. R., look, just tell me one thing, are you fucking Dee?' I said, 'No, I've got a girlfriend in there,' and he said, 'Look, you can tell me the truth, you had her before I did.' And I said, 'No, I'm not fucking her, Kosta.' So he let me up. And I walked in and I said, 'That's my girlfriend, Dee's not my girlfriend.' I said we were just here partying, and he didn't say no more. But he wasn't kidding around. If Kosta had thought I was fucking Dee he would have killed me for sure."

The other girl who was in the apartment recalls Deidre's

reaction to the incident. Deidre, she says, was happy and excited. She was flattered that Kosta would shoot somebody out of jealousy for her. After Kosta had gone she said to the others, "Oh, it's lucky for you that I was here. If I wasn't here he would have killed you all. But I was here and I would be a witness, so he didn't."

When Kosta was sure he could trust Deidre he told her that he had killed eight people and he wanted to initiate her into the Hunters and Killers Club. The club was a group of assassins and various operatives who did what he called "political jobs." To get in you had to murder somebody and have it videotaped. The videotape would be kept by another member as blackmail to prevent you from turning in any other members of the H and K Club. In turn, you would receive the videotape of a murder being committed by the other member.

(No evidence has since surfaced to indicate that the H and K Club existed anywhere outside of Kosta's imagination. Perhaps he got the idea from some of his guns that were made by Heckler and Kote and known as H&K's.)

If Deidre was at all skeptical about this H and K business, she was probably persuaded when Kosta made her watch a film of him torturing another man who was tied to a chair. Though this tape has never been found, Deidre is probably telling the truth about it. Torturing somebody and videotaping it is certainly consistent with what we now know about Kosta Fotopoulos. Also, there is at least one other person who says he saw tapes and films that were meant to be kept secret.

Gus Moamis, who at twenty-four was one of the oldest of the boardwalk habitués, recalls:

"I walked into Dee's house one day. When I walked in the front door they [Kosta and Deidre] were watching this movie. All I caught was a quick glance of somebody shooting somebody and then Kosta flipped the tape off real quick and he got all over me; shit about me being there, what the hell was I doing in the house and why didn't I

knock and like that. Kosta had a rule, where Dee was staying you weren't allowed. To be there you had to be there
while Kosta wasn't there.

"The next morning I was over there and Dee had a box,
a little steel box, it was pushed under the bed. When I
come into the room she had the box opened because I had
bought her—well, let's just say I had bought her a toy—
and I was getting ready to go through the tapes and she
slammed the box real quick on me and locked it. It had a
lock on it and she pushed it back under the bed. The next
time I seen that box it went from her to Lori, [Lori Henderson, Deidre's friend and lover] and then it went to Kosta.
I never seen it no more but I believe there were more tapes
than just that one."

No one but Kosta knows what happened to the man
being tortured in Kosta's film, or how many others met a
similar fate. J. R., for one, has a rather grim view of the
possibilities.

"There were a lot of kids disappearing from that boardwalk," J. R. says, "maybe one a week. I think Kosta might
have been taking them in the woods and shooting them."

While J. R.'s comment is an eerie echo of Kosta's joke to
Dino about cleaning up the boardwalk by "taking a few
bums into the woods and shooting them," there is no evidence that this was happening. Certainly there were kids
who would hang out on the boardwalk for a few weeks
and then disappear, but that is to be expected among such
a transient population.

While Kosta was violently jealous of any man who slept
with Deidre, he apparently was not threatened by having
his friend Peter Kouracos go out with her. In fact, he
encouraged it.

Kouracos took Deidre out twice. He says he did not single her out or have any special attraction to her.

"I didn't have anybody else to take out," he says, "and
Kosta made it clear that she was available."

The first time Peter took Deidre out it was primary night

for the local elections. To Deidre, the street kid and high school dropout, this must have seemed like pretty heady company. Kouracos, after all, was a good-looking guy, bright and articulate, whose large vocabulary made conversations more interesting. He was always well groomed and well dressed, favoring three-piece suits. Furthermore, Peter was plugged into the local power source. He had worked in several local Republican campaigns, and among his friends he counted city commissioners and State Attorney John Tanner, for whom Kouracos had once worked as an unpaid aide. To Deidre's eye, Kouracos must certainly have seemed like a fellow who could have squired any number of young ladies about town, but he had chosen her.

Kouracos, who was licensed as a firearm dealer, told Deidre that he had met Kosta at an International House of Pancakes, where Kosta had been introduced to him as a fellow gun enthusiast. Kouracos took Kosta outside and showed him a new shotgun, and before long they were fast friends. "I was an usher at their wedding," he told her.

Kouracos and Deidre went first to City Hall to watch the vote count come in, and it was there that Kouracos observed what he would regard as Deidre's finest quality: her ability to do arithmetic quickly in her head. As the votes came in from different areas Deidre was able to immediately move them to the correct columns in her head and call out the totals for each candidate.

"She had an incredible facility for juggling numbers in her head, and counting votes," Kouracos says.

Later they went to a party at the home of City Commissioner Bud Asher. Asher and his wife, Dawn, were taken with Deidre, who had worn an alluring new dress for the occasion. Later, the Ashers told Peter that Deidre had been the life of the party.

Peter wasn't so sure. Just before the couple left the Asher home that night, Deidre did something to embarrass Kour-

acos in front of his friends. Dawn Asher had bought dozens of submarine sandwiches at The Subway for the party.
Now, as the party wound down, Deidre asked if she could
take home the leftovers. Dawn Asher told her she could.
"Great. I'll cut them up into smaller pieces and sell them
for a buck each at Top Shots," Deidre announced. Peter
turned red. Later, Deidre told him that she had been only
kidding. But Peter thinks she was serious. Kouracos says
he didn't want to take Deidre out again.

But he did take her out, this time for the general election.
He took her, he says, because she was good with numbers.

If Deidre Hunt had taken a minor role in the lives of
Daytona's establishment Republicans, she had during that
same strange autumn of 1989 been cast as leading lady,
opposite Kosta Fotopoulos, in an unfolding drama that was
complicated enough to make any soap opera seem like *Ses-
ame Street*. The people in Deidre's new social circle smoked
crack, sniffed cocaine, swapped sex partners, passed counterfeit money, blew up automobiles, mugged tourists, burglarized motel rooms, sold guns, bragged about murders,
engaged in sex-booze-drug orgies, and got drunk on a regular basis. They were this girl's new boyfriend, that boy's
ex-girlfriend, guys who had run away from home, girls on
probation, cell mates, and lovers. Some of them had jobs
and obeyed most laws. Others were hookers, dope dealers,
thieves, and con artists. And what seems most surprising,
until you stop and think about it, is that they were for the
most part children. Few of them were over twenty-one.

But Jack Levin says we should not be surprised that most
of the criminals who hung out on the boardwalk were kids.

"Adolescence is a period of rebellion," Levin says, "and
at the extremes you find a lot of teenagers who turn our
mainstream values on their head. We had beatniks, hip-
pies, the counterculture, punks, and now we've got skin-
heads. Their reason for being is to rebel against peace,
harmony, brotherhood, and love. You could argue that
almost every teenager is a sociopath, but only for a few

years. The teens are violence-prone years. Teenagers commit the majority of violent crimes."

Levin has both good news and bad news.

The good news: "Most adult criminals have had juvenile records, but most juvenile offenders don't continue to be adult criminals."

The bad news: "Teenage crime is a growing problem in America and I think we have to blame the baby boomers. During the early seventies all the emphasis was on telling your kids that excessive guilt was bad. Look up the psychology books of that period. Almost all of them advise people to be assertive and not feel guilty when doing the wrong thing. Some people on the edge might view that as a license to kill. We might have created a few more sociopaths."

In the beginning all these kids, the ones who were sociopaths and the ones who weren't, liked Deidre.

"She was like a hero to us," one of them says.

Deidre, who was known on the boardwalk as "Cherri," was a fun girl, a regular spark plug. And she was a good dancer. During this time Deidre had plenty of money, which she got from Kosta, and it was money that she gladly shared with her friends. People who know Deidre will tell you she is a generous kid, always quick with a favor or a few bucks if a friend needs it.

Among Deidre's new Daytona friends, in addition to J. R., were:

Mike Cox, age eighteen, whose real name was Matthew Eugene Chumbley, and who was known as "Matt." Matt was down from his home state of Kentucky, where he had spent time in correctional schools for being a runaway and committing thefts.

Mark Kevin Ramsey, eighteen, worked for Kosta at Top Shots. Kevin had sidelines, though. Among them: drugs, prostitutes, blackmail.

Yvonne Lori Henderson, seventeen, known as "Lori,"

was Deidre's lesbian lover and constant companion during the summer of 1989.

Teja Mzimmia James, seventeen, known as Teja, or "T. J.," was Lori's black boyfriend, an expert on explosives.

Bryan Chase, eighteen. Bryan Chase, who lived with his father and stepmother in Daytona Beach, had a job and no police record. He was, according to his friends and folks, "a nice kid."

There were dozens of others, characters like: Peaches and Tiger, hookers; Rick, described by one friend as "a truly great car thief"; and Joey Tat (short for "Tattoo"), who told everybody on the boardwalk that he was an undercover cop, which gives you an idea of how bright he was.

So it was in this world, among these people, that Kosta lived out his secret life, bragged of his exploits with the CIA, made elaborate plans for heists, and plotted murder.

For a long time Kosta got away with dealing in counterfeit money, with running prostitutes, with insurance fraud, and with crimes far more hideous, not because he so carefully hid the truth, but because the truth was so farfetched. The fact is that Kosta told dozens of people what he was up to. The people who believed him were not the sort who would go to the police. And the people who would go to the police didn't believe him. They were like the bank teller who thought Kosta was so funny when he looked at the counterfeit hundred she showed him and said, "Must be one of mine."

Vinnie Speziale, for example, thought little of it when he and Kosta used to sit at the bar at Top Shots and sketch out elaborate plans for robberies.

"I heard him say things like, 'I'm going to plan an armed robbery.' He wanted to rob McDonald's, wanted to knock over armored cars. Okay? But this was the same gentleman that every morning when I would go down to open Top Shots, I would first go by Joyland and he'd be at the end of the counter reading five dollars' worth of guerrilla warfare comic books. Okay? And I said, 'Kosta, why do you waste your money reading those stupid comic books?' 'Because they give me good ideas,' he'd say, 'I get a lot of good ideas.' I'd say, 'Fine.' I thought he was a kid in a man's body is what I thought.

"Now I think if you got those comic books, everything he did was probably in those comic books."

With Speziale, as with others, Kosta often admitted to crimes or intended crimes, all the while smiling like a kid and practically daring people to believe him. At one point after Speziale and Kosta had caught Kevin Ramsey stealing from the bar Kosta told Speziale that he was going to have Kevin Ramsey killed. But again Speziale took it as just talk.

"Kosta was going to have everybody killed," he says. "You know, he'd say, 'I don't like that son of a bitch. He's stealing from me. I'm going to kill him.' I mean that was the way the man talked. That was his way of putting it. Every other word was, 'I'm going to kill that person.' Whether he was trying to intimidate me or impress me, I don't know."

Jack Levin says that this casual talk about murder is typical of sociopaths.

"When Kosta or any other sociopath talks like that, he might be testing," Levin says. "He may be trying to find some acquaintances who have the same need. By talking about something so gruesome in a light, humorous way, he doesn't attract attention to himself. He can test out people to see if they have the same interest, but he knows that if they don't, people aren't going to take him seriously."

Kosta also told Speziale that he had tapes of him torturing people. He offered to show them to Speziale, but Speziale, thinking it was just crazy talk, declined. Kosta even confided to Speziale what would turn out to be Kosta's deadliest secret, and the deed for which he would become most infamous.

"During the course of the relationship between Kosta and Deidre Hunt, they were getting kind of hot and heavy," Speziale says, "and I kept seeing him doing ignorant stupid things that I thought would end up getting him in trouble with his wife, causing him to have a divorce or marital problems. He was very blatant about the things he did, always thinking he was making a big secret of it when everybody was knowing what was going on, leaving a trail behind him like bread crumbs, flaunting with her.

"I tried to talk to him. I said, 'You know, this girl's going to get you in a lot of trouble.' I said, 'Look what you have and look what you're sacrificing for.' I felt Kosta was a respectable businessman, a well-to-do man with a beautiful wife, with a wealthy wife with a good family, the whole nine yards. I just thought that he was throwing it all away.

"So I said, 'You know, this girl could bribe you, she could do anything to you.' He said she could never do anything to him because he had a tape of her. He said he had a tape of her killing somebody.''

8

The Affair

The Joyland Amusement Center is on the northern end of the boardwalk, literally in the shadow of the vast new forty-seven-million-dollar Marriott Hotel complex. Joyland is a clanging, blipping, whooping arcade of coin-operated games with names like Cyberball, Chase HQ, Operation Thunderbolt, and Pole Position. When business is good and the place is filled with teenagers and families zapping Space Invaders, wheeling around hairpin turns, and firing make-believe Uzis at make-believe gangsters, the arcade sounds like a convention of R2-D2s.

On the left side of Joyland as you walk in off the boardwalk, there is a long snack bar, where you can sit on a stool, eat a hot dog with sauerkraut, and stare out at the ocean. Directly across from the snack bar is an old-fashioned shooting gallery with rifles that fire strobe lights at a piano man, a dodo bird, and various other targets.

Going deeper into Joyland on the right side, there are basketball hoops, where teenaged boys can indulge their Larry Bird fantasies by sinking as many baskets as they can for a quarter before time runs out. Beyond that there is a bank of Skee-Ball games, an attraction from the earliest days of the boardwalk that now seems quaint in a room full of high-tech entertainment. Way down at the back of the arcade there are glass cases filled with the prizes you can buy with the tickets you win by rolling up big scores on the games. All in all, the place is a lot of fun.

To the right of the prize counter, behind a locked door, there is an L-shaped office. It is a cramped, unexquisite place. Lit only by overhead fluorescence, it has no windows. Strictly functional, the office is cluttered with a couple of heavy old desks and chairs, odd parts from broken games, a new machine that counts and rolls quarters, and the blizzard of paperwork it takes to run a business.

Early on the night of Wednesday, October 25, 1989, the evening of her second auto mishap, Lisa was sitting at her desk, paying bills. She fidgeted as she added up the checks she had just written. Usually she liked working with numbers. There was something reassuring in the long columns that would always come out the same if you did it right, just as they had when she was a little girl adding up her father's numbers. She liked to believe that if you did the right things life would come out okay, too. But tonight as her fingers rapidly tapped out the numbers on her calculator, Lisa wasn't doing it right. She was making mistakes. Because of the second incident with the pickup truck, she was rattled.

So when the phone rang, it startled her.

She looked up to see if her husband would answer it. Kosta was standing at the front of the office, talking with Peter Kouracos. Kosta glanced at her, then went back to his conversation. Lisa grabbed the phone. Little did she know this was the call that would change her life.

"Joyland," Lisa said.

"Lisa, it's Elena."

"Hi, Elena," Lisa said. It was Elena Speziale, Vinnie Speziale's wife. Since Vinnie had taken the job managing Top Shots, Lisa and Elena had become friends. They had gone shopping together and taken in a few movies. They weren't best friends, but they were close enough to share personal things. Now Elena sounded troubled.

"What's up?" Lisa asked.

"There's something I have to tell you," Elena said.

"What?"

"I think you should have your husband watched by a private detective."

"Kos . . . ?" Lisa started to say, before she cut herself off, realizing she would draw Kosta's attention. She changed her tone and lowered her voice. "What? What are you talking about?"

"I just think you should, that's all," Elena said.

"Why? Elena, I don't understand, what are you getting at?" Lisa's fingers, no longer tapping out numbers, were now rapping nervously on the desktop.

"Are you alone?"

Lisa glanced up. "Well, no," she said. Kosta was flashing a new issue of *Soldier of Fortune* magazine in front of Peter. Neither man seemed to notice Lisa.

"Thirteen-round, staggered-column, box-type magazine," Kosta was saying. It was gun talk, the kind that Lisa often joked was all Greek to her. "Kosta and Peter are here," she said. "What's going on?"

"I just think you should have Kosta watched by a private detective, that's all," Elena said.

Lisa reached around to her pocketbook, which was slung over her chair. She fumbled in it until she came up with a pack of cigarettes. She pulled one out and lit it. Kosta gave her a disapproving glance, then turned back to his conversation. This was making Lisa nervous. Jesus, was Kosta into something illegal? She looked up at her husband, who, smiling in his boyish way, was laughing with Peter. He's such a kid, Lisa thought. No, he couldn't be doing anything illegal. It's impossible.

"Elena, are you at home?"

"Yes."

"Stay there. I'll call you in a few minutes."

108

Lisa's hands were shaking as she put down the phone, then slammed shut her ledgers and her business checkbook. She placed her bills and other papers in neat piles and slipped them into the top drawer of the desk. Even if she was going to leave the office a mess, she wanted the work at hand to be orderly.

"I have to go out for a little while," she announced to the men, her voice stiff. Kosta and Peter barely glanced at her, and in a moment she was out of the office. She strode across the back of the noisy amusement center and up the short flight of steps that led from the back of Joyland to Ocean Avenue, where she always parked the Porsche. As she moved along the sidewalk to her car she heard a group of teenage boys whistle at her. Men, she thought. If Kosta is doing anything illegal I'll leave him.

Lisa drove up North Atlantic Avenue, took a left at Seabreeze, and then a right on Halifax Avenue. The tourist trade in Daytona Beach only runs two blocks deep from the ocean, and Halifax is a residential area, a lovely and affluent tree-lined street where stylish houses stand beyond deep and well-groomed lawns. Five minutes later Lisa steered the Porsche into the long horseshoe driveway of her mother's house on Halifax, where she and Kosta had been living since Steno had died. Even now, with so much on her mind, she could not pull up to the house without thinking about her father. It had been two years since his death and she still missed him terribly.

Once inside the house, Lisa rushed upstairs to her bedroom, where she quickly dialed Elena's number.

"I'm alone now," she said. "What the hell is going on? Hire a detective? What do you mean, hire a detective?" While she spoke Lisa fidgeted with her pack of cigarettes. She pulled out a fresh one and lit it. "You've got me shaking like a leaf here."

"Look," Elena said, "I don't want to get in the middle of anything, but you're my friend and . . ."

"It's okay. You're doing the right thing. Just tell me what it is."

"Well just do what I'm saying. Hire a private detective and have him watch Kosta, that's all."

"Elena, for God's sake! Don't make me hire a private detective and wait a week before I find out what's going on. You're my friend, tell me."

"Okay, but you have to promise me one thing."

"What?"

"That you won't tell Kosta who told you."

"Okay, I promise," Lisa said. "Told me what, what?"

"I mean you really have to promise," Elena said. "You just cannot tell Kosta that it was me."

"I promise, I promise."

There was a long silence. For a moment Lisa thought the line had gone dead. Then Elena said, "I think Kosta is having an affair."

Lisa went cold. She couldn't speak. She felt a pain in her chest, like a clenched fist crushing her heart. He's going to break my heart, she thought, he's going to break my heart. "An affair?" she whispered. "How? With who?"

"One of the girl's at Top Shots," Elena said.

"Is it Holly?" Lisa said. Holly, one of the barmaids at Top Shots, was the only name that made sense. Holly was pretty. Holly was smart. Holly had class.

"No," Elena said. "It's Deidre."

"Deidre?" Lisa said. "No, that can't be. What the hell has Deidre got that would attract anybody?"

From a woman's perspective, Lisa's question made a certain amount of sense. Deidre Hunt was a street girl, sometimes vulgar, often pushy. She was not exactly the kind of gal a fellow wants to bring home to mom. But a man would certainly have seen the enticing things about Deidre that were lost on Lisa. Deidre was quite an attractive young woman, with a slim and curvaceous body, a beautiful face, and a pair of seductive brown eyes that could lure many men away from home for at least a few hours. That which

110

was "low class" about Deidre to most people might easily translate into "earthy" for a man who had fallen under her spell. And in the right light, accompanied by a whiff of perfume, "pushy" could certainly be mistaken for "flirtatious."

"Deidre?" Lisa said again, disgustedly. If Kosta was having an affair with Deidre, he had compounded the sin of adultery with that of poor taste.

"Don't say anything," Elena urged. "Find out for sure. Hire a private detective."

"I don't know," Lisa said.

"There's more," Elena said.

"God."

"He's buying her clothes. He keeps her in an apartment."

"Who's saying these things?" Lisa asked.

"Deidre. She's shooting off her mouth about it."

Lisa hung up the phone. For the second time that day, she was a wreck. She paced the bedroom, her arms wrapped around her aching chest. "Okay God, don't you think enough is enough!" she said out loud. After she had paced and prayed for this thing not to be true, Lisa did what she would predictably do in such desperate times. She tried to find Dino. Dino would help her, he would give her good advice.

Lisa called Joyland to see if Dino had come into the office. When Kosta answered the phone Lisa hung up. She called Dino's friend Timmy but there was no answer. She called their cousin, also named Dino. She called her cousins Vicki and John to see if they knew where Dino was. But Dino was not around. Probably playing basketball with Timmy, she thought. She considered going downstairs and asking her mother where Dino was, but Lisa was afraid that her mother would spot the quaver in her voice, the sadness in her eyes. Ma would know that something was wrong, and then the questions would never end.

Next Lisa called her aunt who owned a gift shop on the boardwalk. Do you know anything about Kosta seeing another woman? The aunt knew nothing. Lisa was relieved.

Usually every Greek in town knew what every other Greek in town was up to. Perhaps there was no affair, after all.

But maybe there is, she thought, again holding herself tightly because there was no one else there to hold her. Maybe he is seeing that woman, she thought. She cried. Maybe Kosta is about to break my heart. What will I do?

She sat on her bed, soaking her hands with tears. *Deidre*. Lisa had seen Deidre many times at Top Shots and had never sensed any rivalry with her, except that Deidre often admired Lisa's clothes and jewelry. In fact, Deidre had once told Vinnie Speziale that Lisa was her idea of a "real lady." Lisa was flattered when Vinnie told her about the comment. But now, in light of this rumor, an odd incident from a week earlier, the night after the first auto mishap, took on new meaning. Lisa pulled tissues from the box on her night table and wiped at her eyes while she thought about it.

"It was eleven-thirty at night and I was watching *Simon and Simon*," Lisa remembers. "Kosta said, 'Honey, I'm going to take a ride on my bike.' It seemed a little weird to go for a bike ride at that hour but I said, 'Okay, fine.' About a half hour later he calls me. 'I'm at Top Shots,' he says. 'We're going to close in a little while, okay, honey?' I said, 'Fine.' I didn't care, I was watching my TV show. Then a little before twelve-thirty he calls again. 'Hi, honey, now I'm at Angelo's. And Peter's here, we're just hanging around and watching movies, do you mind?' It was just getting to the good part on *Simon and Simon,* so I said, 'Fine fine, talk to you later,' and I hung up. Next thing I know, Kosta comes running in. I said, 'I thought you were at Angelo's?' He says, 'I was, but I came home. I thought you were mad at me.' At that moment my mind clicked and I thought, ah, guilty conscience. I said, 'No, I'm not mad at you. I was just distracted because I was watching the show.' So Kosta says, 'You're not mad at me?' 'No.' 'Good,' he says, 'then I guess I'll go back.' 'Kosta,' I said, 'I'm not mad at you, but I don't think it's very nice that

112

you came all the way home and now you're going back and you're not even going to invite me to join you.' 'Oh, you want to come?' he says. 'Yes,' I said. By this time it was one o'clock in the morning. So we went over to Angelo's, and Peter's there. And Deidre is there. So that's what the guilty conscience is about, I thought. I didn't make any connection that anything was going on with Kosta and Deidre, but I thought, He feels guilty just that there's a girl there at all. So everybody is drinking beer and Angelo decides he'll make spaghetti at two in the morning. I talked to Deidre for a while. She started talking about, 'Gee, if you ever divorced Kosta you could take him for fifty percent of what he has.' And then Peter spoke up. 'Yeah,' he says, 'but the problem is it's not Kosta's stuff, it's all Lisa's.' We all laughed over that. Then Deidre started telling me about what they were doing earlier. They were calling all of Peter's friends and leaving dirty messages. This is how they were having fun. Deidre turned to me and she says, 'You know what I said?' I said, 'What did you say?' She wouldn't tell me. 'Come on,' I said, 'what did you say?' She was embarrassed to tell me. She wouldn't tell me, but I kept saying, 'Oh come on, tell me,' and finally she said, 'Well, I said . . . ,' and she blurts out this incredibly outrageous thing she had said. It was real suggestive. I was shocked, and I don't shock that easily.

"When I got in the car with Kosta to go home I told Kosta, I said, 'I can't believe a person would say a thing like that. You couldn't pay me a million dollars to say those things over the phone to someone, even if they didn't know me.' Kosta just thought it was kind of funny."

By the time Lisa's tears had dried, she had decided to confront her husband with the accusation.

She and Kosta had planned to go to a late movie that night with Peter Kouracos, who often was the third wheel when they went out. But Lisa managed to pry Peter out of the date so that she could confront Kosta during the drive to the theater.

As they drove west across Volusia Boulevard toward the theater complex Lisa rehearsed in her mind different versions of what she would say. Should she be subtle? Should she just blurt it out? Should she try to somehow trick Kosta into admitting that he was an adulterer? She was still on edge, although a shade or two calmer than when she had spoken to Elena. They were in Kosta's BMW, which meant she was not allowed to smoke.

"Kosta," she finally said while they were waiting for the light to change at Ridgewood, "somebody called me today and said you are having an affair with Deidre."

She stared right at him. What Kosta did or said now could signal the end of her marriage. The idea of divorce horrified her, but the idea of living with a cheat horrified her even more. Would he admit it, she wondered. Would he lie?

More than anything else, Kosta looked startled. His eyes flashed with anger. But that told Lisa nothing. Her words would make him angry, whether the charge was true or not.

"Deidre?" he said, forcing a smile. "No. She's too fat."

"Look," Lisa said, "if you're having an affair, you'd better fess up to it now. I know I always told you I would leave you if there was another woman but maybe there's a chance we could work it out if you tell me now."

"It's not true," Kosta said.

"But if it's true," Lisa went on, "and you don't tell me now, then I'll definitely leave you, because then you'll be a liar as well as a cheat."

Lisa was bluffing and she figured Kosta knew it. The truth is there would be no second chance for any husband of hers who slept with another woman. If Lisa knew that she was married to a man she couldn't trust, she could never feel whole, she could never have a baby. Much as she loved Kosta, Lisa knew she would be crushed by a life of jealousy, that she would be made bitter and hostile by the knowledge that her love was being given to a man who

114

placed so little value on it. No, if this thing was true, she would not continue. She would send Rambo packing, pure and simple.

Kosta turned to her now. He flashed his handsome smile. He laughed.

"I'm not seeing any other women, you have my word on that." He reached across the seat, patted her hand. "But, Lisa, I want you to do something for me."

"What?"

"I want you to give me the name of the person who told you this. It's some sort of misunderstanding. I'll get it all straightened out."

"I can't do that," Lisa said.

Kosta's hand on hers suddenly felt cold.

"Who told you this?" Kosta said.

"Is it true?" Lisa asked.

"Of course it's not true. But you have to tell me who told you this."

"I can't do that."

"You have to," Kosta said.

"Why?"

Kosta looked straight ahead at the traffic. "Because," he said, "it's like someone is shooting at me from across the street, trying to ruin my life, and I don't know who it is."

"Kosta," Lisa said, "a person told me this because that person cares about me. I'm not going to betray that by telling you who it is."

Though Kosta did not get the name he wanted, he had succeeded, as he had so often before, in changing the focus of the conversation. The couple spent the rest of the drive arguing not about the alleged affair, but about whether or not Kosta was entitled to the name of the snitch. Kosta, who, of course, had rarely shown emotion during the four years of their marriage, was volatile. It was as if he had been the one stabbed in the back.

At the movies Lisa and Kosta held hands uneasily. Both could feel the tension between them. In the car on the way home the discussion began again. Kosta insisted so vociferously that someone was telling lies about him that by bedtime Lisa was completely confused. Maybe she should hire a private detective, she thought. Maybe it really was all a mistake.

The next day, Thursday, October 26, Lisa, who had always trusted Kosta and had always let him go his own way, became the clinging vine. When Kosta went to the 7-Eleven for a six-pack of Coke Lisa went with him. When Kosta went to the bank to make a Joyland deposit, Lisa went with him. Lisa, the woman who didn't have enough hours in the day for all her work, suddenly had nothing to do but follow Kosta around like a probation officer.

All day long they squabbled about the Deidre thing. Lisa insisted that they have a real conversation about the alleged affair. Kosta refused to talk about it, except to deny the affair and demand the name of the person who had told Lisa.

That night Kosta, still steaming about the fact that she wouldn't give him the name, was in the Joyland office with Lisa. At one point Kosta picked up a small wooden coffee table and started banging it up and down. He smashed the table into bits, demanding the name of the person who was out to get him. Lisa had never seen him like this.

Lisa was unrelenting. She refused to turn over the name. Finally, Kosta gave her a fiery-eyed stare and said, "If you don't tell me who said I was seeing Deidre I will kill your brother."

It was a shocking thing for him to say, even though Lisa could not even imagine at the time that the man she loved was capable of murder.

"How can you say an awful thing like that to me?" she asked.

"Because the only way I can get you to tell me is to kill the person you love most in the world," Kosta said.

The message was clear: you love Dino more than you

116

love me. And also, typical of Kosta, it shifted the focus from one of his sins to one of hers.

Kosta did give in to Lisa on one point, but acquiescence was itself damning. He agreed to fire Deidre. "Okay," Kosta said, when Lisa asked that the girl be fired. To Lisa that was almost a confession that he was having an affair, because it was unlike Kosta to agree so quickly to anything. He was not a man who surrendered. Usually he would insist that he was right and that everybody else was wrong. Kosta had always taken the view that he was smarter than everybody else. Though he had never said it in so many words he had always left the impression that he thought he was even above the law.

The next night, Friday, October 27, Kosta and Lisa ate at Denny's on Broadway, the very location that Kosta had wanted to buy for his own Denny's franchise. Things were less combative than they had been at Joyland. Lisa, hopeful to the point of self-delusion, was a long way from being positive that an affair really existed, and she wanted to make peace. Kosta had agreed to fire Deidre and that was a step in the right direction. She brought it up again while they waited for their meals. Kosta, dripping charm from every pore, had seemed genuinely sad that such turbulence had come into the marriage. He had spent the day trying to please Lisa. "I'll make sure she's out," he said now. He jumped up from the table and went to the pay phone to call Angelo at Top Shots. After a minute Kosta waved to Lisa to come to the phone.

"Here, speak to Angelo," he told her.

Lisa got on the phone. "Did you fire her?" Lisa asked.

"Well, no," Angelo said. "See, I talked to Dennis."

"Dennis?" Lisa said. "What's Dennis got to do with it?" Dennis was an officer with the Daytona Beach police department, a regular on the boardwalk beat.

"Dennis asked me not to fire her," Angelo said. "The cops want to watch her."

"I don't care if the police want to watch her," Lisa said.

"Let them watch her somewhere else. There's talk that Kosta is seeing Deidre and . . ." The words caught in Lisa's throat. All day long she had been hiding her sadness with anger and now she was near tears. "I just want her out of our lives, that's all."

"Well, I can understand that," Angelo said. "But I want to help the police in any way I can."

"Have Dennis talk to me," Lisa said.

The next day, Saturday the 28th, Dennis came to Joyland to talk to Lisa and Dino in the office.

Lisa describes the meeting this way: "He said, 'We'd really prefer it if Deidre stayed at Top Shots.' I asked him why. 'Well, we think she's selling drugs and we want to catch her. We think she's a prostitute, too.' I said, 'Oh, great, you're telling me you want to keep her on the job because you want to bust her?' Meanwhile here I am, Miss Clean-Up-the-Boardwalk, and I'm supposed to keep a dope-pushing hooker in my husband's employ. What kind of example would I be setting? I didn't want anybody working for us who even took drugs, never mind sold them. I said, 'Dennis, if she's as bad as you say you'll catch her doing something.' "

In one sense that conversation was a great relief to Lisa. Until then she had felt terribly guilty about having Deidre fired. What if the girl wasn't fooling around with Kosta? Now it didn't matter; there were other reasons to fire her.

"One other thing," Dennis said that day.

"What?"

"We've heard that she carries a silver pistol in her pocketbook. You know anything about that?"

"No."

"You won't let her stay?"

"No. I'm sorry," Lisa told him. "There are personal reasons why I want her out and I can't risk the boardwalk's reputation or my husband's."

The next incident involving Deidre occurred that same night. There was a Greek dance at the Hilton Hotel on

118

South Atlantic. It was a yearly event, but this one was special; they were burning the church's mortgage.

Instead of floating around and talking to friends as he normally would, Kosta stayed close to Lisa. Brimming with affection, he tended to her every need. *Another glass of wine, honey? You look great in that dress.* The aunts and cousins who were sitting at the same table made the old jokes about how jealous it made them. It was the first time in ages. Lisa was very touched by all the attention. He's trying to show me he loves me, she thought. He knows I'm afraid about the affair and he's trying to make it up to me.

After the dance somebody suggested that everybody go to Razzles, the popular Daytona Beach nightclub that is owned by a Paspalakis family friend. Going to Razzles was a regular thing with Lisa's group of friends, most of whom, like Lisa and Kosta, were in their late twenties. But, lately, it had been unusual for Kosta to join them. This time he thought it was a great idea.

"What's with Kosta?" Dino asked. "All of sudden he wants to go to Razzles."

At Razzles, Kosta's attention and his affection continued. Lisa had a wonderful time. The only distressing moment came when they were on their way out with Peter Kouracos. Deidre came over and asked Peter to stop and talk with her. Lisa, ignoring the younger woman, left with Kosta.

"On the way home I told Kosta that I was worried about Deidre. We were scheduled to go back to Razzles a few nights later for a big Halloween party. But now that I knew that Deidre went to Razzles I was afraid that she might be there on Halloween and she might make a big scene in front of my friends and family. After all, I had gotten her fired."

When Lisa and Kosta got home it was already early morning of the 29th and at two A.M. the phone rang. It was Peter Kouracos calling for Lisa.

"You're probably wondering what Deidre and I were

119

talking about," Peter said. "Deidre was upset that you believed she was having an affair with Kosta. She doesn't understand how you could believe a thing like that and she says you got her fired. She says Vinnie Speziale made up those things about her selling drugs and having a gun in her purse."

While Kouracos's phone call was intended to put Lisa's mind at ease, it had the opposite effect. The new hope she had been building in her mind now came tumbling down. Kosta was the only person to whom she had described her and Dino's conversation with Dennis about the drugs and the gun. Also Kosta had told Lisa that her name was not mentioned when Deidre was fired. Yet, now Deidre knew all of those things. Only Kosta could have told Deidre. Why would he tell Deidre those things unless he cared about her?

In an attempt to recapture the feelings of a few hours earlier Lisa curled up next to her husband, who was still sleeping. She put an arm under him, cast a leg across him and burrowed in deeply, wishing she could just hold him like this forever. Kosta loves me, she told herself. He truly does. She couldn't bear to lose this love, yet she saw it slipping away. She thought about the night shortly after her father died, the night she had come completely apart, screaming and crying, in the bedroom with Kosta. And she thought about how Kosta had held her and comforted her, and cried with her. Now, with her husband sleeping beside her, Lisa remembered Kosta's soft and gentle kisses. Of course, he loves me, she thought, he must love me, and she fell asleep.

On Sunday, the 29th, Lisa and Kosta went to a home show together at the Ocean Center. They talked about how they would furnish the house that was being built for them in Ormond Beach. Kosta told Lisa that he wanted his workshop in the new house to have a secret wall panel that only he could open by pushing a hidden button, and he

Lisa and Dino Paspalakis *(photo by Steve Notaras)*

Lisa with her brother, Dino, and mother *(photo by Steve Notaras)*

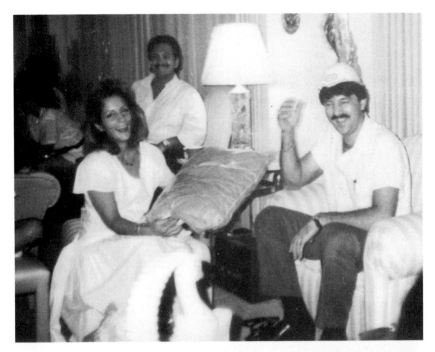

Lisa and friends help
Kosta celebrate his
thirtieth birthday.

Lisa and Kosta, dressed
for Halloween, 1989

Dino and Lisa outside the Joyland arcade *(photo by Steve Notaras)*

The Paspalakis home on North Halifax

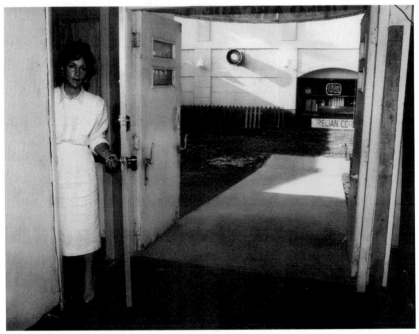

Lisa at the arcade office, where T. J. accosted her *(photo by Steve Notaras)*

Kevin Ramsey, at seventeen

A police officer at the crime scene where Ramsey was tied to a tree and murdered *(photo by Daytona* News Journal)

Mike Cox *(photo by Daytona* News Journal)

T. J. James *(photo by Daytona* News Journal)

Lori Henderson *(photo by Daytona* News Journal)

Deidre Hunt *(photo by Daytona* News Journal)

also wanted bulletproof glass on the windows to his work-shop. Lisa was amused.

"Bulletproof glass? Really, Kosta. What do you think, Al Capone's boys are going to drive by and try to assassinate you?"

It was fun to tease Kosta. They held hands as they walked the floor at the home show. Again, Lisa's pain was easing.

Later that afternoon the fist was back, crushing her heart.

"I was talking to Dino on the telephone. It was a rainy Sunday afternoon and next thing, I noticed that Kosta was gone. So I hung up with Dino and I got in my car and I went down to where Deidre lived, because Pete had told me where she lived."

He's with her, Lisa thought. Lisa drove the rain-slicked streets to the house Deidre lived in on Lenox Avenue, nine blocks south of the boardwalk, a quiet residential street of palm trees and small pastel houses. Kosta's BMW was in the driveway. Lisa pulled over and stared at the house. Her stomach was a knot. Should she go in, she wondered. Should she burst in, guns ablazing, the outraged cuckolded wife? Or should she be the quiet little woman who sits idly by while her husband fucks some vulgar dope-dealing bitch. Before Lisa could decide what to do, Kosta came out the front door and got into his car. As he pulled out on Lenox, Lisa followed him.

Kosta, apparently spotting Lisa in his rearview mirror, drove faster. At the first corner he signaled left, but turned right. Lisa pushed the Porsche as hard as she dared on the corner. She caught up with Kosta, her bumper almost kissing his BMW. Kosta slowed at a yellow light, then sprinted through it. Lisa ran the light. What the hell is he going to do, she wondered, try to lose me and then deny it was him? Kosta took a left; she went after him. He took a right, then another right. She followed him. Then she came around a corner after him. Moving too fast she lost control of the Porsche for a moment and almost crashed into Mac's

121

Famous Bar. What's happening to me, she thought, I'm in a high-speed car chase with my husband. When she got the car back under control she had lost Kosta.

Lisa, cautiously now, and taking deep breaths to calm herself, drove up and down the streets around Lenox, thinking Kosta might have turned back and headed for the shelter of his girlfriend's house. But there was no sign of Kosta's BMW. He had gotten away. "Son of a bitch," she muttered. She turned the Porsche around and drove back to the boardwalk.

A few hours later Kosta showed up at Joyland.

"Damn you," she said, "Damn you. You were with her. Don't deny it."

He admitted he'd been at Deidre's but said he had no idea that Lisa had chased him. He explained that he had gone to Deidre's to tell her to stay out of their life.

"I know she's not interested in me," he said, "but I told her you were jealous, that you thought there was something going on, and I told her to stay away."

Once again Lisa's certainty was shaken. She'd been obsessing about this Deidre thing. Maybe she was just getting paranoid. What Kosta was saying was plausible.

"You could have called her on the telephone," Lisa said. "You didn't have to go there." But she knew that going there was Kosta's style. He liked to confront things head on. Was he or wasn't he having an affair with Deidre? This was driving her crazy.

Before long Kosta deflected the conversation. A few days before this he had gone into the woods to dig up some guns he had buried, and he couldn't find them, which Lisa thought was hilarious. "Some survivalist," she had teased. "You can't even find your guns." Now, at Joyland, Kosta explained that after leaving Deidre's he had gone to rent a metal detector so that he could look for his guns. The reference to the lost guns put Lisa in a better mood. Sometimes Kosta was a bit of a buffoon and when Lisa was reminded of that, it seemed that only a woman who truly loved him, the way Lisa did, would be after him. Would a woman like Deidre really have an affair with a man who couldn't even remember where he buried his guns?

"Come on, I'll show you the metal detector," Kosta insisted. He led Lisa out to his car, popped the trunk, and proudly showed her the metal detector.

"See, I wasn't lying," he said smugly, as if the fact that he really had rented the metal detector somehow proved that he hadn't been in bed with Deidre earlier.

Later, at home, Lisa told Kosta that she'd been obsessed with this Deidre thing and she had to talk about it. "I mean really talk," she said. "Not just brush it off."

She also told Kosta that she did not want to go to the Halloween party at Razzles.

"I'm just so afraid that this girl is going to make a scene in front of all my friends and family," she said. "I mean what does she care, she's a street person. I don't want a scene. I don't want all those people knowing my business."

Kosta insisted that Lisa go to the party. Everything would be okay, he said. He insisted that she call Deidre.

"I'm going to call her," he said. "You'll see that there is nothing to worry about."

Kosta called Deidre, and put Lisa on the phone.

"Deidre said to me, 'I can't believe you'd think I'd have an affair with your husband. I wear purple tights and pink tops and I dance like a nigger.' I said, 'Huh?' She said, 'I'm not his type. Kosta is a classy guy. Anyway, I wouldn't do that sort of thing.' She told me if I didn't believe her I could ask her mother. She said, 'I would never get involved with a married man. You didn't have to get me fired.' So I said, 'Well, I'm sorry if I'm wrong, but employees are easy to find. And you can always get another job. But if you might be causing trouble in my marriage I have to get you out of there.' 'Well, I can understand that,' Deidre said. 'If it were my husband I'd probably do the same thing.' So we talked for a few more minutes. Deidre told me there were no hard feelings, that she would get another job somewhere. She said she'd appreciate a nod if I saw her. I hung up, thinking it had been a real woman-to-woman talk and that Deidre had been rather pleasant about the whole thing."

The conversation with Deidre went a long way toward lowering Lisa's anxiety level. Perhaps I'm just on edge because of everything, she thought. The car accidents, the redevelopment talks, Elena's call. More and more Lisa was feeling that this crisis could be put to rest if she and Kosta could have just one decent conversation about it. She just needed to express her feelings without Kosta telling her she was crazy or demanding the name of the person who had called. She just needed to know that Kosta loved her, that this marriage of theirs was real, that it meant as much to him as to her. There had been grief between them since the miscarriage. Maybe, if they could just have an intimate conversation in which she told Kosta how much she loved him, and he told her how much he loved her, and gripes were aired, they could recapture the feelings that had brought them together.

Once more she insisted that they talk. This time Kosta agreed. "Okay," he said, "we'll have a good talk about it. November fourth."

"November fourth?"

Kosta reminded her that he and she were scheduled to go SCUBA diving with friends on Key West on November 4th.

"It's a three-hour drive," Kosta said. "If you promise not to bring it up until then, I promise you we will talk about it on the drive to Key West."

"Fair enough," Lisa said, and they shook hands. Kosta kissed her gently. "Good girl," he said.

He also asked her to please go to the Halloween party. It was very important to him that she go.

The Halloween party, on Tuesday night, was, from Lisa's point of view, of no particular significance, except for her anxieties about Deidre. Later Lisa would learn that she had been marked for murder at that party, that she had been within inches of a man who held the knife that was supposed to be shoved into her.

"I wore a cowgirl costume with shorts," she says. "Kosta wore his graduation robe, with the black hood, and he also had a brown devil's mask that looked like a face carved on a totem pole. We went to a private party first, then to Razzles. There were a lot of people there whom I hadn't seen for a while, so I was talking with people at my table, and at the bar. I was always with people. When I went to the rest room there was always some other woman who went with me, the way women do. So I was never really alone. I didn't know that somebody was trying to kill me."

At one point, when they first got to the party at Razzles, Lisa noticed someone wearing a Freddy Kruger costume and made a comment to Kosta about how easy it would be for someone to kill someone on Halloween, since they could wear a mask without raising suspicions.

If there was anything odd at all about the party it was the fact that Kosta, so attentive a few nights earlier at the Greek dance, now kept his distance. All through the evening he floated around the room, talking to this one and that one and staying, it seemed, as far away from Lisa as possible.

Lisa's fears about Deidre were not realized. Deidre was at Razzles with her friend Lori, but did nothing to embarrass Lisa.

The following afternoon, Wednesday, November 1, Lisa was alone in the Joyland office. Dino had gone to the bank to make the daily deposit, a regular Wednesday chore of his because Kosta always took Wednesdays off. At around two o'clock there was a knock at the door. Lisa had been going over repair bills for some of the video games, and the knock was a welcome distraction from the distressing numbers. As always she looked first through the peephole of the locked door. Through it she saw the face of a young black man. She didn't know him, but the face did look familiar. She had it in her head that this was some acquaintance of Kosta's, perhaps looking for him. She opened the door, cautiously pressing a foot against the bottom of it, and holding it so that it would not open wide, as she normally did when opening the door to strangers.

The young man was tall and good looking. He looked to be no more than twenty. He had a pleasant smile, but he looked nervous. Immediately Lisa knew that something was wrong. It was a hot day, but the young man was wearing a heavy overcoat. And then she saw it. The man had a gun in his right hand. Lisa froze. The young man shoved the gun into her stomach.

"Get inside," he said, "or I'll shoot you."

Lisa stood her ground. She knew that if she let him into the office, she might never come out of the office alive. In various ways she had envisioned this moment many times, even planned for it. She often worked alone in the office, where cash was handled daily. It had always seemed to her that the office was the perfect place for a robber to do his thing. No windows. Only one door. And worse, a victim could scream bloody murder and no one would ever hear it above the noise of the video games. Kosta, aware of the danger, had even given her a gun for her desk drawer. Lisa had thought about all these things and she had always known that if this moment came the gun would not guarantee her survival. She simply could not allow herself ever to be trapped inside the office with an armed robber. She would be at his mercy.

All of this flashed through Lisa's mind in an instant. She even thought of going for the remote control alarm, but it was at the back of the office, and if this guy didn't shoot her, it would give him time to come inside and lock the door. The gun was pressed against her ribs. The young black man was glancing around, telling her to get inside the office. She yanked her foot from the door and let it fly all the way open. It was like having a cane kicked from under her and she fell forward to the floor. The young man jumped back, pointed the gun at her.

"For a second I just sat there," Lisa remembers. "My heart was pounding. Which way should I run, I wondered, which way should I run? To my left was the stairway up to Ocean Avenue. But to my right, and a lot closer, was the doorway that led out to the sidewalk next to the Marriott. The guy with the gun was shouting at me, 'Get up and get in there.' He was nervous and he kept waving his gun and kind of glancing around to see if anybody had seen him. 'No,' I shouted at him. I jumped up. 'You get in there,' I said, and I ran for the door on my right. God, he could shoot me in the back, I thought as I ran down the sidewalk and behind the Marriott."

But there were no shots, no dashing footsteps behind Lisa. She ran until she got to Grecian Corner, the restaurant run by her aunt and uncle.

"Someone tried to rob me," she told them. "He had a gun."

From the restaurant she called the police. When they arrived Lisa described the incident and the young man who had assaulted her.

"But I left out the part about thinking that the guy was some friend of Kosta's," she says. "I wanted to protect Kosta. I didn't want the police to think he knew people like that."

Later, when she told Kosta about the robbery attempt, his concern was very touching. He held her close and told her everything was all right.

"Honey," he said. "You could have been killed."

9

J. R.

The phone call that Lisa received in October, and the divorce talk that followed, did not trigger the plot to kill her. It only added urgency to a plan that had already been hatched. During the latter part of 1989, well before October, literally dozens of people knew, at the very least, that Deidre Hunt was involved in a plan to murder a woman. Some, of course, knew who the woman was and who was paying for it. Many of them were asked to commit the murder, and have since recalled their part in the drama.

While all of the events certainly took place between July and early November of 1989, the exact chronology is difficult to come by for a variety of reasons. These were not the sort of people to keep appointment books, or to write everything on a calendar the way Lisa Fotopoulos did. Furthermore, many of these people were bombarding their brains with crack, pot, and alcohol. And beyond that there is the simple problem that all of them are accomplished liars and have various reasons to lie, shade the truth, or leave out facts. The result is that clandestine meetings, illegal schemes, and deadly secrets become, in the words of one boardwalk kid, "a jumble." Nonetheless, while no one

128

report can be viewed as entirely reliable, their combined memories do add up to the truth.

The motive for the murder was money. By the summer of 1989 Kosta Fotopoulos was eighteen thousand dollars in debt. He had run ten credit cards up to their limit. He had invested in Top Shots. He and Lisa had bought a duplex in Edgewater, but it was his project and he was responsible for the mortgage. Though Lisa didn't know it, one renter had moved out of the duplex, and the other was stiffing Kosta for the rent. From his counterfeit money transaction Kosta had probably netted no more than thirty thousand dollars in real money, with another twenty thousand or so of funny money still buried in the woods. The money he made from stealing cars, running hookers, and selling drugs didn't seem to be enough to keep up with a lifestyle that included his BMW, expensive weapons, several girlfriends before Deidre, and a habit of picking up checks at restaurants.

Furthermore, even before his wife accused him of having an affair, Kosta must have foreseen the prospect of a divorce. Lisa had been unhappy with him ever since the miscarriage and the opening of Top Shots. Clearly, if she found out about any of these secret activities, she would leave him. And then he would have nothing.

But if Lisa were to die, Kosta figured he then would have everything. In the long run, if he allowed some time to go by, and then murdered Dino and Mary, he would have the house, Joyland, the gift shops, everything that Steno had accumulated.

(In fact, it appears that Kosta had always planned to kill the whole family, or had at least fantasized about doing it. But, except for his possible involvement in Steno's death and his alleged propositions to Bill Markantonakis, we don't know of any specific actions he took to accomplish this before the summer of 1989.)

In the short run, Kosta believed, he would have seven hundred thousand dollars in life insurance money. However, this figure of seven hundred thousand dollars was incorrect. It was based on Kosta's belief that Lisa had a double indemnity clause in two life insurance policies, and that the insurance companies would pay double if she were murdered. In fact, Lisa's death would have brought in three hundred fifty thousand dollars from insurance, and half of that would go to Dino. Nonetheless, seven hundred thousand is the figure that Kosta believed in and seven hundred thousand is the amount that he and Deidre talked about when it was agreed that she would help him find someone to kill his wife, so that they could live together in peace and love. (Though Kosta knew that Dino would get half of the insurance money, he talked about the money as if all of it would go to him.)

In the summer and autumn of 1989 at least five people accepted the job of murdering Lisa Fotopoulos. The first, of those that are on record, was J. R., the nineteen-year-old burglar from Virginia who became Deidre's first Daytona boyfriend. The word on J. R. was "he doesn't give a shit," which meant he would do pretty much anything.

Though Deidre didn't care for J. R. at first, it turned out that he knew the five kids she was living with in a house on North Oleander, and she saw him when he came over there to drink. But it wasn't until she met him at the Ocean Club in the Whitehall Hotel that they hit it off and started dating.

Deidre hadn't yet started working at Top Shots and what J. R. knew of Kosta was mostly what he had heard from Kevin Ramsey. Ramsey worked for Kosta and seemed to both like and fear the Greek. Ramsey, who had recently gotten arrested for buying weed from an undercover cop, told J. R. that Kosta had bailed him out. J. R.'s own impression of Kosta at this time was that Kosta "was quiet and seemed like he could be dangerous."

When Deidre started dating J. R. she moved into the apartment on Beverly Court where J. R. lived with four other guys. Sexual fidelity was foreign to both of them, so

130

after a month or so they stopped dating, but J. R. let her stay at the apartment until she got the room at the Casa Del Mar.

During Deidre's week at the Casa Del Mar, J. R. and others dropped by several times to party in the Jacuzzi. Deidre had money. She told J. R. she was running cocaine for some guy. "Every day she would drop a package off in a bus station locker," he says.

J. R. says that Deidre also told him that she was running a prostitution ring for Kosta.

"She said she was like the head of it. She would call the girls and tell them where to go to meet people. She said she ran the chain. She said Kosta gave her the numbers.

"She talked a lot about guns, too," J. R. says. "She said that Kosta was training her and that he was taking her to gun shows in Orlando. She said he was a master when it came to weapons and that he knew martial arts."

During this time Deidre told J. R. that Kosta was connected to the CIA. She told him also that Kosta wanted him to steal cars. And it was at the house on A1A that Kosta first brought up the subject of murder.

"We were just sitting at the table, me and Dee and Kosta. My friend James was there but he was in the bathroom. We were having an ordinary conversation when Kosta just sort of interrupted and said, 'I'd like you to do a job for me, for ten thousand dollars, so I can inherit some money.' He never mentioned no names. I said, 'Yes' and he didn't say another word. He just changed the subject. Later he gave us all a ride back up to the boardwalk and dropped us off."

A few days later J. R., along with three other guys, spent the night at Deidre's place. J. R. and a guy named Ron had been negotiating with Deidre about stealing three cars for Kosta. "Ron steals cars," J. R. explains. "And Deidre said Kosta wanted three cars stolen in Florida. One of them was a Ferrari Testarossa. Kosta would pay us twenty-five thousand dollars and give us guns and suits and everything."

After Ron left, Deidre told J. R. that Kosta wanted his wife killed for ten thousand dollars.

"It was the first time the victim was named," J. R. says.

Again J. R. said he would do it, and Deidre said she would pass the word along to Kosta. But again, there was no follow-up.

During this time J. R. says that almost every day Deidre was giving him money from her Top Shots tips, or money that Kosta had given her to get her nails done or her hair done.

"I got money all the time. If I kissed her, I got it. I got money all the time, not just when I kissed her or we had sexual intercourse. She acted like she cherished the ground I walked on. Because I treated her like shit, but she liked it, I guess."

The next time the proposed murder came up was a week after Deidre moved to Schulte Avenue. J. R. and his new girlfriend, along with a couple of other kids, were with Deidre, who was thumbing through a gun magazine. This time Deidre sang a slightly different tune. Instead of asking J. R. to do the murder, she announced that she was to do it.

"She told me and my girlfriend that Kosta wanted her to kill his wife, and she showed us the gun she was getting," J. R. says.

J. R. was skeptical. The car theft deal hadn't gone through, the murder for hire had not been followed up. J. R. was beginning to think that Kosta was all talk.

Another week went by. One night, J. R. says, he and his new girlfriend were at the Schulte Avenue apartment with Shannon and Larry, two more boardwalk characters. Deidre told J. R. in front of the others that Kosta still wanted J. R. to kill Lisa.

"Now the price was upped to a hundred thousand dollars," J. R. says. "She was talking about how much money she had and she said she was going to get seven hundred and something thousand just for setting it up. Then Larry

132

and Shannon went into the living room and Deidre said to my girlfriend and me, 'You know, the reason I want to kill people is for the power and the money.' "

This last conversation took place in late September, and according to J. R., the murder of Lisa Fotopoulos was not brought up again until the night before Halloween.

J. R. and Bryan Chase had just gotten back from a trip to Virginia. They were walking along the boardwalk when Deidre came running up to them. She was with Lori Henderson. Lori, daughter of a Daytona Beach assistant public defender, was Deidre's female lover, and each girl had her own male lover. Lori, eighteen, plain looking and fairly bright, was dating Teja James, the only black kid in this social circle.

"Deidre said, 'Let me talk to you,' " J. R. recalls. "So she pulled me to the side and she said, 'Kosta wants you to kill Lisa.' " J. R. says Deidre also said, 'J. R., do you know how it feels to grab somebody by their head and just blow their brains out?' " He adds, "She was happy about it. She expressed it with excitement."

By this time J. R. had been shot at by Kosta in the closet of Deidre's apartment, and he had been warned by Kosta to stay away from Deidre and to stay out of Top Shots. So the possibility of a Kosta double cross was certainly on his mind. But J. R. was a guy who "didn't give a shit," and chances are he would have signed on for the murder if it hadn't been for Lori Henderson.

That night J. R., Deidre, and Lori stood out on the board-walk in front of Pizza King while Deidre outlined the plan to murder Lisa Fotopoulos. Lori was silent throughout, then suddenly she said, "No."

"I knew something was going on when Lori said, 'No,' just out of the blue," J. R. says. "She said, 'No, not him.' I picked that up as meaning that something was going to happen to me. Dee said to Lori, 'That's all right,' and Lori walked away. She got some cigarettes and came back."

Of course, only J. R. knows for sure whether or not he

would have gone through with the murder of Lisa. He says that he would never take a person's life, that he just went along with all this, thinking it was a joke. But he also says that it was Lori's, "No, not him," that persuaded him to bail out, a seemingly contradictory statement. More likely, J. R. just saw that he was involved in something that could lead to money, either through a murder, or perhaps a ripoff of Kosta, and just played along day by day without a clear picture of what he would do. In any case, J. R. agreed to meet Kosta at Popeye's chicken restaurant to discuss the murder, but J. R. did not show up. Weeks later he talked to Lori about her warning.

"She told me she was there when Kosta and Deidre had the conversation and that whoever came into the house was going to die, and she didn't want me to be the one," he says. "She wanted it to be somebody she didn't know very well."

10

Moamis

During the time that J. R. was being courted for the murder of Lisa Fotopoulos others were being interviewed for the same job. One of them was Gus Moamis, the twenty-four-year-old car thief who says he came in on Kosta and Deidre when they were watching the torture film.

On September 12, 1989, Moamis was released from the Volusia County Branch Jail, where he had been serving short time for breaking into motels. From the jail, located west of town out on Volusia, Moamis hitched a ride to the boardwalk, where he looked up his old jail pal, Kevin Ramsey. Ramsey, eighteen, was working behind the bar at Top Shots.

Moamis soon fell in with the Top Shots crowd—Deidre Hunt, Lori Henderson, Ramsey, Mike Cox, Ron the car thief, Teja James, J. R., and assorted underage hookers. Moamis was one of several wayward young people who sometimes sacked out at Deidre's place.

In fact, as Moamis tells it, on his first visit to Deidre's, after a game of football with the others, he accidently climbed into the shower with Deidre, where he says there was "a little sexual contact, but no intercourse." Moamis does claim to have had sex with Deidre on other occasions,

135

which would make him less than unique. Many of the people in this group, male and female, slept with Deidre at one time or another.

It was at Top Shots that Moamis met Kosta.

"At first I thought he was a cop," Moamis says. "He asked me something and I said, 'Man, I don't want to talk to you, you are a cop. I don't want to talk to cops,' and he said, 'I am not a cop,' and the conversation went on a little bit, and about half an hour after we stopped talking, Deidre came over to me and she said Kosta wants to talk to me at the bar."

Gus Moamis, it should be noted, has never been considered a highly reliable witness to the events of 1989. David Damore, an assistant state attorney for the seventh Judicial District, says of Moamis, "I think he tells you some truth and then he adds his own details for effect."

As Moamis tells it, Kosta met Moamis at the bar, bought him a drink, and asked him what he had been in jail for and how old he was. Moamis clammed up.

"So you think I'm a cop?" Kosta said.

"Yeah," Moamis told him. "I seen you talking to the cops outside your place."

Then Kosta asked, "What would it take for me to prove to you that I'm not a cop?"

"I don't know," Moamis said.

Kosta paused. "I want you to do something for me," he said.

The two men walked into the office at the back of Top Shots and, as Moamis tells it, Kosta laid ten one-hundred-dollar bills on the desk. "I want you to get a car," he said to Moamis, who was an experienced car thief. He described the car, a Chevrolet Z-28.

"He told me where it would be parked," Moamis says. "The keys would be in it. Go down there, pick the car up and bring it back to him. That's how I actually got involved with the whole deal."

This car theft that Kosta hired Moamis for is known as

an "insurance job." It's a common scam in which the car keys are left in the ignition by an owner who has paid to have his car stolen so he can collect the insurance money. According to Moamis, there were eight or nine such insurance jobs that he did for Kosta. He or his partner would steal the car, keep it for two days, then blow it up or set it on fire.

"There were times, two times that I can remember, where a person actually come in and sat and talked to Kosta in the office and he pulled me in the office and said, 'Well, you are going to go here this time and get this car.' There was one car, a red Vette, from the airport parking lot. We blew it up in Boca Raton."

According to Moamis, car theft was not the only crime Kosta put him up to. Later on that first night, Moamis says, Deidre Hunt asked him and four other boardwalk characters if they wanted to make some quick money.

"She said she knew where there was some money at and we went and robbed a motel room. We got a couple of movie cameras out of it, a Rolex watch, a small amount of money, and some jewelry."

Moamis says that Kosta knew where certain guests were staying at various Daytona Beach motels and what they had in their rooms.

He says, "you can go in some hotels after midnight and reach behind the counter and they have numbers of all the rooms, all of the keys are sitting right there. Kosta would say, 'You get room two oh two.' It would be that simple. Go rob the room and bring the shit back to him. He would sell the shit to a couple of people that came down there and bought small things, small necklaces and bracelets and stuff like that. Sometimes it was set up so that the key would be there, buried next to the fifth or sixth tree, or by the trash can, or whatever."

Moamis also says Kosta was running prostitutes out of Daytona Beach hotels and was working a two-for-one deal where he would give two one-hundred-dollar bills to kids on the boardwalk and tell them to bring him back four hundred. The kids, according to Moamis, would use the two hundred to buy drugs, then resell the drugs for enough profit to pay back Kosta and still make some.

Cocaine selling was, according to Moamis, another of Kosta's illegal activities.

"If Deidre was behind the counter and somebody come in and wanted a gram of coke, they would get ahold of somebody in the bar, you know, has anybody got any coke, go tell Deidre. Deidre would go get it from Kosta. Deidre would bring it to whoever and sell it to them. The second day out I bought a gram from them. It was always there."

Gus Moamis, a Greek-American, sensed, as did J. R., that Kosta was dangerous. "He was quite violent," Moamis says. "He was the kind that he could do anything at any time. He told me a story one time, though I took it as a joke, about a person that he killed somewhere in some river. He cemented their feet in a tool box and dropped them off in some lake and videotaped them drowning. He threw them over the boat and he had on some stuff and went in the water and taped them drowning. I don't know if he got that out of a book or what."

On September 16, as Gus Moamis tells it, he went into the Top Shots bar.

"Deidre was working behind the bar. It was about nine o'clock at night and I came in and she said, 'Kosta wants to talk to you.' I said, 'Okay, fine.' I went in the back. He said, 'Have a seat,' went out and got us a couple of beers and we were sitting there talking and he got real serious and he asked me if I would ever kill anybody and I said, 'I don't know, if the money was right.' It wasn't in a joking manner.

"He leaned across the desk and said, 'How much would it cost for you to kill somebody?'

"I said, 'I ain't got no idea.'

"He took a briefcase from the floor next to the desk and

put it on the table. He opened it up and said, 'There is seventy-five thousand dollars in there.' There were little stacks of thousands lined up all the way across the briefcase.

"I said, 'You're serious, ain't you?' He said, 'Yes.'

"We sat there and talked a little more and I kept asking who it was and he wouldn't tell me. I said, 'Somebody here, guy, girl, or what?' and he wouldn't tell me. He asked me again how much it would cost for me to kill somebody. He said, 'I want to give you a little time to think about it before we discuss who it is. If you want to do it, the money is here. You get half the money before and half afterward.'

"We discussed a few ways I could do it, take them somewhere out in the woods and kill them, and he asked me, 'How would you do it?'

"Before I left, Kosta paid me thirty-five hundred dollars he owed me for a couple of cars that were stolen earlier that day."

Moamis says he thought seriously about doing the job.

"Yes, I thought about it. Who wouldn't with seventy-five thousand dollars looking you in the face? If I had a gun right there, he wouldn't have had the money no more the way I looked at it.

"I spent that night at Dee's and I come out of the bathroom and she was lying in bed and she asked me if Kosta talked to me and I said, 'Yes.' And she said, 'Did you tell him yes or no.' Then it dawned on me what she was talking about and I asked her, I said, 'Do you know about this?' and she's the one that told me it was Lisa. The next day I got arrested, so nothing really ever happened after that."

If Moamis had taken the job, he says, he probably would have killed Kosta, too.

"It was plain right from the start that whoever killed Lisa was going to be killed, bottom line. I wouldn't have walked in the house and shot the lady of the house first and leave the guy sitting there, especially when I know he loved guns."

But Moamis also says, "I am not the kind of guy that can just go kill somebody, especially when I found out that it was Lisa. That shocked me. I know Lisa from talking to her at the bar and at Joyland, but I don't know her real well. She seems like a super nice girl to me."

11

Mike

The third person to bail out of the Lisa Fotopoulos murder plan was Matthew Chumbley, who was known on the boardwalk as Mike Cox, a name he had invented. "I used it," he says, "whenever I was beating people."

"Beating" people in the lexicon of Mike Cox does not mean hitting them. It means taking money from them by selling them real or bogus LSD, conning them, stealing from them, doing whatever it takes. Most of the money Mike stole went to feed a serious drug monkey that had been on his back since early childhood.

Mike, who would discover Christ after all of this was over, had spent much of his youth at juvenile camps. In his home state of Kentucky he had been arrested for marijuana possession and carrying a concealed weapon. For that he had done "like forty-two hours or something," he says. In early September of 1989 he hitchhiked to Daytona Beach with a friend.

Mike and his friend migrated from motel to motel on the beach before moving into a small apartment where they rented a mattress on the floor for twenty dollars a week from a guy who worked on the boardwalk. After their host got thrown out of his place for selling crack, Cox descended to the streets, where he slept in abandoned motels and smoked a lot of crack.

At Top Shots he met Deidre, and through Deidre he met Kosta Fotopoulos, whom he regarded as a formidable personality.

"I was not afraid of Kosta, personally," he says. "I was afraid of the power he had."

Mike's first business transaction with Kosta was to be a gun purchase, but the deal fell through. It had begun when a friend told Cox that he needed some protection during drug deals. Cox suggested to his friend that Cox and J. R. get machine guns and go along as armed escorts on the drug sales. The friend thought that was a fine idea. Cox asked around on the boardwalk. The question was: who do you go to for guns? The answer was: Kosta.

"I was trying to buy two Uzis," Mike Cox says, "and Kosta told me it would cost me, I think, eight thousand dollars or something like that. I'm not sure of the price. But he told me he could have them for me in an hour with silencers and all the ammunition I needed."

The deal collapsed because the price was too high, but the negotiations had planted Mike Cox in Kosta's mind as one more young man who would do illegal things for money.

"Kosta always called me the Assassin after that," Mike says. "I didn't like that. You know, 'Hey, Mr. Assassin.' That's what he called me every time he seen me."

Sometime in October Kosta told Deidre to feel out Mike Cox for the job of murdering Lisa. Deidre found Cox and asked him if he would like to make ten thousand dollars.

"When she asked me did I want to make ten thousand dollars, I thought she was was joking. I said, 'Who do I got to kill?' And she said, 'Somebody.' And I said, 'Who?' And she said, 'Well, it might be a woman. I can't tell you right now.' And then she said, 'I have to talk to somebody.' "

Mike

At nine o'clock on Thursday, October 26, Mike Cox met Deidre at G. B. Reef's bar, just a few blocks north of the Marriott. His memory of what occurred that night is consistent with Deidre's.

Cox says that he did not trust Deidre and did not find her attractive. (Though he does proudly recall joining a sex orgy with Lori: "She was giving Buck head, and Tiger was eating Lori, and I was behind Tiger.") He does remember that things were pretty lively at the bar that night. Some of the guys at the bar were having a beer bust. Pay a dollar and get all the draft beer you can drink until somebody gets up to take a piss, then the beer bust is over.

The murder Mike was being hired for, Deidre said, was to be carried out in an office. (When J. R. and Gus Moamis were approached about murdering Lisa they were told the murder would take place in the victim's house.)

"You've got to go into this place, knock on the door to the office and ask for somebody," Deidre told Mike that night at the crowded bar.

"Who?"

"I can't tell you who, not yet. You'll be let in the door. Just shoot the woman. There's a bathroom in the office. Somebody will come out of the bathroom and give you the ten thousand."

"No way," Mike told her. "I want to see the money first."

Deidre thought about it. "Okay, I can arrange to have it out on the desk."

The details were still vague to Cox. But Deidre was drinking, and as she drank, Cox pestered her for more information.

"It's a lady who's trying to blackmail Kosta," she finally told him.

"Who's going to be coming out of the bathroom? Kosta?" Mike asked.

"Yes," she told him. "And you've got to shoot him, too, in the shoulder."

143

Deidre assured Cox that he would get his ten thousand dollars, and he told her he would do the job. Deidre told him to meet her at Top Shots the following afternoon, Friday, at two o'clock. She would set the whole thing up for him and give him a gun.

"And a silencer," Mike said. "I want a silencer."

"I can't," Deidre told him. "It would be too hard to dig it up."

"Dig it up?"

"The silencers are buried in the woods with other guns," she explained.

With that settled, Deidre, now almost drunk, began to shoot her mouth off about the Hunters and Killers Club. She made it sound to Cox as if the H and K Club was her and Kosta's organization, but was somehow linked to the Mafia and other organized crime. She told Mike about the videotape requirement, said that there was a videotape of her doing a murder and that she had a videotape of someone else committing a murder.

"Do you want to see it?" she asked.

"No," Mike said.

"If you're interested in joining you could make ten thousand dollars a week," she told Cox. She told him she had a Swiss bank account with over half a million dollars in it that Kosta had put there. Cox liked what he heard. It sounded glamorous.

"Besides," she told Mike, "if you ever get caught you'll only get three years at the most."

"Three years?"

"It's all political," Deidre explained. "There's lots of high up people involved. It's all got to do with politics."

At one point Deidre started talking about the murder again and she said something that troubled and confused Cox. She told him that it was okay for him to kill the person who came out of the bathroom.

Cox says now, "It messed my brain up. I was like, what

144

the hell's going on. I guess she didn't realize she had told me it was going to be Kosta coming out of the bathroom."

Though Mike Cox didn't catch on at the time, the plan, of course, was for Kosta to kill Mike. Specifically, Kosta would hear shots, come out of the bathroom, discover that some lowlife had shot his darling wife to death and he, Kosta, would shoot the hoodlum to death. This is more or less what would have happened to J. R. or Gus Moamis if they had gone through with the murder. "Kosta liked people who were expendable," Deidre says.

Like J. R. and Gus Moamis, Mike Cox gave serious thought to committing the murder. However, like those two, he was to be plucked from harm's way. On the morning after his meeting with Deidre at G. B. Reef's, Mike Cox was arrested for trespassing and was safely locked up in the Volusia County Branch Jail.

12

Kevin

Deidre would have to kill somebody. That's what Kosta told her. If she wanted to be a member of the Hunters and Killers Club, she would have to kill. Furthermore, she would have to let Kosta videotape the murder.

All of this was explained to her certainly by early October 1989, when Deidre was recruiting potential murderers. As each new murder conspiracy unraveled, it became more and more clear that Deidre herself might have to murder her lover's wife. If that was to be the case, she would first have to prove that her heart was as cold as his. He told her she would have to show him that she was capable of murder.

Lori Henderson recalls, "One day Deidre was telling me about Kosta wanting to have his wife killed, and then all of a sudden she started saying, 'He's going to have me kill someone to make sure that I can do it, to prove to him that I can kill his wife.' Deidre wasn't really decided on who she would kill. She thought Kosta was in love with her and they were just going to be happy together after his wife was gone.

"Kosta gave Deidre a Beretta. [Note: others recall that

Deidre was supposed to get a beret, so it is not clear whether Kosta gave her a cap or a pistol in this instance.] She was supposed to get an H and K on it or something like that, once she had completed everything. She was supposed to kill someone so she could take responsibility for killing Lisa."

The person Kosta picked for Deidre's initiation into murder was Kevin Ramsey.

Kevin Ramsey grew up in Wilmington, North Carolina, in three different homes, his mother's, his father's, and his grandmother's. His parents say he was a good kid, but easily persuaded into mischief.

His father, Terry, an electrician in Wilmington, recalls, "Kevin always went along with the crowd, he was easily led. As a teenager he went joyriding one time in another kid's car with three other kids. The judge made him do community work, put him on probation, and told him to stay in school. But he was a good kid, never a violent kid. He wasn't big, but he was strong and he would wrassle with other kids, but he would never hurt them."

Kevin liked to play basketball and he liked to draw cartoons. "Could really get the details down on cars and motorcycles," his father says.

Kevin quit high school in his sophomore year when he was sixteen. "Got involved with a girl and moved in with her," his father says. He later broke up with the girl and tried his hand at a variety of jobs, but when he got restless, the idea of going to Florida took hold of his imagination, and nobody could shake it loose. His mother, Vicki McLamb, recalls, "He said there had to be more opportunities in places other than Wilmington. We begged him not to go. He just wouldn't listen."

Kevin was a jolly kid, his mother says, always clowning around. He loved to joke, laugh, and run after girls.

"Yet," she says, "he was very sensitive." He often wrote poetry.

Shortly before he left for Florida Kevin wrote a sadly prophetic poem and gave it to his sister, Tonia.

To those whom I love,
if I should ever leave you whom I
love to go the silent way,
Grieve not nor speak of me with tears.
But laugh and talk with me
as if I was beside you there. . . .

When Kevin first got to Daytona he was arrested in a stolen car, but later released. Like other aimless kids, he gravitated to the boardwalk. He called his mother periodically to tell her he was okay. He lived for a while in the same group as J. R. In fact, he and J. R. were good friends until Kevin, then eighteen, got a job as a bartender at Top Shots. "Then," says J. R., "he got too big for his britches."

Vinnie Speziale, who was Kevin's boss at Top Shots, says, "Kevin, aside from the fact of what I would classify as being a punk, was a decent kid. By that I mean he would help you out with anything you needed. If you needed the trash emptied, you know, with no remuneration he'd do that. We had an instance where our beer cooler went out, and this kid lugs these huge cooler things all the way up to the end of the pier, upstairs to be stored. You know, just things like that.

"He seemed to be a messed-up kid, you know. He looked up to Kosta like a father or a brother. He worshipped Kosta. He worshipped the ground Kosta walked on. Kosta confided in Kevin more than he did in me. They were very close. Maybe he confided in him too much."

J. R. also remembers that Kevin looked up to Kosta. "Kevin always talked good about Kosta," says J. R., "about Kosta always giving him money and stuff. Kosta bonded him out of jail one time when Kevin sold weed to an undercover cop and was arrested. Kevin liked Kosta, and he feared him. He was always like, 'Don't do this, Kosta will get mad.' He appeared to be in awe of him.''

Not surprisingly, Kevin's image on the boardwalk was at some variance with the one of the sensitive, poetic teenager that the folks back home in North Carolina recall. Though he worked hard at his Top Shots job Kevin also, it seems, was constantly on the lookout for a fast buck.

Gus Moamis, for example, says Kevin Ramsey was running prostitutes. Others say Kevin was selling acid. And, though his parents say Kevin was incapable of violence, Mike Cox says, "I knew Kevin was robbing people on the beach at night. He told me he would hide up against a wall and lay down and wait for people to walk by and jump up and beat the shit out of them with a two-by-four or something and rob them.''

Kevin Ramsey was a poet. And he was also a hustler. And it was his hustling that got him in trouble with the local psycho. When Kosta Fotopoulos decided that Kevin Ramsey would be the person Deidre would kill, it was not a random choice. Though Kevin might have adored Kosta at one time, through the fall of 1989 there were steady signs that the relationship was deteriorating.

For one thing, Kevin stole money from the man he looked up to.

"Kevin was stealing from the business,'' says Speziale. "I brought it up right in front of him and Kosta. He said, 'I swear to God, I never took a penny out of that register.' I said, 'The goddamned money never made it to the register, did it, Kevin?' And he goes, 'No, it didn't.' I mean he didn't take it out of the register. It never made it to the register. So, he admitted to the stealing.''

Kosta fired Kevin and told him never to enter Top Shots again.

When Kevin stole from Top Shots he had betrayed the Greek, but that, apparently, was not enough to earn him a death sentence. Even after the firing, Kevin and Kosta seemed to get along well. But when Kevin betrayed Kosta a second time, by running prostitutes of his own, Kosta started with the death threats.

Gus Moamis says, "I personally on two occasions seen Kosta threaten to kill Kevin if he didn't stop running prostitutes, because Kosta was losing money. His girls were going from Kosta to Kevin and he told Kevin, you know, if you don't stop it I will kill you. He was serious, too."

However, it was probably neither the stealing nor the pimping that sealed Kevin's fate. Kevin was marked for death because he was planning to blackmail Kosta, and he made the mistake of telling Deidre Hunt about it, which was roughly akin to broadcasting it on Daytona's largest radio station.

Kevin's boardwalk friend Teja James, recalls, "After Kevin found out that Kosta was passing counterfeit money, he said he was going to blackmail him. He asked me did I know anything else about Kosta. I was like, 'Well, dude, that's out of my league, you know. I don't want to be involved with it.' He just said he wanted a couple thousand dollars off Kosta or he was going to go to the police. I don't think he ever told Kosta that. But he told Deidre. I'm pretty sure she told Kosta."

That's a pretty safe assumption. Later, when Deidre found out that Kevin was to be her victim she told her friend and lover, Lori Henderson.

It was the night of October 20, five nights before Lisa would get her dreadful phone call from Elena Speziale. Deidre spoke to Lori while Deidre waited on the boardwalk for Kevin and Kosta.

"Deidre told me that it was going to be Kevin," Lori says. "She told me that Kosta had set it up with him, that he was supposed to meet him down at Joyland to talk about getting his job back or something, and Deidre was waiting on him to get there. She told me that Kosta had picked Kevin to be the victim and that they were going to meet him on the boardwalk. Deidre wanted to kill Kevin. She wanted to find out if she could kill someone. I didn't

150

think she was capable of it, but Kosta, yes. Deidre was afraid Kevin wouldn't show up. Then kind of jokingly she asked if he doesn't show up, then, you know, who should she kill or something like that. She said if Kevin didn't show up she would take Tiger into the woods. Tiger is the girl down on the boardwalk, a little sixteen-year-old girl. It was just joking."

It's incredible that Kevin Ramsey walked so willingly into this trap, because clearly in the days preceding it he believed that his life was in danger.

Robin Bergdorf, a twenty-three-year-old nurse's aid who was one of Kevin Ramsey's girlfriends in Daytona, recalls that when Kevin was living with her in her trailer on Ridgewood Avenue he came home drunk on the night of October 18 and said he was afraid he was going to be killed or badly hurt because he had learned too much about Kosta's business.

"I said, 'You ain't got nothing to be afraid of,' " Bergdorf says. "Then he said that he was afraid because of something that he had done with Kosta Fotopoulos or knew about him. Supposedly, he was selling drugs for him. This was after he stopped working in Top Shots. He said he learned too much while he was working for Konstantin.

"I took it he was quite afraid when he started crying. He cried through the whole conversation and afterward for about an hour."

For the next two days, Bergdorf says, Kevin was his normal self. And then he disappeared.

Kevin had not, however, skipped town, though that would seem a prudent thing to do under the circumstances. There is no saying why Ramsey didn't just run away from Daytona. But one reasonable explanation is that Kosta had found out where Kevin's relatives lived and had threatened to kill them if Kevin left town.

Kevin also turned to Raymond Smith, a security guard who was sometimes assigned to the Krystal's hamburger joint, one block east of the boardwalk, where many of the boardwalk kids hung out.

"Kevin didn't seem like the kind of kid who was in big trouble," Smith says. "Seemed like he'd been pretty much on his own for a long time. He asked for my phone number once when I was working. He told me thirteen- and four-teen-year-old girls were going in the pool hall and he thought there was something sexual going on and it had something to do with Fotopoulos. He was concerned. He wanted me to investigate. I told him I'm not a police officer, I can't investigate."

One night in mid-October Smith was at home when Kevin called.

"Hey, Ray, this is Kevin."

Ramsey sounded excited. "What's up?" Smith asked.

"I'm scared," Kevin told him.

"Scared about what?"

"I don't want to talk about it on the phone."

"Well, give me an idea," Ray said. "What are you scared about?"

"Somebody's after me," Kevin told him.

"How do you know?"

"I just . . . think somebody is after me," Kevin said. He sounded spacey. He wasn't making much sense.

Kevin asked Smith to meet him.

"So we agreed to meet at Krystal's," Smith says. "It was nine-thirty at night. I'm sitting there and this blue Mercedes with tinted windows pulls up. Kevin gets out of the passenger side. He comes in. He was really petrified that somebody was after him. 'Someone's after me, someone wants to kill me,' he says. I said, 'Like in a movie?' He said, 'No, I'm serious.' I was surprised because Kevin was the type of guy, nothing would scare him. He didn't tell me who would try to kill him. He said it had something to do with the pool hall. 'Well, how did you find this out?' I asked him. 'Somebody told me,' he says.

"He wanted a bodyguard. I said I can do it but I've got

to go through the office and it will cost money. He said he'd call me.

"He had me confused. This didn't make any sense. I said, 'Whose car is that?' and he said it was his dad's, which was hard to believe. I had never seen him in a vehicle before, he was always on foot. The car was like silver blue, with dark purple tinted windows so you couldn't see in, nice wheels. I said, 'You're moving up in the world.'

"I asked him why someone wanted to kill him. He said he didn't know, he would talk to me later. He looked like he was really in a rush to get out of there. He got back in the car on the passenger side. I couldn't see who was driving."

The Mercedes and its driver remain a mystery, as does Kevin's reasons for staying in Daytona when he was so certain that someone wanted to kill him.

Equally mysterious is Kevin Ramsey's love life. While Robin Bergdorf describes herself as "a very close girlfriend" to Kevin, and says he was living with her up to the time he disappeared, Diane Nelson, another girl who hangs out on the boardwalk, and says Kevin was "like a brother" to her, tells a different story. "Tiger and Kevin were supposed to get married in about three months," Diane says. "They broke up, but they didn't really break up. They were playing some kind of scam where he was going with some girl to get her money and after getting her money he would pick up with Tiger again. Tiger was a prostitute."

Add to this a third girlfriend, Diamond. After Kevin vanished, it was Diamond, according to several of the boardwalk kids, who put out a story that Kevin had gone to work for her father in Orlando, and then had stolen a truck and split. Some believe that Diamond was paid to spread this story. But that seems unlikely. What would be the point of paying someone to spread a cover story when Kevin's killer was proudly telling half the county about how she killed Kevin?

What follows is a description of Kevin Ramsey's murder,

based on the confession Deidre Hunt gave to the police, and the recollections of the people to whom Deidre described the murder before she was arrested.

On that Friday night, October 20th, Deidre finally met Kevin at Popeye's, a franchised fried chicken restaurant. Kevin knew he was to meet Kosta there and he was not afraid. Kosta had told Kevin that all was forgiven and that Kevin would be initiated into the Hunters and Killers Club.

When Kosta arrived, the three of them got into Kosta's car and drove west toward the wooded area along Williamson Boulevard, not far from the Strickland shooting range, where Kosta often practiced. Along the way Kosta explained the night's initiation. They would go into the woods and he would shoot at Kevin's feet. Kevin would have to remain perfectly still. This would somehow show that Kevin was qualified to go into Europe to do hits and face enemy fire. Kosta also explained that when Kevin went to Europe to commit these high-priced murders, he would be given a Russian rifle. "That's what the terrorists use," Kosta explained. "That way when they find the bullets they'll think it was a terrorist, not just some guy who came into the country to do a hit."

Perhaps there is no better example of how persuasive and charming Kosta Fotopoulos could be than the simple fact that Kevin Ramsey felt safe enough to go into the woods at night and stand by a tree and let Kosta point a gun at him and fire it, simply because Kosta assured him that he was no longer interested in killing Kevin.

When they got to Williamson Kosta pulled over. From the trunk of his BMW he removed an AK47 automatic rifle, an eight-millimeter video camera, a flashlight, and a .22 caliber pistol with a silencer. The trio walked into the woods. When they were far enough from the road, which was virtually untraveled at this hour, Kosta handed the .22 to Deidre. He pulled out some rope.

"He tied Kevin to a tree," Deidre says. "He said, 'Kevin, this is just a precaution so you don't move, because you

154

don't want to get hit.' Kevin's hands were behind his back around the tree and Kosta tied his hands together. Kosta walked to the left. He took out the video camera and pointed at me and he said take the .22 and shoot him. I shot Kevin three times in the chest and once in the head, in the left temple at close range. Then after that Kosta shot him again with some kind of Russian gun. He had it on semiautomatic I guess because it only shot one bullet when he pulled the trigger. He made me catch the shell. He untied Kevin and took the rope, so Kevin's body was like scrunched. He said, 'Sorry, man,' and he said, 'Come on,' so I just followed him. We went back to the car and left."

The preceding quotes from Deidre Hunt are taken from the confession she gave to police after she was arrested. They are the parts of the confession that are consistent with the recollections of Lori Henderson, Teja James, and others to whom Deidre described the murder before she was arrested. The full confession to the police contains many self-serving details, which the others don't recall hearing when Deidre was not in custody, and which must be considered suspect.

For example, in her confession Deidre says of the .22, "I don't know why he gave it to me. He said 'Carry this,' and I did what he said." And after Kosta told her to shoot Kevin, Deidre says, "I didn't know what to do. I was scared by this point and he could just as easily have shot me." Of the video camera, Deidre says, "I didn't know it was a video camera until afterward. I just thought it was a flashlight he had."

Deidre's story in a nutshell is that Kosta forced her at gunpoint to kill Kevin and that, furthermore, he threatened to kill her family if she didn't do as told. It's likely that Kosta threatened Deidre's family. That was one of his ploys. But the idea that Deidre killed Kevin strictly out of self-preservation is at odds with every other story surrounding the events of those troubling days, and with her demeanor on the videotape.

With any murder there will be discrepancies large and small between stories told by comurderers, and between different versions told by one murderer. But the basic facts of Kevin Ramsey's murder cannot be refuted because, uniquely, they were captured on videotape.

The videotape that Kosta made that night is fifty-seven seconds long. It begins with Deidre Hunt standing in the dark woods with only the light of Kosta's flashlight on her. She looks at the camera and tells Kosta, "Don't shine it in my eyes. Hold it down." Then she says, "Ready?"

We hear Kosta say, "Come closer. I can't see you." Kosta, apparently, points to where Deidre should stand. "Stand right there," he says. Deidre moves closer to Kevin, who is tied to the tree. The camera pans to the face of Kevin Ramsey and then back to Deidre. Again she says, "Ready?" Kosta says, "Okay." Then Deidre lifts the gun and points it at Kevin Ramsey's chest. She fires three times into the left side of his chest. Kevin moans in pain. He says, "God." Then he makes another sound of agony, like, "Ahhh," and he lifts his left leg in pain. His head is down now. Diedre walks over to him. She grabs his hair and pulls his head up. She puts the gun to his left temple and fires once more. Kevin falls forward. We can see that his hands are tied behind him with a rope. The video ends.

After Kosta shut off the video camera that night he picked up his AK47 and shot Kevin one more time.

Lori Henderson recalls, "Deidre told me they had tied him to a tree or something and shot him a couple of times in the body and then she told me that she picked up his head and she shot him one time in his head, and then she had to hold a jacket to catch the shell because Kosta said something about Kevin not being all the way dead or something and so he shot Kevin with a big gun. She told me he had videotaped it."

After Kevin was dead, Deidre Hunt did not act as if she had done something to be ashamed of. Her descriptions of the murder to friends have about them the quality of a boast. She had, it seems, done something of which she was proud.

During the days following that night in the woods off Williamson Boulevard Deidre told at least four people about the murder, and probably more. She told Lori Henderson. She told Mike Cox. She told J. R. And she told Kevin's friend and Lori's boyfriend, Teja James. She told Teja because after J. R. had turned her down and Mike Cox got arrested, there was still the matter of Lisa Fotopoulos to be dealt with. Kosta wanted his wife dead and, as much as she had enjoyed killing Kevin, Deidre did not want the job of killing Lisa. She wanted Teja to do it.

Teja, twenty-one, had lived in Daytona off and on, and now had been down from Brooklyn since June, long enough for him to have fallen in with Kosta and the kids who hung out at Top Shots. Of all those kids, he was closest to Lori, who was his girlfriend, and Kevin Ramsey, who was his drinking pal.

Sometime during the last week of October Teja recalls being in Deidre Hunt's apartment on Lenox. He sat on the bed with Deidre in her bedroom. Lori was in another room.

"Do you remember what I told you and Kevin that time?" Deidre said, referring to one of the many times she had shot her mouth off about Kosta's various rackets.

"About the counterfeit?" Teja asked.

"Right," Deidre said. "The counterfeit. And you remember that Kevin was going to blackmail Kosta."

"Yeah," Teja said, "I remember him talking about it." He remembered Kevin trying to find out if Teja knew other things about Kosta.

"Have you seen Kevin around lately?" Deidre said. She smiled.

"Come to think of it, no," Teja said. "Kevin hasn't even been in town lately."

"No, he hasn't," Deidre said knowingly.

"I wonder where he went. His girlfriend told me he was in Orlando."

"He's not in Orlando," Deidre said. "He's in Daytona."

"Daytona? Where?"

"He's dead," Deidre said.

"Right," Teja said. "Sure he is."

"I'm not kidding," Deidre said. "He's dead. I killed him."

"Yeah, right, Deidre. Right," Teja said.

"I'll show you," Deidre said.

Teja watched as Deidre climbed off the bed and walked to her closet. What she was telling him was ridiculous, but she didn't look as if she were joking.

"Yeah, right," he said again, nervously. "Kevin's dead. Sure."

Deidre came back to the bed carrying a pair of her shoes. "See," she said. She thrust the shoes forward with one hand and pointed to the red crusted stains on them. "That's his blood."

Teja could feel himself getting tense. His heart was beating faster. He was starting to believe this shit.

"Oh, come on," Teja said. "This is a joke, right?"

"No joke," Deidre said.

"It's got to be," he said. "Tell me it's a joke."

Then Deidre called Lori into the room.

"Lori," Deidre said, "tell Teja that Kevin's dead."

Lori looked at her boyfriend.

"Well?" he said.

"He's dead," Lori said.

Teja knew Lori well enough to realize this was no joke. He was shocked.

"But why?" he said. "How?"

Deidre and Lori sat on the bed like two girls at a pajama party and told Teja how Deidre and Kosta had killed Kevin Ramsey and why it was videotaped.

"Deidre told me how they went about it," Teja says now. "Told me where the body was, how many times he was shot, what he was shot with, what he had on, what he said, the last thing he said, and that the only thing they regretted about it was that his last spoken words, before they turned on the video camera, were 'I'm hungry.' I was pretty pissed off about it. Kevin was my friend."

Perhaps the thing that shocked Teja most that day was the fact that his girlfriend knew about the murder in advance. In fact, on the night of the 20th, while Kevin was being tied to the tree, Lori was at Top Shots with Teja, knowing what was going on.

"The whole time Lori was sitting with me at Top Shots, saying that she was waiting to go meet Deidre at a bar, was when it happened," Teja says.

When the girls finished telling their tale in Deidre's bedroom that day, Teja was numb. Kevin dead? It was hard to imagine. And then Deidre began her pitch.

"He's coming to talk to you next, you know," Deidre said.

"Who?"

"Kosta."

"Kosta?" Teja said. The name itself had begun to sound frightening.

"What are you going to do?" Deidre asked. "He's going to ask you to work for him."

"Or?" Teja asked.

"Or, you know, end up like Kevin," she said.

13

Teja

Teja Mzimmia James had arrived in Daytona Beach in June of 1989. A tall, good-looking, light-skinned black, with a broader vocabulary than many of his boardwalk cohorts, Teja had come down from his home in Brooklyn, he says, "for another spring break," and to work, hanging drywall for his father, who lives in the Holly Hills, a neighboring community. He didn't plan to stay long, but when he fell for Lori Henderson he decided to stick around.

Teja started seeing Lori. He moved in with his father. Soon he was haunting the boardwalk as he had in past years. He and Kevin Ramsey became drinking pals.

Teja is a friendly enough fellow, part of the great majority of juvenile delinquents who are not permanently sociopathic, but like the other boardwalk habitués, Teja cultivated an image as a tough guy. He explains it much the way the others would.

"See, on the street I learned to carry myself. You have to be a tough guy when you're around a crowd of people, or somebody is going to always aggravate you or bother you or, you know, put you down or something. But when people know that you will strike and you will get violent if they cross you in the wrong way, then they'll leave you alone. That's the image that most people know of me."

Part of being a tough guy, for Teja, as it had been for J. R., and Mike Cox, was putting word out on the street that he had committed murder. All three of them had made that claim to at least one person one time, and that was enough to get it around. In all three cases it got around to Kosta and gave him reason to think he had found his assassin. Whether it is true in any of those cases is not known.

In June Teja worked for three days making change at Joyland. There he knew Kosta Fotopoulos as "the man who owned the building," but didn't meet him. It was in July, through an incident at Top Shots, that Teja got to know Kosta.

Teja was shooting pool at Top Shots late one afternoon when some guy who had swallowed too many beers at the bar started loud-mouthing to Kevin Ramsey. Ramsey, not wanting to get in trouble with the boss, kept cool. The customer grew gradually more obnoxious and abusive. Finally Teja decided to help Kevin out by leading the boozer to the door.

"Get your hands off me, nigger," the customer said, and that was enough. Teja made short work of the customer. "Two hits, it was over," he says.

Kosta, who had watched the incident, was impressed. He came over and complimented Teja on his fighting skills.

Apparently their short conversation was enough to convince Kosta that Teja could be trusted, because a few days after the skirmish Kosta told Teja about a major narcotics sale that was going to go down at a Daytona warehouse.

"So?" Teja said.

"I want you to steal the payoff money," Kosta told him.

"He freaked me out with this warehouse thing, because he just came out of the blue with it," Teja says. "He asked me to go into the warehouse with an Uzi, kill everybody there, and bring the cash to him. I could do with the dope whatever I wanted to."

Though Kosta spoke to him in serious and conspiratorial tones, Teja suspected that the warehouse existed only in Kosta's imagination, and, indeed, the plan might have been nothing more than the plot from one of Kosta's comic books.

"I came back to him later and asked whatever happened to that deal," Teja says, "and he told me, 'Ah, the license plate turned out to be the wrong one,' or something."

Though Teja might not have taken the warehouse job seriously he learned quickly that it could be a deadly mistake not to take Kosta seriously.

"People were afraid of him. I was afraid of him when I wasn't carrying a weapon. Deidre told me about the time Kosta was going to kill this one dude that was in her house, not J. R. This is a guy that's got a permanent burn mark on his neck from the barrel of a gun."

Teja also tells this story of a confrontation that helped fortify Kosta's legendary image on the boardwalk.

"One night a guy threw a cue ball at Kosta after Kosta had asked him to leave the bar because he was drunk and belligerent and causing a problem. And when the guy threw the ball, Kosta politely walked over to him. The guy went to swing at him, and Kosta did something to the guy, but before you could blink your eyes, the guy was on the ground with the 9 millimeter in his mouth, you know. After that people just stopped bothering Kosta."

The fact that Kosta was a dangerous man is Teja's explanation of why, when Kosta suggested in late October that Teja kill Lisa, Teja felt that he was being told, not asked. He knew that bad things could happen to people who didn't do what Kosta asked. He knew because of that conversation in Deidre Hunt's bedroom, when she had shown him the blood-crusted shoes and told him about the video-taped murder of Kevin Ramsey.

Teja says that it was a few days after that conversation that Kosta approached him about killing Lisa, though it wasn't immediately clear what Kosta wanted.

They sat at a table in Deidre's apartment on Lenox, just Teja and Kosta. Kosta had prattled on for quite a while, spinning tales of valor and adventure in the CIA and describing in detail hits he had made. "I've killed many people," he told Teja, "but never for less than two thousand dollars. If it's under two thousand dollars I won't mess with it." Then Kosta stopped talking suddenly, as he sometimes did. He stared across the table at Teja. "I know you know about Kevin," he said. "I don't know how you know, but I know you know."

Teja felt his body stiffen. He didn't know what to expect.

Kosta leaned back in his chair and relaxed, as if to say there was nothing to worry about.

"How would you like to do a few things for me and get paid for it," he said. He allowed a few silent beats, then added, "Instead of going down the other road?"

Teja knew what the other road was. It was the road Kevin Ramsey had taken into the woods off Williamson.

"I could do some work for you, sure," Teja said, squirming in his seat. This is one dangerous son of a bitch, he thought. Teja wished he had a gun with him, because Kosta sure as hell did. He remembered Lori telling him about Kosta's torture tapes.

"Good," Kosta said. "I want you to be a sort of middle man for me."

"Middle man?"

"Sure," Kosta said. "When people have a problem with me, they come and talk to you and you bring their request to me."

"Okay," Teja said. He didn't know what Kosta was talking about exactly, but that was fine. He wanted to know as little as possible. Kevin had known too much. The way Teja figured it, the more you knew about Kosta's business, the greater your chances were of ending up tied to a tree with a flashlight shining in your face and an AK47 pressed against your skull.

"One other thing," Kosta said. "Don't try to leave town on me. I know where your family lives."

Teja knew this was true. Kosta had once given him a ride to Teja's father's house in Holly Hill.

While Teja, like the other boardwalk characters, undoubtedly shaves his stories to make himself less villainous, his description of Kosta's proposition has the ring of truth to it. Deidre, Bill Markantonakis, and others have reported that Kosta used threats against family as leverage. Even Lisa, though she didn't take it seriously at the time, got a taste of it that night in the Joyland office when Kosta battered the coffee table, demanded the name of the person who had called her, and shouted, "If you don't tell me who told you, I'll kill your brother."

When Kosta finally got to what he really wanted, he told Teja he would pay him ten thousand dollars to shoot Lisa at Joyland and make it look like a robbery. Teja said he would do it.

The first time that Teja was supposed to meet Kosta and get specific instructions Teja chickened out. After that, Kosta came up with a new plan. He called Teja on the phone, and told him to get a knife and stab Lisa to death at the Halloween party at Razzles.

Kosta's explanation of how the murder could be committed without detection in a crowded nightclub is a clear indication that he never understood that dastardly deeds could be done much more neatly in adventure movies and comic books than in real life. His scenario would have worked in a James Bond film, but likely would have developed a few hitches at Razzles.

"He told me about the knife, three ribs up," Teja says. "You know, I forget the name of the muscle, but it contracts your lungs so you can't breathe. The diaphragm, that's it. And I was supposed to go three ribs up from the back, stab her once, pull it out, stab her again one rib down, turn it, and bring it out. That would stop all talking, all screaming, all breathing. Just sit her down in the chair, fold her arms in front of her and lean her head down so she appeared drunk."

With this impractical plan in mind Teja and Deidre went to the Pic N' Save, where they bought a knife to kill Lisa with.

On Halloween night Teja went to Razzles with the knife hidden in his sleeve. Incredibly, he wore no costume on the one night of the year when he could hide behind a mask and not draw attention to himself. There were hundreds of people in the glitzy, raucous nightclub, which attracts locals and tourists. Lisa, in her cowgirl outfit, sat at a small cocktail table surrounded by friends in bear suits and Batman costumes. On the other side of the dance floor, beyond dozens of gyrating partyers, Teja saw Kosta, wearing his black hood. Yes, Teja thought, he's staying as far away from his wife as he can get.

"I was going to do it at first," Teja says, "because it seemed like a now or never thing, you know, that you do something and stop b.s.'ing around, or you end up like Kevin. I was standing by Lisa for like five, ten minutes, but then I left and went over to where Deidre and Lori were. And Deidre said, 'Go to the bathroom and Kosta's going to follow you.' "

When Teja got to the men's room at Razzles Kosta was waiting. When the two men were alone Kosta stood by the sink and pulled off his dark hood. He reached into a pocket and pulled out a small piece of paper.

"You know what this is?" he said. He held the paper over the sink.

"A check," Teja said.

"A check for ten thousand dollars," Kosta said. "See. Look." He jabbed at the check. "Look who it's made out to."

Teja looked again. His own name was on the check.

"Me," he said.

"Right," Kosta said. "Now here's what you do." Kosta stood behind Teja, wrapped his left arm around Teja's chest, and with his right thumb poked at the spots on Teja's back. "You get behind Lisa, see, and you stick the knife in, three ribs up."

Kosta went through the murder plan again, detail by detail. Then he gave Teja a friendly pat on the back, and sent him out to murder Lisa.

This time Teja was determined. Get it over with, he thought, take the money and get the hell out. Now the music was really thumping and the crowd was getting soused. For a moment it wasn't hard to imagine murdering somebody there in the dark nightclub amid the noise and excitement, and actually walking away without being noticed. Again Teja worked his way through the crowd. He moved close to Lisa. He could feel the knife in his sleeve, the small handle pressed against his palm. Just stick it in her back, he told himself, three ribs up. Pull it out. Stick it in again. He moved closer. Lisa was laughing. The music was throbbing. It was so loud that Teja could hardly hear himself think. People were out on the dance floor, hundreds of them now, pressed so tightly they could barely wiggle their bodies. They were dressed as elves and devils and pirates and princesses. *Just sit her down, people will think she's drunk.* He stood behind her, pretending to stare out at the dancers. It was so crowded that people were bumping into him when they passed by. The moment of truth was gaining on him. What would Kosta do if he chickened out? He had to do it. But as he got closer and the handle of the knife grew more slippery from the sweat on his hand, the whole idea became less real. The crowd, which moments ago had seemed to promise cover and anonymity, now seemed to stare back at him, a thousand witnesses. How the hell could he knife a woman in this madhouse? He couldn't do it. No. Not here, not with all these people.

"I looked at Deidre and Lori. I said, 'Man, I can't do this. I'm too nervous. There's too many people watching me.' And Deidre's like, 'Oh shit, Kosta's going to be mad. Oh, fuck.' "

A few minutes later Deidre met with Kosta in a stall in the men's room and told him that Teja was afraid to put the knife in Lisa's back.

When Kosta came out of the men's room he told Teja, "Don't worry about it. I'll call you tomorrow morning between eight-thirty and nine."

The next morning Kosta called Teja and told him to meet him in the parking lot of the Texan Hotel. There Kosta got into Teja's car.

They drove to Deidre's apartment. Kosta and Deidre went into the bedroom and had sexual intercourse for half an hour. When Kosta came out he told Teja how he was to kill Lisa.

The new plan was a return to the old plan. Teja was to kill Lisa in her office at Joyland.

"The three of us drove up by the boardwalk. Kosta showed me where I was going to go. He showed me where Dino's car is parked, where his wife is going to park, what time Dino leaves, what times she's supposed to be there, where we're going to wait so we can watch Dino's car and where Deidre is supposed to pick me up after I'm done."

By this time Teja already had the gun he was to use on Lisa. It was a .22 caliber pistol. The friend who sold it to him had warned Teja that the gun always jammed after one shot. Teja had planned to fix the gun, but says he never had a file small enough.

In the car that morning, Kosta, as was his style, gave Teja very specific instructions about how to kill the woman he had married. "When you get in the office punch her in the face," Kosta said. "Knock her back into the office, then step in and close the door. Pull the gun on her, take her to the back of the office. The gun won't be heard through that wall.

"When you get her back there, order her to take off her jewelry. Don't rip it off. It's Greek gold and I want it back.

167

Don't touch anything metal. Also, there's a little box that looks like a remote control door opener. Don't let her get to it. It's an alarm that can be placed anywhere in the office. Shoot her two times in the back of the head and leave."

At one-thirty on the same day, Wednesday, November 1, Teja and Deidre pulled into the parking lot of Hog Heaven, a popular barbecue spot on the west side of Atlantic Avenue. From where they sat they could see Dino drive off. When Dino drove away, at around two-fifteen, Teja knew that Lisa was alone in the office.

What follows is Teja's version of what happened that day.

"I got out of the car, walked through the Hog Heaven parking lot, across A1A, and across the dirt mound, down the steps into the game room. And I sat there at a game. It was this jet fighter game where you sit there and play. I was playing the game because there was this guy making change right by the door. He left and walked off. I stopped playing the game. I went and knocked on the door and she opened the door. And I put my hand on the wall and I said, 'Is Kosta here?' And she said, 'No.' And I said, 'Do you know what time he's coming back, I'm supposed to talk to him about a job.' And she said, 'No, what is it you want?' And then I noticed that she looked down and she saw the gun, and then she looked back up at me and she sort of cringed a little bit, you know, like she was scared or something.

"And that's when I pulled out the gun and said, 'Get back in the office.' She dove on the ground and she said, 'No.' I told her, I said, 'Get up, bitch.' She got up and I said, 'Get in the office' and she said, 'No, you get in the office.' I'm like, 'What are you, crazy? You get in the office.' She said, 'No, you get in the office.' And then I told her something and then she ran off. She came back and said, 'Get in the office.' I said, 'No, you get in the office.' She said, 'No, you get in the office,' and we went through that ordeal again. And I cocked the gun and I aimed it at her, and then she finally took off.

"I put the gun back in my jacket, walked by the lady at the cashier, and waved at her and kept walking."

When Teja got out on A1A Deidre picked him up.

"How did it go?" she asked. "Is she dead? How many times did you shoot her?"

"I didn't kill her," Teja told Diedre. "She got away."

"Oh, shit. Kosta's going to be mad."

They drove back to Deidre's place and waited for Kosta to call.

When Kosta learned that his wife was still alive, he was frantic. "How am I going to deal with this? How am I going to deal with this!" he said. He told Teja to go home. "Don't leave your house until I call you," he said.

So Teja, like Mike Cox, and J. R. before him, saved his own life by not committing the murder of Lisa Fotopoulos.

In his original court deposition Teja claimed that before knocking on the office door he went into the men's room and pulled the clip from the gun. He later admitted that this was not true. However, there are indications that Teja was less than zealous about killing Lisa Fotopoulos. Even before he was arrested he told some of his boardwalk friends that he didn't want to kill her and had deliberately botched the Joyland attempt.

"I went there with the intention of doing it," he says. "But when I was playing the video game I realized I couldn't. I was like, man, I can't kill this lady. If she had gone back into the office when I told her to, I would have been fucked."

Certainly it is self-serving for Teja to say this even if it is not true. On the other hand he did miss the first scheduled planning session with Kosta. He did avoid killing Lisa at the Halloween party. And on this occasion he did have a clear shot at Lisa, but let her get away. So maybe Teja really was taking each plan only as far as his conscience allowed, in order to avoid being shot himself. This scenario is made more credible by the fact that the next assassin acted in similar fashion.

David Damore, the assistant state attorney, believes that of all the kids involved in the plot to murder Lisa, Teja is the one most likely to straighten out. "He's the one I am most hopeful for," Damore says. "There is a certain likability about Teja. He's young enough, resourceful enough, that he will have a lot of opportunities. He's a handsome young fellow, and I grew to like him, though not his actions. I want to call him a scoundrel. If you didn't know what he got involved with you could like him very much. He's a friendly kind of fellow, he's got an aura about him. It takes a while to get him to tell you the truth, but once you get him to tell the truth he's charming. He has recanted his story about the gun not being loaded. The gun was loaded and Lisa did come within an inch of her life."

14

Edgewater

"**G**od, you could have been killed," Kosta said to Lisa after he learned that some young black man had assaulted her. He seemed extremely agitated. Lisa was touched by his concern. Almost immediately, Kosta went to work installing a security system that would protect his wife from another incident like the holdup attempt. At the office he put in an intercom so that anybody ringing the buzzer on the door would have to speak into the intercom and identify himself before the door would be unlocked.

"He got me a walkie-talkie set," Lisa says. "I could give one to whoever was working the floor. That way if I had any trouble I could call for help. He gave me a rifle, too. He said I could scare off people with it."

For the rest of the day Lisa was extremely edgy. Kosta stayed with her, hammering out his security system and boasting that it was foolproof.

At one point Lisa opened a drawer and noticed that her gun, the one she would have needed to save her life if the holdup man had gotten her alone in the office, was missing.

"Kosta, do you know what happened to my gun?"

171

"Gun? What gun?"

"My gun, Kosta. The one you gave me. The one I keep in the office."

"Oh, that," Kosta said. "I lent it to somebody."

"Who?"

"A guy I know," Kosta said.

While it was unnerving to realize that her life might have depended on getting to a gun that wouldn't have been there, Lisa found nothing particularly suspicious about the fact that the gun was gone. It was typical of Kosta to lend someone a gun. He passed guns around the way other people pass around popcorn. Lisa accepted his explanation without comment. Besides, she had a gun in the glove compartment of her Porsche. She would just bring that gun into the office tomorrow. All these guns, she thought. I went my whole life without ever even seeing a gun and now I'm surrounded by them.

It was after dark on that same night, November 1, when Lisa and Kosta left Joyland. As usual, they walked up the back stairs to Ocean Avenue, where both of their cars were parked. She took deep breaths; that was supposed to calm you down. She could hear the sound of the ocean, a block away. She studied the sky above it, now gone gray in the twilight of a November evening, and thought wistfully that it would be great if she and Kosta could just get away for a while to someplace safe. Maybe she and Kosta could patch things up if they had some time away from the pressures of family and work. November 4 was just three days off, and she looked forward to a good talk on the drive to Key West.

As they walked out of Joyland and headed for their separate cars, Kosta gave Lisa an affectionate hug. "I know you're still upset about the holdup attempt," he said. "But everything's all right now." Then he told Lisa that he wanted to watch a war film that night, so he said he was going to stop at the video store to rent a film. Lisa knew that her mother and Dino were out, and still shaken by the days events, she did not want to go home to an empty house.

"I'll follow you in my car," she told Kosta.

Kosta, in the BMW, took a left down the small hill to Atlantic, then right. Lisa, in her Porsche, followed him.

Almost from the beginning of the drive Lisa had the eerie feeling that she was being followed. She couldn't quite be sure. For a long time they drove straight up Atlantic Avenue, so there was nothing really unusual about having the same car behind her all the time. There were hundreds of cars driving up and down Atlantic Avenue. This was the dinner hour, and the people who weren't heading home for supper, were scouting out restaurants. But the car behind her, with its high beams bouncing off her rearview mirror, seemed intent on something else. It seemed to have a purpose, a purpose that involved Lisa.

Lisa couldn't see the driver or even what kind of car it was. But it troubled her. The car seemed always too close, and she got the feeling that the driver was intent on keeping up with her. It's paranoia, she thought. Nerves. The young black man with the gun had invaded some part of her inner life and left it open to fear. It's just nerves, she told herself. Nevertheless, when Kosta stopped at a light and Lisa fell in line behind him, she reached over and snapped open the glove compartment to get the gun.

She felt around for the .38 caliber revolver. At first it seemed not to be there and that scared her. Then she felt it, the reassuring heft of the gun. Protection. She pulled the gun out and held it on her lap.

On the other side of the intersection was a pickup truck with two good old boys hooting and hollering and playing their radio too loud. Those are the kind of people who are supposed to be carrying guns in their cars, not me, she thought. She patted the pistol once before the light changed. This is nuts, she thought, what am I going to do, shoot somebody? It was a holdup attempt. It had nothing to do with me, personally.

173

But still she was on edge. In a two-week period she had had two auto mishaps and a holdup attempt. On top of that, she had been told that her husband was sleeping with another woman. Yes, she thought, we definitely need a vacation. More deeply in the past, but still weighing heavily on her, were the deaths of her grandmother, and her father, and the miscarriage. She put the gun on the seat beside her. She put her hands on the steering wheel, then grabbed quickly for the gun, testing to see how fast she could get it into her hand and in a firing position if need be.

The video store was on Granada, a simple left off Atlantic, but before they got to Granada, Kosta took a different left and then a right onto a dark and quiet neighborhood street. Lisa followed him. It was a way to get to the store, but it wasn't any shorter, so it didn't make sense to her that he would take it.

In her rearview mirror she saw the lights swinging around the corner behind her. The car was following her. Her heart started pounding. Oh God, what is going on, she thought. She reached over for the gun. Kosta slowed down, forcing her to slow down. The car behind her came closer, its lights blinding her. *Oh, my God, someone is trying to kill me, someone is trying to kill me.* She was at once terrified by the thought, and struck by how absurd it was. She squeezed the gun in her right hand. She felt as if she were crushing it. Then Kosta picked up speed. At the end of the block he turned right. Lisa hurried after him. The car behind her turned left. Through her rearview mirror she watched its rear lights grow smaller in the distance until it was out of sight.

By the time Lisa pulled in next to Kosta's car at the video store in a small plaza, she was near panic. She sat in her car, hyperventilating. Slow down, take deep breaths, she told herself. For a moment she thought about taking the gun into the store with her, but decided no, that was crazy, and she shoved it back in the glove compartment. Her hand ached from holding it. Her face was sweating. She got out of her car and rushed to her husband.

"I think I was being followed," she said.

Kosta laughed. "Are you serious, honey?" he said.

"I know, I know, it's crazy, but I think someone's following me."

Kosta laughed again and put an arm around her. "Nobody's following you," he said. "You're just imagining things. You're shook up over what happened today."

Lisa knew he was probably right. It was just her mind playing tricks on her. Not surprising. Why wouldn't she be a little paranoid. She'd had a loaded gun pointed at her just a few hours earlier.

After Kosta picked out a film, they left the video store and drove home. Lisa again had the feeling that she was being followed. It's all in your mind, she told herself over and over. When they got home she rushed into the house and quickly set the alarm system.

The drive to the video store was not the last strange incident of the day.

Lisa made supper and she and Kosta talked for a while about the holdup attempt. Kosta assured her that she was now protected. She had an alarm, she had a walkie-talkie, and she had a husband who packed a gun. She told him she thought the gunman was someone he knew, someone she might have seen around Top Shots, but Kosta took little interest.

Later, Peter Kouracos came over to watch the movie with them. They got into a debate about something or other—Peter tended to be argumentative—and by ten o'clock they still hadn't shoved the film into the VCR. Kosta excused himself. He stood up and walked out of the room, leaving Lisa and Peter to chat. Kosta went to the basement, where he had a gun workshop.

A few minutes later Lisa heard loud noises coming from the back of the house. She went downstairs and opened the door to the backyard.

"Kosta was over by the barbecue area," she remembers. " 'Kosta,' I said, 'Let's watch the movie. What are you doing?' He said, 'I'm burying something.' He was over by the barbecue pit, digging with a small shovel. It was dark and I couldn't tell what he was burying, exactly, but it looked like some sort of brown briefcase. Oh, boy, Rambo strikes again, I thought."

Lisa didn't ask Kosta what he was burying that night. She had gotten used to this eccentricity of his. Though he had never buried things at home before, he, of course, had often buried guns and other survival equipment in the woods. Kosta, the great survivalist, had also marked trees, drawn maps, written codes. He liked to think that he could survive under any circumstances, and this business of burying guns and supplies was, as best she could figure, just one aspect of what ultimately had to be seen as a hobby. Since Kosta seemed in all other respects to be normal, all this had to be viewed as boyish mischief. On this particular night, Lisa thought maybe Kosta had used his metal detector to find the guns he had misplaced and was now reburying them near the barbecue pit so that he wouldn't lose them again.

On Thursday, November 2, Lisa identified Teja James as the man who had assaulted her from a photo lineup that the police brought to her house. When Dino pointed out that Teja had worked at Joyland and was someone whom Kosta and Deidre knew, Kosta played it down. "Yeah, Teja, that's right," Kosta said. "I guess I do see him around sometimes, yeah, you're right." Kosta left immediately.

That afternoon Lisa and Kosta drove in Kosta's car to Edgewater, a forty-five-minute drive south, on the other side of the river. They owned the duplex there, which they had purchased jointly but which Kosta managed. While Lisa didn't know about the tenant who wasn't paying the rent, she knew that the other unit was empty, and this trip was to meet a man who wanted to take a look at the vacancy.

By this time Lisa was a wreck. It was extremely upsetting to realize for sure that the young man who had attacked her was someone who knew Kosta and Deidre. She had an uneasy feeling that there could be some connection between Kosta's affair and this attack. But she also understood that she was tense and that it was natural for her to be making paranoid connections. After all, only eighteen hours or so earlier, she had been certain that someone was following her.

She had been trying along the way to nail down Teja in her head. She knew he was from around the boardwalk, but she couldn't quite remember him.

"Oh, you know Teja," Kosta kept saying. "He's the fellow worked at Joyland for a while." He said it several times, always connecting Teja to Joyland, more than to his own circle of acquaintances.

"Yes," Lisa finally snapped, "I know Teja, he's the boy who damn near killed me."

Then she stared out at the highway, trying to make sense of things. For a long time she felt as if she had done something wrong and didn't know what it was.

"Kosta," she said, when she was finally ready to talk about her fears, "you don't think Teja's going to try to hurt me, do you?"

When Kosta spoke his voice was strangely cold. "You can identify him," Kosta said. "If I was Teja I'd track you down and kill you."

"Gee, thanks for the reassurance," Lisa said. His words chilled her. She had wanted comfort from her husband, for him to say, "No, honey, that's crazy, he won't hurt you."

The more Lisa thought about it, the more it troubled her that the man who had pulled a gun on her was a friend of the alleged other woman in her husband's life.

"You can't tell me that Deidre didn't know Teja was going to come and rob me," she said.

Kosta didn't answer. He drove along, one hand on the

177

wheel of his BMW, and one hand on his jacket where he
carried the gun, his usual driving posture.

"I know," he said excitedly a few minutes later. "Maybe
somebody hired Teja to kill you!"

"Hired someone to kill me? That's crazy. Who would do
a thing like that?"

"Alfred Fuller," Kosta said. Fuller was one of the top
people at the Marriott.

"Al Fuller?" Lisa shrieked. "Kosta, are you out of your
mind? Al Fuller is a respectable businessman. What are you
talking so crazy for?"

"Well, you know he's always talking bad about you and
the boardwalk people," Kosta said. "He wants to build a
hotel there. He thinks you and Dino are all that's stopping
him. Maybe he thinks if he had you killed everybody else
would give in."

Lisa couldn't believe that Kosta could even suggest such
a thing. The fact that he did only brought closer to the
surface of her thoughts the festering fear that Kosta, himself, was somehow involved.

It is difficult to say at what level Lisa now considered
the possibility that her own husband was somehow connected to the holdup. Certainly that idea, so far unspoken,
was a presence between them all during the drive to
Edgewater. The idea that maybe Kosta was trying to kill
her was, on the one hand, so logical, and on the other, so
unthinkable and dramatic, that Lisa could neither dismiss
it, nor take it seriously. It became for them on that drive
something like a loaded gun in the hands of a child. It was
something they could play with, but it was something very
dangerous.

They were driving along with this wordless tension
between them when suddenly Kosta pulled his hand away
from his jacket. Lisa panicked. She jumped forward in her
seat. "What are you doing?" she shrieked. In an instant
she realized that Kosta had reached up to adjust the rearview mirror.

"What's the matter with you?" Kosta said. "What did you think, that I was going to kill you?"

"Well, yeah," Lisa said, and they both started laughing. Lisa laughed long and hard, letting all the pent-up tension come out in giggles. "God, I thought I was a goner there for a minute."

When all her laughter was spent Lisa tapped her husband playfully on the shoulder. "For all I know," she said, "you could be behind this whole thing. You could be taking me somewhere to shoot me."

"Nah," Kosta said. "I wouldn't shoot you."

Now they had shifted into a tone of baby talk, a kind of playful way of speaking that was something special between them when they were first married.

"Oh, you wouldn't, huh? Why not?"

Because I love you, she wanted him to say.

"Because I would get blood all over my car," he said.

"Oh, thanks."

"Besides, why would I?" Kosta said.

"For the insurance money."

"No, it wouldn't be worth it," Kosta said. "I'd have to share the money with Dino."

It was not the answer Lisa wanted to hear. It made her uneasy. It sounded as if Kosta had actually thought about it.

15

Bryan

On the night of November 1, when Lisa was terrified because she thought she was being followed to the video store, she was not just being hysterical. She really was being followed. The young man in the car behind her was Bryan Chase, age eighteen.

Bryan Chase was, by all accounts, cut from different cloth than the other boardwalk drifters. For one thing, he was a local kid, not a disgruntled runaway from a city to the north. He was a big and easygoing kid, a bit of a hayseed, somewhat immature, and easily manipulated by other people.

Mary Mullaley, one of J. R.'s girlfriends, recalls, "Bryan was real nice. He wouldn't do anything wrong, he wouldn't steal or anything. He was a totally different person from the others."

Bryan came from a broken home, something he had in common with Deidre, Teja, J. R., Mike Cox, Kevin Ramsey, Lori Henderson, and virtually every other boardwalk malcontent. He had grown up in a small West Virginia town that had a population smaller than that of the Marriott Hotel during speed week. In Daytona Beach, Bryan lived

with his father, David, and his stepmother, Amber Cysneski.

Bryan, according to his father, never got in trouble with
the law. "He was a pretty good, likeable kid, didn't get in
fights with people, no, sir," says David Chase. "Yes, he
could be manipulated by the wrong crowd, no doubt about
that, and he could be easily intimidated. He would give
you the shirt off his back, but when it came to the ladies
he would have no willpower."

The lady for whom Bryan had no willpower in October
and November of 1989, the one who could play him like a
fiddle, was Deidre Hunt. In fact, he told a number of
friends that he was smitten with Deidre and wanted to
have sex with her. He told one friend that he was dating
Deidre and that she was a nymphomaniac.

"A woman could manipulate Bryan real easily," says
Amber Cysneski. "He liked older women, that's all he ever
talked about. J. R. and them told me he liked Deidre, that
he was infatuated with her. I'm sure he could be manipulated by her."

Bryan, however, might have been more dreamer than
coxswain. J. R., who considered Bryan his closest Daytona
friend, says, "Bryan never got laid in his life. He wanted
to be like me, get laid. But he did not have a good style
with the girls."

Deidre Hunt, in any case, was among the new cast of
characters who entered Bryan's life in the fall of 1989, when
he started hanging around the boardwalk. By the time
David Chase and Amber Cysneski met Deidre briefly on
November 2, they had become concerned about Bryan's
new friends.

"He would sneak them in the window of his room at
night, in and out, in and out," Cysneski says. "I saw them
a few times in the living room, but they didn't stick around
too much when we were around. He was hanging around
the boardwalk a lot. I knew he was going to get in trouble.
It's not unusual for a boy his age to have kids over a lot,

but he was working and they weren't. They weren't any good, I could tell that. They read him out real easy, them kids knew he wasn't like them."

At the boardwalk Bryan was friends with Kevin Ramsey, who sometimes did repairs on Bryan's car, and J. R., who once spent a few days living in the Chase apartment.

Though David and Amber were troubled by the fact that Bryan hung around Top Shots pool hall on the boardwalk and had made so many friends from that area, there was really nothing so awful that they could point to in his behavior. David and Amber both worked long hours, and they had a new baby to take care of, so they saw little of Bryan. Besides, Bryan had always been a good kid, and he worked as a houseman at the Desert Inn Hotel, where his father was employed. It wasn't as if he were a bum, even if some of his friends were.

"I didn't know Bryan's friends so well," David says. "Now I wish I would have."

Though he saw little of his son, during the month of October David saw enough of him to notice that Bryan seemed to change.

"Normally he would joke," David Chase says. "But now he would kind of snap back if you said something, not take it the way it was meant. If you asked him something he would be kind of like, it's none of your business."

The reason Bryan was so moody during these days was that he had agreed to murder Lisa Fotopoulos, and it was tearing him up. Though Bryan's lust for Deidre Hunt undoubtedly played a part in getting him drawn into the plot (she either gave him sex or held out the promise of it) it is likely that the glue that held Bryan to his murder commitment was the threat of his being murdered by Kosta. Bryan, according to Robert Rinehart, who worked with him at the Desert Inn, "was afraid of his own shadow."

And he was, according to his father, "not a violent person at all." "He was macho," David Chase says. "He had a stocky build. He worked out and he'd wear tight-fitting clothes to show his muscles. But it was more of a look than a reality. He was not gunwise. I had lots of guns in West Virginia, but Bryan never even liked to hunt or fish."

After the Teja Joyland fiasco, according to Deidre, Kosta was "pissed." He told Deidre that she had two hours to arrange Lisa's death.

"He wanted me to steal a car and hit her with a car, and then shoot her," Deidre says.

Lori Henderson recalls, "Deidre was sitting on the kitchen floor crying because Teja hadn't killed Lisa. She said that since Teja hadn't done it, Kosta would make her do it. I told her just leave, you know, go back to Massachusetts, and all of that, and she was crying and she was afraid of him. She thought Kosta had all this information from the CIA and all this stuff, and he had the tape of her killing Kevin."

Deidre, not wanting to murder Lisa herself, turned to Bryan.

"I asked Bryan if he wanted to do it and he said yes," is the maddeningly simple way Deidre put it to the police in her November 7 confession.

Lori Henderson recalls, "Deidre went to Bryan's house looking for J. R. J. R. wasn't there, but Deidre stood there talking to Bryan for a while and then she came back downstairs and she said, 'Bryan is going to do it.' "

Deidre gave Bryan the gun that Teja had used in his failed attempt. She had gotten it back from Teja and had been keeping it in a sock under the front seat of a Ford LTD she had rented from Cheapo Rent A Car. "That way," she explains, "if it was found it would be thrown out of court, because anybody can leave a gun in a rental car."

By this time nearly everybody, except Bryan, knew that the gun would jam after the first shot.

While Kosta, apparently, did not rig the gun this way (it was like that when Teja got it) he made no effort to repair or replace the gun. One might think that Kosta, since he planned to shoot Bryan after Bryan shot Lisa, took great comfort in knowing the gun could not be fired a second time. However, as Deidre tells it, Kosta never got it through his head that the gun would jam, even though she and Teja told him several times. He kept saying that Bryan should shoot Lisa "four times in the head." While it is hard to imagine that Kosta would want a loaded gun in the hand of a man he intended to kill, it is equally hard to believe that he would want his entire murder scheme to depend on a single .22 bullet fired by a nervous and inexperienced teenager. David Damore agrees that Kosta probably never digested the information that the gun would jam. "Kosta thought he knew everything," Damore says, "and he wasn't going to listen to these people. When he was told the gun would jam, it probably went in one ear and out the other." However, as Damore sees it, even with only one bullet, the death of Lisa Fotopoulos seemed certain.

"This gun, this twenty-two," Damore says, "is the perfect murder weapon. It takes one slug in the brain to kill somebody. The .22 is a devastating round going through the body. It bounces around in there like a pinball."

Bryan Chase's first set of murder instructions was to watch Joyland on the night of November 1 and follow Lisa when she left. He was to follow her in his car and crash into her. When Lisa got out to exchange licenses Bryan was to shoot her and kill her.

This, by the way, is the earliest reference by Deidre, Lori, or any of the others, to the use of an auto accident as the ruse to kill Lisa. None of them report any knowledge of the two auto mishaps Lisa had in October, and Kosta, of course, still denies any attempts on Lisa's life. So it will probably never be known whether or not the two earlier accidents were bungled murder attempts or just bizarre coincidences unconnected to the later attempts on Lisa. Possibly they were genuine accidents, but they gave Kosta the idea of committing the murder this way.

In any case, Bryan, on the night of November 1, watched Joyland from the McDonald's across the street, and Deidre and Lori watched Bryan from the parking lot. "He was supposed to hit her Porsche and say, 'I'm sorry, lady' and go over and shoot her," Deidre says. This was the night that Bryan followed Lisa almost to the video store. Later, he explained that he had turned off because of some confusion in signals. Most likely, he just chickened out, or was confused by the fact that Lisa's car was following Kosta's to the video store instead of heading for the house on Halifax, as he'd expected.

On the night of November 2 Bryan followed Lisa all the way home and still didn't ram her. Clearly, Bryan was trying to avoid this murder. But he never quite threw in his cards. Whether he was kept in the game by dreams of sex with Deidre or nightmares of death by Kosta is a matter for speculation.

About this unrealized attempt, Deidre says, "Bryan followed Lisa all the way home and didn't do it. Lori and I were following him, we were like two or three blocks behind but we ended up getting lost. We ended up on John Anderson because Halifax turns into John Anderson. We went all the way up to Ormond because we thought we were still on Halifax."

Again it seems Lisa's life was spared because the people who wanted her dead, as treacherous as they were, sometimes behaved like Keystone Kops. Perhaps if Lori and Deidre had been nearby, instead of getting lost in their rented car, Bryan would not have backed out that night.

"We went back to McDonald's," Deidre says. "Bryan was there and he told me, 'I can't believe this, I had a chance.' He was telling us about the chance that he had and he fucked up. I said, 'Fuck it, go home.' I told him it had to be done and we'd probably get back to him tomorrow. The next day Kosta said, 'What happened,' and I said, 'Well, he didn't get a chance, his car didn't make it there.' So Kosta was mad. Kosta wanted him to come in the house and do it while she was sleeping. Kosta said, 'Okay, all right, we have to find a way, since we got this kid involved we've got to make him do it, and he's expendable, too.' Bryan was going to live if he had done it with the car. Kosta told me he wanted Bryan to get in the house, shoot her in her sleep, and he would shoot Bryan on the way out.''

Kosta told Deidre that Bryan would have to come through a window, because an alarm would go off if he came through a door.

During the forty-eight hours before Bryan actually got into the house there were a couple of fruitless murder missions concerning the window. The exact details are uncertain because Deidre's memory of them is hazy and because Bryan was probably lying to her, anyhow. Obviously, he was trying to botch this murder, buy some time, and maybe find a way out.

The first time Bryan went to the house under the new murder plan, he came back and told Deidre he could not break the window. He was then supplied with a glass cutter. Next he came back and said that he had been scared off by the sound of neighbors. In all, Bryan Chase managed to fail to kill Lisa at least six times, probably more.

By the night of Friday, November 3, the window plan had been altered. Instead of breaking a window at the front of the house, Bryan would go to the back of the house. At the back, facing the swimming pool, there is a grid of small square windows. The windows almost certainly would be too small to accommodate a strapping young man like Bryan, and we have to assume this was obvious to Kosta. So the plan, it seems, was that at some hour early Saturday morning, while the house was still dark, Kosta, certain that Lisa was asleep, would sneak downstairs and turn off the basement light to signal the waiting Bryan to come into the house. Kosta would then turn off the alarm and unlock the sliding glass door at the back of the house so that Bryan could get in. Bryan would break one of the small

186

windows at the back, to create the appearance that a burglar had come through the window. But, in fact, he would
slip through the open door. (One alternative theory on this
is that Kosta really thought Bryan could fit through one of
the small windows and only unlocked the door after he
heard Bryan struggling with the window.) Bryan would
move through the house to the upstairs bedroom, directed
by Kosta. He would shoot Lisa in the head at close range,
killing her while Kosta watched. (In fact, according to Teja,
Kosta wanted to videotape the murder of his wife, but
decided it would be impractical.) Then, Bryan would steal
some valuables to enhance the appearance of a burglary
and get out. That probably is what was to happen, as Bryan
understood it.

16

The Suspicion

At three o'clock on November 1, after the apparent holdup attempt, Dino Paspalakis returned to Joyland from the bank. As soon as he walked down the back stairs into the arcade he saw police and knew something was wrong.

"My sister," he said. "Where's my sister?"

"I'm okay," Lisa called from the doorway of the office, where she was talking to one of the policemen. She rushed to Dino, slipped into his arms, and cried.

"There was a man with a gun," she said. "He tried to force me back into the office. Dino, I was so scared." Dino held Lisa for a long time. She was sobbing and trembling. "It's okay," he told her. "You're safe now."

At eleven o'clock the next morning, Thursday, November 2, Dino paced nervously in the living room of the house on North Halifax. Along with Lisa and Kosta, he waited for Detective Bill Adamy of the Daytona Beach police department to arrive with photos of suspects. Dino's hands were still shaking. How close had he come to losing his sister, he wondered. After all, the holdup man carried a gun. Maybe the tall young black man was some crazed heroin addict who could kill without conscience. Dino had heard of such people. Maybe if Lisa had handled it differently she would be dead. It was an incredible thought, the worst thing Dino could imagine. The crime had shaken him badly. More than ever, he realized how much Lisa meant to him.

Lisa had always been Dino's soul mate. As kids they had fought rarely, certainly not like other siblings they knew. They did have their rivalrys, but they were always friendly. Lisa would sometimes howl when Shootin' Sam would outdraw Dino at Joyland—"by the time you got your gun out of your holster you were dead for half an hour," she would say—but she would always admit that she had been just as slow with a gun.

Later, when they were both teenagers dispensing quarters at Joyland, they would now and then challenge each other at pinball. Though Lisa would never play racquetball, and certainly not basketball, with Dino, they did go places together—picnics, movies, concerts.

When the boys started flocking around Lisa, she told Dino which ones she liked and which ones she didn't. She wanted, she said, to meet a boy as nice as Dino. And when Dino worried about his looks, it was always Lisa who told him that he was really quite a good-looking kid, which was true. And when he wondered if girls would like him, she said, "Are you kidding? They'll be crazy about you."

"Really?"

"Well, sure," Lisa would say. "Look at you, you're big, you're handsome, you've got sexy brown eyes. Let's face it, you're"—she would put a hand to her mouth and giggle—"a nice Greek boy." Which did not entirely please Dino, because he definitely was not in the market for a nice Greek girl.

Even college had not diluted their closeness. When Lisa went off to the University of South Florida, she called often from Tampa, talking to Dino, who was still in high school, for hours about her professors, her grades, and her friends. Later, Dino went to the same school, and after he graduated with honors, he went on to law school at the University of Miami.

Only Lisa knew the truth, that Dino had never wanted to go to law school. He did it for his parents, who wanted their son to become a lawyer. It didn't take Dino long to develop a deep hatred for law school. Dino didn't like the uncertainty of legal cases. Like his sister, he preferred the yes or no of accounting. Either things add up or they don't, no ambiguity. When he was in law school he would call Lisa.

"I hate it here," he told her. "I feel like I'm in the Florida state penitentiary."

"Then withdraw," she told him.

"But what about mom and dad?"

"What about them?"

"Oh, no big deal or anything. It's just that I will destroy their biggest dream, that's all."

"They'll be hurt," Lisa said, "but it's your life, Dino, you've got to do what's best for you."

"Maybe I should finish one more semester and then tell everybody how I feel."

"That's a great idea, Dino. There's a big call for people who finished one more semester of law school before quitting."

"Huh?"

"Dino, the hell with it. Just quit. You're unhappy. You should leave now."

So Dino dropped out of law school and he never regretted it. Steno and Mary were upset and there was much drama at home for a while, but Lisa stuck up for Dino. Dino sometimes wondered, if Lisa hadn't been there for him would he have had the strength to drop out or would he be working at a profession he hated?

Now, on the morning of November 2, Dino felt that Lisa needed him to be there for her, but he wasn't sure why he felt that way. Was she in danger? Was that it? Who was this young black man with a gun? Would he try it again?

190

Dino was anxious for the police to catch the guy. And that's why Adamy was coming, to show Lisa a photo lineup of possible suspects. Maybe Kosta can help, Dino thought. After all, he knows every bum on the boardwalk.

When Adamy arrived he laid out one big sheet of photos on the coffee table in the center of the living room. It showed a dozen mug shots of young black men.

"We don't know if your man is among them," he said, "but he might be."

Lisa stood in front of the photos. Kosta and Dino stood just behind her.

As Dino stared down at the lineup of photos he realized that he recognized one of the men. It's Teja, he thought, staring at the photo of the young light-skinned black man. Dino remembered that Teja had once been thrown out of Walk-In Charlies, an arcade run by a friend of Dino's, for fighting. In fact, he remembered that Teja had worked at Joyland for a few days. Dino's manager had hired Teja in Dino's absence, and though Dino didn't like Teja he could see no reason to fire him. But in less than a week Teja got himself fired by constantly making remarks about Dino in front of the manager. Teja also hung around Top Shots, so Kosta certainly knew him. Kosta, also looking at the photos, said nothing. Why doesn't Kosta say something, Dino wondered. He must recognize Teja.

"It's him," Lisa suddenly said. "That's the one."

She was pointing to the photo of Teja.

In that moment, when Lisa pointed to the photo of Teja, it was as if she had given Dino the final number he needed to balance an accounting problem. It was also the most shocking realization of his life. Dino stood behind his sister, and beside his brother-in-law, dazed, as if he'd been hit over the head, and in seconds his mind reviewed a series of facts leading to a conclusion that perhaps had already been there waiting to be discovered.

Lisa had, of course, told Dino about the affair Kosta was supposedly having with Deidre. Although Lisa was not certain it was true, Dino was. He had once seen Kosta and Deidre shooting pool together at Top Shots. It was an innocent enough thing on the surface, and so he had never reported it to his sister. But even at the moment it happened, there was something in it that troubled him. It had seemed as if Kosta and Deidre, in their smiles and their body language, had made too much effort to say "We're only playing pool" when they hadn't been accused of anything else. When Lisa had told Dino about Elena's phone call, the rumor of an affair had resonated with that moment in the pool hall, and he had been certain that Kosta and Deidre were lovers.

Now Dino made more connections, terrible connections. He was sure that Kosta was having an affair with Deidre. He knew that Deidre's closest friend was Lori Henderson. And he knew that Lori's boyfriend was Teja. (Dino also made another connection at the time, which, though it was incorrect, shows that his instincts were to link the Kosta-Deidre romance with the assault on Lisa. Lisa had mentioned that the man who came to the office had a silver automatic pistol, and Dino remembered being told by Dennis, the police officer who asked Lisa not to fire Deidre, that Deidre carried a silver automatic.)

Other small things now seemed significant. He remembered a moment once when Lisa had confronted Kosta about being seen with Deidre. Kosta had explained that he had picked "them" up at a bus stop and given "them" a ride home. Now Dino remembered who "them" was—it had been Deidre and Teja.

All of this went through Dino's head while Lisa stared at the photo of Teja and told Adamy she was sure that was the man. And Dino was almost certain of something else: Kosta was trying to kill Lisa.

Dino tried to keep cool. He felt as if he were shaking all over, but nobody seemed to notice. Kosta had gone off to a corner of the room. He seemed annoyed that Lisa had picked out Teja's photo.

"That's Teja," Dino said after Adamy had left. Though he had been too stunned to tell the police everything, he now tried to explain to Lisa who Teja was. "The guy who worked at Joyland for a while," he said, "the guy who hangs out at Top Shots." Lisa didn't know Teja, but Kosta certainly did. At first Kosta tried to stonewall it. "I don't know him," he said. But soon he changed strategies. "Oh, yeah, Teja. They call him T. J. Sure." And then he insisted that Lisa should know him. "Teja," he said, "you know Teja. He used to work at Joyland."

Dino knew what he had to do. He certainly was not going to accuse Kosta. For one thing he couldn't prove it, and his accusations might lead to another attempt on Lisa, or even on himself. For another, if Dino was wrong, he had to go on living with this man in his family forever. After the discussion had grown thin, Dino went quietly upstairs and called his lawyer. "I have to see you immediately," he said. The lawyer told him to come right over. On the way out that morning Dino made a note of the plate number on Kosta's BMW. He also took plenty of cash with him. He would pay the lawyer in cash so there would be no written record of the visit. If Dino turned out to be wrong, he didn't want Lisa to know he had suspected her husband of trying to kill her.

It was 11:00 A.M. when Dino left the house to drive to his lawyer's office, telling no one. As he drove across the river that day and into the sections of Daytona where few tourists go, he realized that there had been something wrong about Kosta all along.

Dino's relationship with Kosta had not begun well. He was against Kosta before he even met him. Kosta was, after all, some man who dared to think he was good enough for Lisa. Lisa was the light of Dino's life, and in all likelihood Dino would have gotten off to a bad start with any man who threatened to come between them.

Worse, the Kosta-Lisa romance seemed to go off almost in secret from Dino, without his blessing, so to speak.

"The first time I met Kosta was the day Lisa got engaged to him, though I didn't even know they were serious at the time. I was living in Tampa and they came over. Until then I really had no idea she was seeing this guy. At one point when Lisa and I were alone, I said to her, 'Lisa, why don't you drop this guy?' It wasn't that I had a bad impression of him. It was just that I didn't have a good impression of him. I didn't know him. Mostly, I guess it was just that nobody was good enough for my sister. After Kosta and Lisa got engaged, the idea of checking him out did cross my mind. But then I thought, what if I check him out and he finds out I checked him out. That's not going to get our relationship off to a great start."

As it happened the relationship did improve quickly, and in time Dino grew to love his brother-in-law. But the love that Dino felt for Kosta was more the perfunctory sort of love that Dino knew he should feel for anybody who was family. Still, they became friends.

"We used to go wave running together," he says. "I had a Yamaha two-man wave runner and we'd do that. And one of the things we did a lot was we'd play this video game at Joyland called Cyberball. It's football in the twenty-first century. We'd each have a screen with our own robots on it. Sometimes I'd win, sometimes Kosta would win, but we always had a great time playing it."

There were times, too, when Kosta's place in the family was perhaps more than Dino would have liked.

"There were times," he says, "when I was kind of jealous of Kosta's relationship with my father, the way they would play cards and stuff. I remember one time the three of us were at Joyland moving games around and I turned to Dad and said, "Why don't we do it this way, put this game here' and so forth. Dad says, 'No, no, Dino, I don't like that.' Then he asked Kosta what he thought, and Kosta said the same thing and Dad thought it was a great idea. Well, that just blew me away. I got upset and told them all off. I just walked out. I realized later it was just a misunderstanding and my father didn't really understand what I had been suggesting."

Dino's lawyer was a man by the name of Thomas Hall, a slim redheaded Van Johnson lookalike who had gotten burned out as a high school teacher and gone to law school. His office on the west side of town was small but welcoming.

"Dino," he said, "what can I do for you?"

Dino came in, sat down in a leather chair, leaned back and took a deep breath. Here it is, he thought. This would be the first time he said it out loud.

"It's my sister," he said.

"Oh. How is Lisa?"

"I think her husband is trying to kill her."

The lawyer waited for more.

"Yesterday a guy assaulted Lisa with a gun," Dino said. "He's a guy named Teja, they call him T. J., a boardwalk guy."

Then Dino went into his story. He told Hall about the affair with Deidre, the Lori-to-Teja connection, the silver gun. He told him about all the insurance money that would fall into Kosta's hands if Lisa died, about the fact that the marriage was troubled. As he spoke, his hands manically gesturing through the air, his thoughts came out in a gush of words, and several times Hall had to tell him to slow down, tell the story calmly. There were tears in his eyes when he thought how close Lisa had come to being killed.

As Dino told the story to the lawyer other things came back to him. He told Hall, for example, about the time he and Kosta had gone shooting.

Kosta's love of guns had always troubled Dino. Like his father and his sister, Dino knew little and cared less about firearms. He couldn't really understand how a person could love weapons so much and spend so much money on them. Nonetheless he had gotten close to Kosta and he knew that sharing his knowledge of weapons was important to Kosta, so when Kosta had asked Dino if he wanted

195

to go in the woods and shoot a submachine gun, Dino had gone. Besides, he thought, he had never fired a gun of any kind, and it might be kind of exciting.

"We went out to the woods off Williamson, along a little dirt trail on the other side of the highway from the gun range. Kosta had what he said was a registered Uzi and he told me it was okay, I wouldn't get in trouble. He shot the Uzi for a while and then he let me shoot it. I didn't really enjoy it. We just shot at a bunch of bottles lined up in front of a mattress or something. But the strange thing was I would stick near him and I would find an excuse not to be the one to go out and set up new targets. It didn't make any sense but I was afraid he might shoot me, you know, and go home and say, 'Oh, Lisa, I'm sorry, but I accidentally killed Dino.' I didn't have anything to base this on. It was just intuition. I guess I thought anybody who was shooting an Uzi and loving it was dangerous."

Dino finished telling his story to the lawyer and took a deep breath. "So that's what I think is going on. I want you to get me a private detective who can follow Kosta and find out what's going on. If I'm wrong, and I hope to God I am, then none of us can ever mention it again. I haven't even told Lisa. I have to live with this guy."

Hall leaned back, thought it over. Dino had been afraid that his lawyer might just think he was hysterical, that there really was no reason on earth to think that Kosta would be trying to kill Lisa. But now Hall wrung his hands together. Clearly, he was troubled by what he was hearing.

"You have a very serious problem here," Hall said. "I'll tell you what I'd like to do. I'll ask around to see who is the best person in town, okay. I'll have somebody in abeyance, in case we need him. But if you hire somebody right now you'll be jumping the gun. If Kosta really just tried to kill Lisa yesterday then he'd be foolish to try again in the near future. We'll hire a private detective, but we'll put him on hold, okay? He'll be just a phone call away."

"Okay," Dino said. But he wasn't at all sure that things

were okay. He would have to keep an eye on Kosta and Lisa himself.

This was the same day that Lisa had driven to Edgewater with Kosta, and that evening when Lisa and Dino were alone Lisa told Dino about her conversation during the drive.

"I said to Kosta, 'How do I know you didn't try to kill me for the insurance money.' You know, in a joking manner."

It was one of the few times that Dino blew up at his sister.

"Lisa, are you out of your mind?"

"What? What are you talking about?"

Now Dino was stuck. He didn't want to reveal his suspicions. "Well . . . well," he said, "what if Kosta really is behind this and he knows you suspect him?" He forced himself to smile, to make it all a joke.

Lisa smiled back. "If Kosta is behind this, then I'm as good as dead," she said.

For Lisa, the idea that Kosta was trying to kill her was still being played at some safe and not quite real level of her mind. It was, after all, a thought too ridiculous to be taken seriously.

For Dino, that was not the case. He took it very seriously. But for now, he would keep his silence. To speak up without evidence might cause Kosta to accelerate his plans. Dino was scared.

17

The Shooting

The next day, Friday, November 3, was the first day of the Greek Festival, a time loaded with heavy emotions for the Paspalakis family because it was during the festival that Steno had died two years earlier. Dino went to the festival, and later had a few drinks with friends at Razzles. As usual he'd had to shout to carry on a conversation over the thumping music. That and the haze of cigarette smoke left his throat sore. When he got home at one-thirty in the morning Lisa and Kosta were still up, watching a cable TV movie with Peter Kouracos. Dino said his hellos, then went upstairs to watch a different movie. Shortly, he went to bed. But, with so much on his mind, he didn't sleep well.

At a little after four o'clock in the morning Dino woke up. His throat was still sore. He was thirsty. He decided to get up and go downstairs for a glass of milk.

He walked down the front flight of stairs, and when he got to the main floor he could see that the light in the stairway leading to the basement was on. When he got to the doorway he could see that the lights in the basement were also on. It was in the basement that Kosta had set aside a portion of the large recreation room as his work-shop. There he tooled his guns and made his own bullets.

"Kosta," Dino called, thinking that Kosta must be down there making bullets. Nobody answered. He walked down-stairs, found nobody there, and flipped the light switch to turn off the downstairs lights. On his way up to the kitchen he turned off the stairway light. When he got to the kitchen he turned a light on, but it bothered his eyes so he turned it off immediately and poured his glass of milk by the glow from the refrigerator.

He returned to the third floor by the formal staircase at the front of the house. Something about the lights being on troubled him. Where is Kosta, he wondered. Is he out of the house, working on some plan? On the third floor Dino walked into the guest bedroom, which faces Halifax Avenue. He stood there in the shadowy light, staring down at the driveway. His car was there, so was Kosta's car, and Lisa's. Everything was as it should be. I'm just on edge, he thought, and he went back into the bedroom with his glass of milk.

Fifteen minutes later he was in bed again, almost asleep, when he heard noises.

When Dino had turned off the basement light Bryan Chase had been waiting behind the house in the dark. Bryan took the turning off of the light as his signal to come in. At a little before five o'clock in the morning Bryan came to the sliding glass door at the back of the house. He smashed a brick against one of the small windows near the door, either in a legitimate attempt to enter the house through the window, or as a ruse to make it appear that a burglar had come that way. Around this time Kosta came down the stairs, turned off the burglar alarm, let Bryan in through the glass door, closed the door, and set the alarm once more. The two men perhaps waited in the dark for several minutes to make sure Dino was asleep.

When the time was right the two men moved quietly up the back stairs, Kosta leading the way. They crept into the bedroom where Lisa lay sleeping. Kosta crawled in next to his wife. He looked at Lisa, then at Bryan. He wanted to watch it happen. Bryan, probably nervous, probably shaking, pulled the .22 caliber pistol from his pocket. He moved very close to Lisa. She was sleeping on her side, so he had to aim the pistol into the side of her head from above. He pulled the trigger, firing a bullet that crashed into Lisa's skull and entered her brain. Immediately blood began pouring out of Lisa's head. Bryan pulled on the trigger again. The gun jammed. He tried it once more. Still the gun would not fire a second shot. He shook the gun and turned around and went to the door of the bedroom, as if he were going to leave. Then he came back and shook the gun some more.

As far as Kosta knew, Lisa was dead or dying. And now it was clear to Kosta that Bryan would not be able to fire another round. Kosta reached under the bed. He pulled out a loaded 9-millimeter, semiautomatic Walther PPK pistol. The light of early morning coming through the windows was more than enough for him to take careful aim at Bryan Chase and fire four bullets into the boy.

We know about Bryan's last minutes from Lori Henderson's recollection of what Kosta told her and Deidre later that morning.

"He just described how it happened," Lori says. "He described in detail, you know, about how he had unloaded the gun into him. He was kind of proud. He was happy he had killed Bryan."

Lisa had been sleeping soundly. She had stayed up late with Kosta and Peter Kouracos, watching a movie on the VCR. She and Kosta had discussed their Key West trip, scheduled for the next day. She had gone to bed sometime after Dino came home, while Peter was still there. At 5 A.M. she heard a noise and woke up momentarily. Her head hurt and she went immediately into a dream. In her dream there was a judge, a huge judge in black and he seemed angry. He smashed down his gavel and it made a terrifying BOOM. Why was he so angry, Lisa wondered. Down went the gavel again, crashing like thunder— BOOM—its noise resounding through her head. It made a terrible pain in her head. Why doesn't he stop? she thought, why doesn't he stop? BOOM went the gavel. Her head hurt so much, and she thought if the judge would stop banging his gavel then her head would not hurt. BOOM went the gavel one more time.

"I woke up or opened my eyes," Lisa recalls, "and Kosta was standing over me like in a crouched position with his arm around me or under me crying his eyes out and I heard my mother in the background screaming, 'Oh my child, my child,' and just screaming at the top of her lungs. And Kosta was crying and he was saying, 'I'm going to kill him, I'm going to kill him,' and I had no idea what happened. And then the next thing I know, my mom came into the room and Bryan Chase was lying on the floor and she said 'Who is this?' and Kosta said something like, 'Well, that's the guy that shot Lisa.'

"At that point I knew I was shot and I knew I was in shock and I thought, What do I do? Do I just lie here or do I come out of shock and tell these people who I love and who love me, that I'm okay? So I came out of shock and I said, 'I'm all right.' And I looked at Kosta and I said, 'Is it Teja?' That's the only thing that made any kind of sense, that Teja would try to kill me to stop me from identifying him as the holdup man. And Kosta said, 'No, it's not Teja, it's Teja's friend from Ohio, he must have hired him, I'm going to kill him, I'm going to kill him.' "

For Dino, who was half asleep at the time, the noise sounded not like a banging gavel but like fireworks. To him it was a constant bang, bang, bang, bang, and he woke up suddenly. His heart was pounding. What the hell is going on? he thought.

Wearing only his underwear, Dino ran into the hallway. *Lisa*, he thought. He charged toward Lisa's bedroom.

"Dino, call 911," Kosta shouted. "Lisa's been shot."

Dino, thinking that the house was being fired on from outside, dove to the floor of the hallway. He crawled along the carpeting until he got to the upstairs bathroom, which had a phone. Still staying low he reached up and yanked down the phone that sat on the bathroom sink.

He called 911. "This is an emergency," he said. "Someone is shooting at us. They're shooting at us, they're shooting at us! My sister's been shot. They're outside the house, shooting at us." The dispatcher asked Dino for the address and told him the police would be right there.

When Dino hung up he ran into Lisa's bedroom. "Lisa, Lisa," he cried. Don't die, he thought, don't die.

Lisa was lying in the bed, awake but dazed. "My head hurts," she said, "My head hurts." There was blood on her pillow.

Then Dino saw the third person in the room. A young man was lying on the floor, slightly forward of the bed, a gun still clutched in his hand.

"I saw a person on the floor with blood, and I remember feeling like hitting this person," he says.

"Don't worry about him," Kosta said. "He's dead."

Dino, still in his underwear, and now realizing that there were no shooters outside, went back to the phone and called 911 again.

"I told them there was a dead person and to send an ambulance for my sister. They told me to stay on the phone until the police arrived."

For Mary Paspalakis, fully asleep one floor below, the sound of gunshots sounded like the slamming of a door.

"I heard boom, boom, boom, boom," she says. "I got up and went to the stairs and started yelling, 'What's going on up there, kids, what's going on?' I thought it was doors that were slamming. Dino called down to me, 'Please go

202

into your room and close the door because there is a crazy person outside, firing shots inside.' I got scared and went inside. Then I thought, What am I doing here, my kids are getting killed upstairs and I'm here. So I got up. I got outside my room again, and I went upstairs. Dino was calling the police. I ran to Lisa's room and I saw the man dead on the floor. I thought it was a rubber dummy, that Kosta was playing a joke. I said, 'What are you doing? What is this, a joke?' Kosta was sitting there in his underwear cradling Lisa and he was crying and he said, 'No, no, no, they just killed Lisa.' Then I saw the blood running down Lisa's forehead. And then I went nuts, I was screaming, 'My child, my child. Help me.' I thought she was going to die any minute. Then Lisa said, 'Don't worry, Mom, I'm okay, don't yell.' "

While they waited for the police to arrive, Kosta cradled Lisa in his arms. She felt thirsty, so he got her a glass of water and helped her gently nurse it sip by sip. There were tears in his eyes. He loves me, Lisa thought, he does love me.

When the police came Dino met them at the door. They told him to come out in the driveway and not reenter the house. Not knowing exactly what was going on, the police refused to go in until the others had come out. They gave Dino a bullhorn and in Greek he told his mother and Kosta to come out of the house so that the paramedics could go in and get Lisa.

Lisa recalls, "I was wide awake and somebody was coming in. At first I thought it was paramedics, but then I could see that it was policemen. They came in like something out of *Miami Vice*, pressed against the wall, guns raised. The police officer opened the door and he looked in and shouted, 'victim in bed, victim in bed.' Then, 'somebody on the floor, he's got a gun, he's got a gun.' They were being real cautious, and I was calling to them, 'Come on in, he's dead.' To me everything was so obvious, I didn't understand why they couldn't see that he was dead.

"Finally the paramedics came rushing in. I told them that my head hurt and they put me on a stretcher that was so hard it felt like a board to me. Then they put me in these shock pants, they were these big things like giant bubbles. I said, 'What do I need these for, I'm not in shock.' They said. 'Calm down, everything will be all right.' They told me not to move, and when they picked me up my neck and head hurt. So they taped my head to the stretcher.

"When we came past my mother, she was screaming and crying. One of the paramedics said to her, 'It's a miracle, your daughter's alive.' "

The fact that Lisa had a bullet in her brain and was still alive and alert was not a miracle; there have been many such cases. It was, however, extreme good luck. Dr. Keith Wilson, author of *Cause of Death*, says that a .22 caliber bullet fired in the back of the head would be the "perfect weapon" that David Damore describes. However, Bryan Chase fired the gun into the side of Lisa's head, into an area that offers more chance for protection from the vital parts of the brain.

Wilson says, "A larger caliber bullet, like a forty-five, would have been devastating from any direction. It would have gone in one side of Lisa's brain and out the other, almost certainly killing her. But a twenty-two shot into the side of the head will expend most of its energy going through the bone, so that it has very little velocity by the time it gets inside. The bullet would then settle either in the fluid that surrounds the brain or (as it did with Lisa) in the temporal parietal lobe, which is so densely fibered that a bullet could penetrate the area without causing any permanent damage."

Dino, still wearing only underwear, stood in the driveway and watched the ambulance take away his sister. "The hospital," he said to one of the police officers, "I've got to go to the hospital."

"Pretty soon," the cop told him. "She'll be all right."

As soon as Lisa was out of the house a police videographer was sent in to make a videotape of the entire house. Dino and Kosta were given paraffin tests, to see if either had fired a gun recently.

Kosta, of course, had fired a gun, as he explained to the police. He had been awakened by the sound of a gunshot in the room, he told them. In the semidarkness he could see the young man who had shot his precious Lisa in the head at close range. Kosta, thinking that the gunman would shoot again, reached under the bed for his gun and had shot the young man four times, killing him.

It was an eminently reasonable story. Kosta had done what any man would have done. Here was his wife, apparently dead beside him, and her killer, still armed, hovered over the bed, perhaps preparing to put a bullet into Kosta's head. Kosta, it seemed, had done the only right thing, and the police had no reason to think anything different had gone on in the house.

But Dino knew better.

Kosta had arranged this murder attempt, he was sure of it. Dino stood out in the driveway in the shadows of early morning and watched in amazement as his brother-in-law charmed the police with the heroic tale of how he had avenged the shooting of his wife. To Dino's eye Kosta looked guilty as hell. But he knew also that to a stranger Kosta looked as innocent as could be. This was not a man who was burdened with guilt. If his hands shook at all it was because his wife had just been shot and he had just killed a boy. If he seemed not as grief stricken as he ought, it was because he was still in shock. No, Dino thought, the police aren't going to see right through Kosta. I have to catch him. I have to stop him.

He scanned his memories for a clue, the proverbial forgotten detail that would nail Kosta. Suddenly an idea came to him.

"Can I make a request?" he said to one policeman. He

explained about his trip downstairs for a glass of milk.
"When I came up I turned the light switch off," he said.
"Can you take a fingerprint from the bottom of the switch
to see who turned it on?" Dino was still somewhat dazed
and confused, and different scenarios of what had happened were able to reside in his mind at the same time. In
this one, he was thinking that Kosta might have turned on
the light earlier to let the gunman in and then gone back
to bed while the gunman hid in one of the dark rooms
before doing his business.

In fact, a light switch is not sufficient surface to yield a
usable fingerprint, but neither Dino nor Kosta knew this at
the time and to Dino's eyes, Kosta's reaction was panic.

"No, no, Dino," Kosta said. "That's okay, there's no
need for that. I think . . . I think I might have left the light
on."

Can't you see it, Dino thought, can't you see how guilty
he is? But the police officers seemed to sense nothing.

Literally within minutes of Lisa's arrival at Halifax
Memorial Hospital the waiting rooms were swarming with
anxious Greeks. The word had gone out over a telephone
network. *Lisa's been shot.* Dino had gotten dressed and
called his friend Timmy. Timmy's mother had called a few
people. Each of them had called others and long before Lisa
went into surgery there were forty friends and relatives
crammed into three waiting rooms at the hospital.

Among this crowd of friends and family Dino felt lonely.
What they shared was a love and concern for Lisa, but
he alone possessed the terrible knowledge that Lisa's own
husband, a friend to all of them, was trying to kill her.

He had tried to tell a few of them, but it was only making
things worse.

"At the house my uncle Stacy had come over while the
police were questioning me and I had taken him aside and
told him, 'Look, it's Kosta who's trying to kill Lisa,' and I
told him the whole thing about Deidre and Teja and the
holdup. And he said, 'Dino, you're delirious, that's crazy.'

206

He didn't believe me. So I told him, 'Look, whether you believe me or not, don't repeat what I just told you.' "

By the time Dino was at the hospital he understood that it was best not to share his suspicions with his Greek family and friends. He loved them all, but he also knew how much they loved to talk, and if he told them what he thought, it would only be a matter of minutes before it got back to Kosta. Kosta, he knew, would laugh it off and then kill Dino to shut him up. When Dino saw his aunt Joyce, his uncle Stacy's sister, he told her what he had told Stacy and said, "Make sure Stacy doesn't repeat it. I'm putting on a facade with Kosta and I don't want him to know I know."

Now Dino set about the more urgent business of protecting his sister. He roamed about the hectic hospital from policeman to policeman. "I want twenty-four hour protection for my sister," he said. He was almost crying. "I want a police officer watching her at all times."

He did not mention Kosta. He presented the reasonable argument that she had been held up by a gunman barely thirty-six hours ago and it appeared that somebody was trying to kill her. The police couldn't promise anything. "Okay, if you don't think she needs it, I'll pay for it," he told them. "Just give her the protection. I'll pay for it." Still, he couldn't seem to get anyone to say, "Yes, Dino, she will be protected."

"But then this woman investigator came over to me," he says. "Her name was Allison Ebel. I said, 'Look, are you an investigator on this case?' She said, 'Yes,' so I pulled her aside into a hallway where nobody could hear us. 'It's Kosta,' I told her. 'It's Kosta, he's trying to kill my sister.' I told her everything. I said if I'm wrong then I don't want to be quoted on this. She said she would see what she could do. Then later when I got home she called me up. 'Dino,' she said, 'you got your protection.' "

18

The Hospital

They were going to shave her head. Lisa was still confused by everything that had happened, but she was no longer in shock, and that much she understood. They were going to shave her head. Oddly enough, this disturbed her more than the fact that she had been shot and the bullet was still in her brain.

Looking straight up at the ceiling because it hurt to move, she lay on a gurney in the emergency room at Halifax Memorial Hospital. "Kosta," she called.

Kosta was right there, just beyond her view. Now he came into her field of vision, blocking out the light above her. "I'm here, darling," he said. He smiled nervously, took her hand.

"Kosta, don't let them shave my head."

"They have to," he said.

"But my hair, my hair."

She knew it must sound ridiculous, even vain, worrying about her hair at a time like this, but it seemed important. It was something she could concentrate on. She remembered the times when people had complimented her on her hair, the times when men had found her sexy. She had

208

never been particularly flirtatious, but still it was nice to be considered sexy. I wonder how sexy they'll find me when I look like Telly Savalas, she thought now. Though the pain was like an anvil pressed on her head, she smiled. She had always been able to make jokes in her mind, even in the worst of times.

"I'm going to look like a bald lady in one of those science fiction movies," she said to Kosta. It was an image that revolted her.

Kosta squeezed her hand. "You'll look fine," he said. "Just fine."

"Why, Kosta?" she cried. "Why do they have to do this?"

"You have a hole in your head," Kosta said. "They have to operate."

"Well, why can't they just shave a little section, where the hole is?"

"Huh?" Kosta said. He seemed to be thinking about something else. "Oh. They can't." He squeezed her hand again. It was small comfort, but at least he was trying. "Bacteria or something. If anything got in the hole it could infect your brain."

"A bullet in my brain," Lisa said. "I can't believe it."

"It's a twenty-two."

"Huh?"

"A twenty-two," Kosta said. "A small caliber." He seemed so proud of his knowledge of guns. "That's what the mob uses for hits," he said. "It's a small bullet but it will rattle around inside the head. Do a lot of damage."

"Oh, great," Lisa said. She was not afraid. But she was thirsty. The headache was awful. Lisa had been asking for a Tylenol, but nobody would give her one.

"What time's breakfast?" she asked.

"Don't worry about that now, honey. You have to go through surgery first."

"How about a cigarette?" she said now.

Kosta frowned. "No," he said. Lisa knew he had never

approved of her smoking, but here in the emergency room, the idea must have seemed absurd to him. Where's Timmy, she thought, he'll give me a cigarette. Or Thea Anna, she smokes. Earlier Lisa had asked a nurse for a cigarette and the nurse had curtly informed her that smoking was not allowed. "Well, then take me somewhere else," she had joked, but her humor had not been appreciated. Now, she thought, Kosta could be a little more sensitive to a woman with a bullet in her brain than simply grunting "no," to her request. What a grouch. But then she remembered that it was Kosta who had saved her life, and she felt bad.

Kosta really loves me, she thought. Maybe he had an affair with Deidre and maybe he didn't, but he really, really loves me. She remembered how Kosta had held her after she was shot, how he had bawled like a baby, how he had sworn he would kill Teja for doing this to her. She had never seen such emotion from her husband, and just thinking about it now brought tears to her eyes. "Kosta," she said. "Things will get better. I love you."

He smiled down at her. She could see that he was terribly troubled by this tragedy. But he smiled. He leaned down and kissed her cheek. "I love you, too, sweetheart," he said.

There are three waiting rooms in the intensive care unit at Halifax and by this time all three were crowded with people who had come about Lisa. The doctor had assured them all that Lisa had a 95 percent chance of living, but had warned them, too, that personality change or memory loss was a real possibility. Many of them wept openly. All of them were more concerned than Lisa was. At one point Lisa told one of the cousins to send Thea Anna to her. When Anna heard this she went rushing madly down the hospital corridor where Lisa lay on the gurney. "Lisa, Lisa," she cried, thinking her niece wanted to say something to her before she died. Lisa looked up. "Thea Anna," she said. "I have to ask you something."

"Oh, Lisa?" Thea Anna cried. "Oh, Lisa."

"Do you have a cigarette?" Lisa asked.

When Kosta had gone to talk with the others, and calm them down, it was Dino who stayed with Lisa then. Dino held her hand and bawled even as he assured her that everything was going to be all right. She told him how gentle Kosta had been and all Dino could do was smile falsely and tell her that was good. This was no time to tell his sister that her husband was trying to kill her.

"She was talking intelligently the whole time," Dino recalls. "I held her hand, telling her how confident I was that she would make it and I was bawling. I was scared, but I was confident she would make it. There were fifty people in the three waiting rooms. They kept coming, one person right after another, the cousins and the aunts were bawling.

At 8:00 A.M. they took Lisa onto the elevator to bring her up to surgery. As soon as Lisa was in surgery, Kosta left.

Kosta had gone to Deidre's house. Deidre and Lori, who had driven by Lisa's house early in the morning and seen the police cars, were waiting for him, expecting to be told that Lisa was dead. It was then that Kosta described how he had killed Bryan Chase and how Lisa had sat up in bed after being shot.

"He said she just sat up and looked at him," Lori says. "She had just been shot. Kosta couldn't believe it. He was disappointed that she wasn't dead."

Deidre Hunt remembers Kosta bragging about how he murdered Bryan. "Kosta just emptied the gun into him. He said he made him meatloaf and laughed."

Deidre also says that Kosta wanted the hospital blown up. "He was mad," she says. "He wanted her dead, even in the hospital."

Deidre says that Kosta ordered her to have Teja place a bomb in a flower pot to be sent to Lisa's room, or sneak in explosives made from detergent and gasoline and put them under her bed.

While Kosta may, indeed, have given such orders, Lori Henderson remembers that it was Deidre who beat the drums most loudly for a bomb plan.

"Dee was making plans for blowing up the hospital. After Lisa finally got shot, and still didn't die, I think Dee kind of lost it. She had gotten completely infatuated with it all and she was just planning that this person has to die, and that person has to die. J. R., because he knew about it. Mike Cox, because he knew about it. And Teja has got to do this, she said, he has to go to the hospital and blow it up. I tell you, she got really crazy."

Twelve hours later Lisa was alone, and the belief that Kosta really loved her was dying fast. Kosta did this to me, she thought. She lay, still dazed and confused as she rose gradually from the drug-induced sleep. She felt as if she were being pulled up from the bottom of a pond. They had explored her brain and decided not to remove the bullet. "We'll leave it in," the doctor had said to her during the day when she was half awake. "We'll keep an eye on it. If it shifts we might have to go in there and take it out some day."

Now it was quiet in the dimly lit intensive care unit. Kosta did this to me, she thought again. It was Saturday night and she could remember that she had had visitors on Saturday afternoon but she couldn't remember who they were or what was said. Kosta did this to me. The facts add up. Deidre is his girlfriend. Lori is her girlfriend. Teja is Lori's boyfriend. Teja tried to kill me. My gun was not in my desk drawer. The insurance money. He was afraid I would divorce him and leave him with nothing. Kosta did this to me.

It was an unacceptable thought. She pushed it away and thought, instead, about the candy apples that her grandfather used to make.

When she was a little girl her grandfather would come from Greece and stay for two or three months at a time.

Each night the dining room table would be covered with fat bags of apples, and Lisa would fall asleep with the smell of apples filling the house. Grandpa would stay up almost all night, and when Lisa awoke in the morning there they would be, rows and rows of bright red taffy apples on the table, on the kitchen counter, everywhere. Steno would take the taffy apples to the boardwalk and sell them at the snack bar.

Kosta did this to me. My own husband tried to have me murdered. No, she thought. She didn't want to have to face this.

She thought about her father. Those days at the beach when she was a little girl. "The Atlantic Ocean," he had said, holding her on his shoulders, and she thought she could see all the way to Greece. The car noises he made, *"Vroom, vroom,"* when he told her about the races.

The man I love is trying to kill me, she thought. The thought kept returning and each time it grew heavier and harder to push away. No, she thought, the facts are deceiving. It's Deidre who is behind all of this, she's doing it behind Kosta's back. Yes, Deidre. But Lisa knew it wasn't Deidre. She knew.

She tried to focus on other things. Cousins, old boy-friends, business. But it kept coming back to her that she was lying in bed with a bullet in her head. *There is a bullet in my brain.* A bullet that should have killed me. I should be dead, she thought. And that's the way my husband wanted it.

That boy, she thought, that boy who came into my room. He's dead. Kosta murdered him. Murdered. What an incredible thought. Lisa could feel the thoughts were coming faster, making more sense. Murder was supposed to be something you heard about on the late news. *Two people in Orlando were found murdered tonight.* Or even, once in a while, *the body of a Daytona Beach man, missing since last week, was found in the trunk of a car near the Halifax River early this afternoon.* But never was murder something that happened

213

in your own house, committed by your own husband. She was shaking off her sense of fogginess. Soon she would be completely awake.

She thought about Kosta, all the cuteness over the years, her funny little Rambo boy burying things in the woods, reading his comic books, collecting his guns. He had always been so adorable. She went over everything, the courtship, the wedding, the good times and bad, thinking that if she just played it all back enough times she would see this terrible tragedy coming at her. She would find a clue. But the clues only made sense after you knew the truth, and the truth was that she had married a monster. The facts add up, she thought, the facts add up. Everything was becoming clear, too clear. Suddenly her eyes opened. She was awake. In the dark she could see everything.

"Oh God," she said out loud. "Oh God, oh God, oh God."

She sobbed for a long time before she fell asleep again.

19

The Brother

On Saturday afternoon Dino drove back to the house with several friends and cousins. The near death of his sister and the knowledge of what was really going on weighed heavily on him and he needed the support of friends, even if he could not tell them everything. Kosta was there, looking properly distressed. Dino showed the group the small window in back, which supposedly was the point of entry for Bryan Chase. The window was barely big enough for a child to get through. It was clear to Dino that the window had been broken for appearances only and that Kosta had probably opened the door for Chase. Though the house alarm had gone off when Dino had opened the door for the police after the shooting, it was Dino's belief that Kosta had turned off the alarm to let Chase in and had turned it back on again afterward. And, in fact, that probably is what happened. But now, on Saturday afternoon, Dino said nothing about Kosta's involvement, just pointed to the window and hoped that what was so obvious to him would become obvious to others.

"A few years earlier somebody really had come through one of those windows and burglarized the house," Dino

215

says. "It must have been a kid or somebody very small. So when I was showing it to people on Saturday afternoon I mentioned that fact and Kosta goes, 'Oh yeah, that's right,' as if he had completely forgotten that. It seemed very suspicious to me that he had forgotten it, because it was such an unusual way to enter a house, that nobody would forget it. I figured Kosta decided to make it look as if somebody had used the small window because the previous break-in would give that scenario credibility."

Also on Saturday Dino asked his friend Jimmy Walls to do some spying. Walls had been friendly with Kosta, and could hang around at Top Shots without unnerving Kosta. Dino and Walls devised an elaborate set of signals to make sure their communications were not heard by Kosta. Dino, when he was visiting Lisa at the hospital during the next few days, would call into Walls's beeper, and leave a code number to indicate it was him. Then he would go take the elevator up to another floor of the hospital to receive the call from Walls, who would report any news. Though in retrospect this method of communicating might seem a bit dramatic, it was at the time no more than reasonable caution. Then, none of the innocent people really knew what was going on. Kosta Fotopoulos was, after all, the proud owner of submachine guns, hand grenades, and various other firepower, so the idea of him directing spies and planting wiretaps was not far-fetched.

By dark on Saturday the cousins and friends had gone. Now it was just Dino, Mary, and Kosta, in the house. They watched the TV news. Every station carried the story of Lisa Fotopoulos, local businesswoman, who had been shot by a burglar, who, in turn, had been killed by Lisa's husband, Kosta. Dino watched in silence, waiting for some hint that somebody somewhere thought there was more to the story than it seemed. But there was nothing.

As the evening wore on Dino became more and more tense. He and Mary would have to spend the night in the house with a man who was capable of murder, and yet he

216

could in no way indicate that he feared Kosta. If Kosta knows that I know, Dino thought, he will kill us for sure. Though Dino didn't know about Kevin or any of Kosta's other videotapes, he had seen the body of Bryan Chase on the bedroom floor. He knew that Kosta could kill.

The family of three ate supper together. Lisa's absence seemed to leave a hole in the room and there were moments of excruciating silence.

After supper Dino stood in the kitchen and watched his mother as she methodically washed dishes and put them away. She seemed to lose herself in her chores, trying to push away thoughts of her daughter. Already Dino sensed that the events of the early morning had damaged his mother in ways difficult to see. The intrusion into her house, the violence to her family, had shaken her trust in strangers, had ignited in her new fears. She seemed, even in the smallest movements, to be somehow more cautious, more fearful that something could strike her suddenly. How will she take it, Dino wondered, when she knows that the violence to her family came from within her family. What would she say when she learned that the man who had tried to kill her daughter was her beloved son-in-law? He dreaded the moment when he would have to tell her.

Just then his mother turned to him. "Dino," she said, "I've been thinking. You should sleep with Kosta tonight."

"Kosta?" Dino said. What an incredible thought. It was like something out of a Woody Allen movie.

"He needs you," Mary said. "He's sad. His Lisa is in the hospital."

It took some doing, but Dino convinced his mother that sleeping with Kosta was not the best thing.

"I should sleep in your room," he told her. "I'll be there to protect you if anything happens."

Still, Dino said not a word about Kosta being the villain. He had adopted the viewpoint that Teja was behind the attempt on Lisa, and that Teja or one of his cohorts, might

217

come in the night. "Kosta," he explained, "can protect himself."

By bedtime on Saturday Dino was a wreck. He had no way to protect himself if Kosta appeared with a gun during the night. What could he do, throw a lamp at Kosta? How much protection could he really give his mother or himself from a man who had more guns than Dirty Harry? The answer, he knew, was none. He and Mary would be as helpless as deer in the forest if Kosta decided to come for them. As he thought on this, Dino thought also that he needed to show Kosta that he believed there was some-body outside of the house who had tried to kill Lisa. If Dino didn't act properly apprehensive about outside dan-gers, then Kosta might realize that Dino suspected him. Then it came to Dino that there was a way to solve both problems. He would borrow a gun from Kosta.

Kosta was in the television room watching the usual shoot-em-up action fare. Dino sat down beside him on the couch.

"Kosta, can I interrupt you for a minute?"

"Sure," Kosta said. He aimed the remote like a pistol and turned off the sound on the TV.

"I've been thinking about Teja," Dino said.

"That son of a bitch," Kosta said. "I've been thinking about him, too. If I catch that black bastard I'll kill him."

"He's dangerous," Dino said. "I think he's behind this thing."

Kosta smiled. He patted Dino's shoulder. "I think you're right," he said.

"Look, I'm a little scared," Dino said, "and I was won-dering . . . do you think I could borrow a gun, just for the night?"

If he doesn't give it to me, I'm in trouble, Dino thought. If he doesn't give me a gun it means he wants me un-armed, so he can come in and shoot me.

Kosta smiled. "Sure, Dino, sure." He left the couch and

walked out of the house. A minute later he came back with the gun from Lisa's car.

He waved the gun at Dino. "This will protect you," he said.

Standing in the living room, next to Dino, Kosta then unloaded the gun and reloaded it with bullets from his pocket.

The son of a bitch is putting in blanks, Dino thought. He's filling it with blanks and he's doing it right in front of me.

He handed Dino the gun. "You know how to use it?"

"I think so," Dino said. "I think so."

"Good," Kosta said. He patted Dino on the back.

All night long Dino stayed awake. He lay, fully dressed, in his mother's bedroom, his heart thumping madly with every sound. He had the door padlocked on the inside, and the gun lay on a night table just inches away. Now and then he would grab for the gun to see how quickly he could get it into his hand. He felt as if he were drawing down on Shootin' Sam at Joyland. Let's hope my aim's a little better now, he thought. Being what he calls "gun illiterate," Dino had no way of figuring out if the bullets in his weapon were blanks. (Later he showed the bullets to Officer Allison Ebel and she assured him that they were live rounds. In fact, Kosta, for whatever reason, had replaced the old bullets with a more deadly type.)

Mary Paspalakis, knowing only that her daughter had been shot by a stranger, finally fell asleep about 2:00 A.M. and Dino could hear the soft sounds of her breathing.

By dawn, just before he fell asleep, Dino decided that he could not go through this again. His mother would have to sleep at a relative's house. The only way he could get her to do that, he knew, would be to tell her the awful truth.

On Sunday morning Dino went out early to get the *News Journal*, Daytona's newspaper. The top story: HUSBAND

Kills Intruder, Wife Wounded in Shooting at N. Halifax Home.

Dino had expected the shooting to make the papers, but he was shocked to see it in big bold headlines, the top story of the day.

The story, by *News Journal* reporter William D. A. Hill, began, "An 18-year-old intruder is dead and a prominent Halifax Avenue businesswoman is in serious condition after a shooting in the woman's home early Saturday morning, police reported."

The article went on to recount Kosta's story about being awakened by a loud noise, seeing the intruder, and shooting him. The front page also carried a photograph of Bryan Chase's body being taken out of the house. Dino took the paper home, wondering how many people in Daytona Beach would see right through it. How many would know what he knew.

Later that morning Dino drove his mother to the hospital to visit with Lisa.

"We were driving along," Dino says, "and I turned to her and I said, 'Ma, there's something I got to tell you. There's a good chance Kosta is involved in all of this. So we can't sleep in the house.' But she refused to accept it. She started yelling at me. 'No, no, Kosta wouldn't do that to Lisa.' She kept saying, 'You're going to kill your sister, telling her a thing like this.' And I kept saying, 'Well, I'd rather have her die from hearing this than from being shot by Kosta, or from hearing that you and I were murdered in our beds by her husband.' But she just wouldn't believe me. I told her, I said, 'Look, Ma, you have to sleep at Thea Loulas' tonight. Kosta doesn't know where she lives.' And my mother, she kept saying, 'No, we will sleep at home,' and I'd say, 'No, you're sleeping at Thea Loulas' and we went back and forth like that.

"But when we got to the hospital, all her friends were there waiting to see Lisa, and I guess they must have suspected something because they all said to my mother,

'Mary, you do what your son tells you, you don't sleep in that house,' and I guess then it started to sink in for her that it really was true and she cried."

Later that day Dino drove back to the house with Kosta in the BMW, to take a break from the hospital while other people visited with Lisa. Along the way Dino brooded about what was happening, most intensely about the fact that Kosta had sat by Lisa's hospital bed and held her hand. He held her hand, Dino thought. He had the nerve to hold her hand. Somehow, it seemed to Dino, that this was the greatest violation, for Kosta to sit there and act like the loving husband after what he had done. It had disturbed Dino so much that he had left the room. Now as they drove along, he took deep breaths to calm himself. His emotions, he would later say, were fighting it out with his intelligence. Intellectually, everything pointed to Kosta. Emotionally, Dino didn't want it to be true. He wrote scenarios in his mind that would somehow explain everything and leave Kosta innocent. But it was difficult. Still, even now, with all this anger broiling inside of him, he would give Kosta the benefit of the doubt. Allowing for what he thought of as "the five percent chance that Kosta is not involved," he turned to his brother-in-law.

"Kosta," he said, "I went to the police."

Kosta turned his head quickly to Dino, then back to the road.

"I told them everything that I know about the Teja-Lori-Deidre connection," Dino said.

"Oh," Kosta said. He nodded his head up and down. "That's good."

Dino studied Kosta for more of a reaction, some proof that he definitely was a murderer or definitely wasn't.

"You know more about these people than I do," Dino said.

"So?"

"Well. You ought to go to the police." He paused. "And tell them what you know."

221

Kosta stared out at the road. He pulled a hand from the steering wheel, reached across his chest, and patted the spot where his pistol was holstered.

"I'm going to take care of it myself," he said.

"Take care of it yourself?" Dino said. "For God's sake, Kosta, this isn't some Rambo movie. You don't take care of it yourself. You go to the police and you tell them everything you know and you let them take care of it."

Kosta just smiled. It was a smile Dino knew well. It meant, I, Kosta, know what's best, and you know nothing.

(Apparently, Kosta really did plan to "take care of it" himself. According to Peter Kouracos, he and Kosta drove around Daytona looking for Teja one night after the shooting. Though Kouracos makes no mention of Kosta's intentions, he does note, "We were both armed.")

In fact, Dino, through Allison Ebel, had begun to keep in frequent contact with the police, who by this time were leaning toward the theory that Kosta was guilty. Dino's suspicions resonated with a few of their own. Why, they wondered, would a burglar walk through a house full of valuable objects to enter a bedroom and shoot a sleeping woman? Furthermore, if the burglar was going to shoot someone, why the woman? Why not shoot the man, who was bigger and stronger, a much more serious threat? Their own investigation was leading them quickly to the same conclusion that Dino had made: Kosta had engineered his wife's shooting. Dino was helping the police by keeping a small spiral notebook in which he wrote everything he heard or remembered about Kosta that might be helpful.

By Sunday night the Jimmy Walls operation was beginning to show signs of success. Kosta, it seemed, was no less paranoid than Dino about wiretaps. Walls reported that Deidre was receiving calls from Kosta at Top Shots. She would speak briefly, than saunter over to a pool table and shoot a rack, before discreetly walking out to the boardwalk, where she would then place a call, presumably to Kosta, on the coin-operated phone. Dino, of course, didn't know what was being said, but all the secrecy didn't do much for the "five percent chance that Kosta is innocent" theory.

During this time there was one other surprising source of information that Dino entered in his notebook. An older black man seemed to be in the intensive care unit waiting room all the time. He slept on the bench while his wife was in the hospital. On Sunday morning as Dino was walking by the elevator the old black man waved him on. When the door was closed the black man looked at him conspiratorially.

"Be careful," he said.

"Huh?"

"Be careful," he said. "Your brother-in-law came looking for you at three in the morning."

"Oh," Dino said. He had no idea what he was dealing with. Was this man some friend of Kosta's? Was it some sort of trick?

"He calls her, you know," the black man said.

"Who?"

"Deidre," the man said. "He calls Deidre."

During this time theories about who wanted to kill Lisa were not hard to come by. There was, of course, the Teja theory. There was a theory, put forth by one of the newscasters who haunted the hospital corridors, that someone high up at the Marriott was trying to kill Lisa, the same theory that Kosta had spouted to Lisa on the drive to Edgewater. It was an absurd idea, but not as absurd as the one that Kosta put to Dino in the hospital on Monday morning.

A few weeks before the shooting there had been a meeting at which a local political appointee by the name of George McGee stood up and made disparaging remarks about Greeks. Specifically, he accused the Greek gift shop owners of having no taste. Their gift shops, he said, were too cluttered. "That's how Greeks are," he said. "I been to Greece and it's the same thing, everything is cluttered."

The comment had caused a small uproar in the Greek community, and days later McGee was obliged to publicly apologize. Lisa led the lobbying to make McGee apologize.

Now, on the Monday morning after the shooting, November 6, Kosta came up to Dino in a corridor at the Halifax Memorial Hospital and said, "I know who is behind this."

"You do?" Dino said, thinking, I'll just bet you do. Dino was trying to get out of the building, but he didn't want to stir Kosta's curiosity about where he was going, because he had an appointment to see a private detective.

"It's not just me who thinks this," Kosta said. "A lot of people are thinking the same thing."

"Who?"

"George McGee," Kosta said.

Dino couldn't believe what he was hearing. The idea was so preposterous that he was embarrassed for Kosta for even saying it.

"George McGee?" Dino shouted. "George McGee?" All the rage he'd been holding in now erupted. "Kosta, what the fuck is the matter with you? What do you think, McGee tried to kill my sister because her gift shop is too cluttered? George McGee."

Kosta said nothing. Dino kept shouting. "It wasn't George McGee, goddamnit, and it wasn't the Marriott and it wasn't Teja. We know who it was, don't we? We know." Now he was screaming and shaking his fists and crying all at once. "I'm getting out of here," he said. He headed for the door. Then he turned and shook a fist at his brother-in-law. "I want you out of my house by tonight. Take all your stuff and your goddamn guns and just . . . just get out." He wanted to walk back and lunge at Kosta and just beat the hell out of him for trying to kill Lisa. But there was another more prudent part of him thinking, Watch it, Dino, this guy's a fucking psycho, he carries a gun. "Just leave us alone," Dino said and he stormed out of the hospital.

By eleven o'clock Dino was in the office of a private

detective. "I want Kosta watched," he told the PI, thinking that if he'd hired a detective on Thursday when he wanted to, by now Fotomat could have processed a dozen glossy double prints of Kosta meeting Bryan Chase and maybe even handing him a gun or something. The private detective told Dino to save his money. The police were on it, he said, and they will solve it. "But if I had to bet money," he said, before Dino left his office, "I'd bet that Kosta is behind this and he's hired other people through Deidre to keep himself clean."

From there Dino went to the bank, where he had Kosta's name removed from the company accounts, so that Kosta couldn't cash a check and fly to Greece. Dino also changed his will, taking Kosta's name off of it.

During these days Dino's closest confidant was his friend Timmy Kostidakis. Timmy had known Dino forever. They used to play basketball together. In more recent times Timmy had been part of a crowd of Paspalakis cousins, both real and nominal, who would get together on Friday evenings and play small stakes poker. Kosta would join in these sessions, too, but Timmy had never found him sociable.

Dino had turned to Timmy for advice as early as Thursday, after his visit to the lawyer. He had met Timmy that night and told him what was going on. Timmy, like Dino, was anxious to give Kosta the benefit of the doubt, but it did not look good. On Saturday morning after the shooting, Timmy was the first person Dino had called, and he came right over. Throughout Saturday and Sunday it was Timmy that Dino called constantly to hold himself together.

After that first harrowing night in the house, sleeping in his mother's room with the loaded gun, Dino started sleeping in Lisa's guarded room at the hospital. He slept there on Sunday night and Monday night.

On Tuesday night Dino met at the police station with police and investigators from the state attorney's office. Surrounded by law enforcement officers he again told everything he knew and suspected. He told them about Kosta and Deidre's affair, about Teja being Lori's boyfriend, and Lori being Deidre's girlfriend. He told them about the window, the insurance, the downstairs light, the phone calls at Top Shots. Though Dino was unaware of it, by this time the police knew a good deal more about the case. In fact, one of the things that the police knew that Dino didn't know was that Kosta had bragged to boardwalk friends that he had murdered Steno Paspalakis. When the discussion was over that evening, Bob Wheeler, the chief investigator for the state attorney's office, and Mike Politis, another investigator who was also a "cousin" to Dino (many friends in the Greek community are called cousins, even when they're not related) went to the hospital.

"We had to go to Lisa's room separately," Dino explains. "Because if Kosta was there, or any of his spies, it would not be good to have me seen with investigators."

That night the investigators told Dino and Lisa that Kosta would be arrested for murder.

20

The Investigation

The police investigation of the Fotopoulos case was the most highly publicized in Daytona Beach history. It began on that Saturday morning, November 4, when officer John Slavin was told to go to 2505 North Halifax.

"I had received information that there was a shooting and I supposed the shooter was still in the house," he says. Slavin, who was soon joined by officers in other cruisers, lit up the house with the spotlight from his car and ordered everybody outside. That's when Dino rushed out in his underwear and had a bullhorn shoved in his hand, so he could tell his mother and Kosta to come outside.

"He said that his sister had been shot and that his brother-in-law had shot a guy. He wanted me to go in. We went through the foyer and up the larger staircase. At the top of the staircase there is a bedroom door facing you. I didn't know if the shooter was still in there. I inched my way in. There was a lady lying in bed. She looked at me. She said something like, 'He's over there and I think he's dead.' I was able to see an individual lying on the floor, head facing east. He had something in his hand, I couldn't tell what. At this point I didn't know that this fellow had expired. I had no idea who he was. I shined the flashlight on his hand. It was a gun. I removed it from his hand. We brought in the paramedics. I said to the woman, 'You're going to be all right.' "

Detective Charles Evans and Corporal Gregg Smith, from the Criminal Investigations Division (CID), came to the house. Like the others, they sensed that the broken window, the dead burglar, and the hero husband did not add up to a solved case. Something had happened in the house other than what appeared to have happened. They drove to the Desert Inn Hotel, where David Chase, Bryan's father, worked. They told Chase that his son had been shot to death. They asked Chase about Bryan's last days. Chase said his son had gone to bed early the night before, and he had never seen him again. He told them about the visits from the two young women, and how Bryan had been moody lately. He told them Bryan had gone out early that morning and left a note by the coffee pot saying he'd be home later. He told them that Bryan had always been a good kid.

The police searched Bryan's room but found nothing that could be used as evidence.

Meanwhile, Mary Paspalakis's house was being invaded by a team of crime lab technicians from Orlando. Of most interest to them was the window at the back of the house.

David Damore, who would eventually prosecute the case, says he is fairly certain that Kosta, after turning on the television loudly enough to drown out the noise of breaking glass, turned off the house alarm and let Bryan in the sliding glass door at the back of the house. However, the findings of the lab technicians do allow for other scenarios.

"The evidence is not conclusive that Bryan Chase actually made it through the window, or didn't," Damore says. "There are two theories available. One is that Bryan Chase was able to make it through the window and, with the knowledge that Kosta had given him, found his way to the bedroom. The other is that Kosta had shut off the burglar alarm and opened the door for Bryan and walked him to the bedroom.

"Bryan was fairly stocky, 178 pounds, and it would be difficult to get through that window. But we did find glass on his clothes. If we assume that he kicked the glass, there would have been a spray, known as blowback, that would have left glass on him. It's also possible that he tried to get through the window, but couldn't fit through. Maybe at that point Kosta came to help him in. That would explain the glass on him."

On Saturday night a 911 call came into Daytona police headquarters from a young man who was in a phone booth. He said he knew what really had happened at the Fotopoulos house. While the young man was on the phone a police car was sent to detain him at the phone booth. Evans and Smith went to pick him up. It was J. R. The two officers took J. R. to the police station and taped an interview. They hoped J. R. could lead them to Teja, who was still at large, but J. R. said he didn't know where Teja was. By this time the "Teja hired Bryan to kill Lisa" theory, which had never been strong to begin with, had been pretty much abandoned. J. R. had good reason for blowing the whistle on Kosta. Bryan Chase had been J. R.'s friend.

"It pissed me off when I found out they had killed Bryan," he says.

Furthermore, it was clear that the four 9-millimeter bullets that went into Bryan's body would have been in J. R.'s body if he had signed on for the Lisa shooting.

The next day, Sunday, November 5, acting on the information they had gotten from J. R., Evans and Smith called on Deidre Hunt and Lori Henderson.

"We went to Hunt's Lenox Avenue apartment," Smith says, "but it was obvious that they weren't going to say much in front of each other."

At one point, when Deidre was out of the room, Lori turned to the police and told them she was willing to talk

229

to them alone. She agreed to come to the police station the next day.

On Monday when Lori didn't show up, the police went back to Deidre's. Deidre told them she had taken Lori to a friend's house.

On that same day police who went to the Paspalakis house to continue the investigation were greeted by Peter Kouracos. Peter and Kosta, they learned, had been sleeping in the same bed, a detail that would inspire some obvious speculation. Kouracos insisted that nothing sexual had occurred, that the men were simply napping.

On Tuesday, the 7th, Mike Cox was arrested on an unrelated prostitution charge. He told Evans that he had information about the Fotopoulos shooting, and what he said corroborated J. R.'s story.

Later that same day the police caught up with Lori and Deidre at Cheapo Car Rental on Volusia, where the two young women were returning a rental. When the cops asked Lori to come with them, Deidre got belligerent.

"She pitched a fit," Evans says. "She did not want us to be alone with Lori."

Finally, Deidre and Lori both went to the police station and Lori told the cops everything. Deidre was arrested. (Lori was arrested two days later.)

By the time Lori stopped talking, the cops had heard enough to arrest Kosta.

21

The Arrest

Though Lisa had come to terms with the truth about Kosta on Saturday night, she would, like her brother, occasionally slip into the "five percent chance that Kosta didn't do it" mentality. And like her brother, she kept what she knew to herself. The last thing she wanted was to have Kosta find out that she knew he was a killer. While the police were busily trying to put the puzzle together and get enough evidence to arrest Kosta, Lisa and her husband acted out their roles of deception. When Kosta came to visit, Lisa recalls now, it was strange.

"We sat and watched TV mostly. We didn't talk much about the shooting. We talked about family and how business was going at Top Shots. The shooting was the one subject we ignored. It wasn't as if I sat there thinking all the time about the fact that this man had tried to kill me. Usually, I just didn't think about it. I kept it out of my mind. I was afraid to think about it. I still believed in the legal system and I knew that things would take their course and that he would be caught. I guess I still couldn't really deal with the betrayal, the fact that my husband had tried to kill me."

On his visits, Kosta often fed Lisa. He held her hand. He tried to be the perfect husband. But he said little.

During this period of Lisa's hospitalization Dino visited constantly, but he and Lisa never acknowledged, in words, what they both knew. Dino, throughout, was afraid that a discussion of the truth would be too much for Lisa to handle. But Lisa knew the truth. She made that clear to him on Sunday night, the 5th.

"I told the police about Teja and Lori," Dino said to her that night. He watched for Lisa's reaction. She seemed okay. "I told Kosta he should go to the police and tell them what he knows about these people, but I don't think he will."

"What did you tell them?" Lisa asked.

"I told them that Teja was Lori's boyfriend, and Lori was Deidre's lover."

"And Deidre was Kosta's lover," Lisa said. Dino was echoing all the thoughts she had had.

"Yes."

There was a long moment of silence. The truth settled in the space between them. Then Lisa took her brother's hand. "Dino," she said, "one plus one is two."

"Yes," he said, "one plus one is two."

And that was it. Neither of them was ready to say out loud such a horrendous thing as, Kosta tried to kill Lisa and murdered an eighteen-year-old boy. And at the time, Lisa never imagined that the truth was far more horrendous. But in the simplest equation they had exchanged the information that Kosta was a killer and that they both knew it.

On Tuesday night, the 7th, Kosta came to visit. He sat on the edge of the bed, as usual, awkwardly patted his wife's head, held her hand, and then fed her. Kosta talked for a while about Top Shots, about another business he might open. But his words were drowned out by the noise of what went unsaid. Turning from each other, they watched the TV news. There were new shootings to be reported, other lives being wrecked. Lisa, perhaps sensing that this was the last time she would ever see her husband as a free man, felt the tears come into her eyes. She wanted to ask him why. She wanted to ask him if he had ever loved her. But she couldn't. Though it would be some time before anybody sat down with Lisa and talked about the meaning of the word *sociopath*, she knew already that she had married a hollow man in whose heart no love lived. If he had loved her at all, it was the selfish love of a child who loves the source of food and presents, not the selfless love of an adult. When he was gone, she knew, she would feel the loss not of the man she had married, but of the one she thought she had married, a man who had never existed.

Later that same night investigators Wheeler and Politis came to Lisa's room and told her and Dino that Kosta was going to be arrested for murder. Before they left they moved Lisa into a different room under a "Jane Doe," so that Kosta could not find her.

Precautions were also taken for Dino.

"You'll spend the night at my place," Wheeler told Dino. "In the morning you'll be assigned a personal bodyguard."

"A bodyguard? Why?"

"There might be a contract on you," Wheeler said.

"A contract? You mean like a hit man?"

"Could be. Kosta might have hired someone to kill you."

Dino asked if he would need a bulletproof vest. Wheeler told him no.

"How long will I have a bodyguard?"

"Just until noon," Wheeler said.

"What happens at noon?"

"If we arrest Kosta tonight, then everybody will know it when it hits the noon news tomorrow. If there is a contract out on you, the hit man will know that Kosta is in jail."

"And the hit man will know that he's never going to get paid," Dino said.

"Right," Wheeler told him.

233

"Okay," Dino said. "Let's hope he watches the news."

(Though it has never been proved that a hit man was hired to kill Dino, Dino's friend Timmy recalls getting strange calls during this time from someone who was trying to locate Dino but refused to identify himself.)

After the two investigators left, it was as if a weight had been removed for Lisa and Dino. Finally, they could talk about it. Dino told Lisa that some of the boardwalk people had told police that Kosta bragged about killing Steno. It was all too much and they talked about the fact that it would take months for them to sort it all out and begin to heal.

"Maybe I'll need a shrink," Lisa joked. She knew she didn't want to go through life being suspicious of every man she met. She would do whatever it would take to put this behind her.

Kosta would be in jail soon and they both felt relieved. Now they could joke about some of the tense moments of recent days. Dino had walked across the hospital parking lot late one night, when an air conditioner made a loud boom. He thought someone was shooting at him and ran for the door. "Even at the time," he told Lisa, "I was thinking, 'Gee, if I've got to get shot, at least I'm at a hospital.' "

There had been another time when Dino had not visited for twelve or thirteen hours, which seemed like a long time to Lisa. He came in and she looked at him oddly and said, "Who are you?" Dino had been tense all along that Lisa would suffer some brain damage from the bullet. Alarmed, he had run to her, almost in tears, "Lisa, Lisa," he'd cried, "it's me, Dino, don't you know me?"

"Of course I know you," Lisa had said. "I just mean I haven't seen you in a while."

They recalled these light moments, knowing that there would be many difficult moments to come. Kosta would be tried for murder. There would be newspaper stories and television shows. Already the videotaped murder was becoming a story around the country, picked up by the

234

wire services and nationally syndicated television shows. And there would be years of explaining to friends and family exactly what had happened.

At a little after midnight on Tuesday, officers Bill Batten and Bob Blackwell, from the street crimes division of the Daytona Beach police department, drove to the house on North Halifax. Kosta was not home, so they parked across the street and waited for him. When Kosta pulled in at around one-thirty in the morning of the 8th, the officers drove over and met him in the driveway.

"You're under arrest," they told him. "We have to take you to the police station for questioning."

Though Kosta looked surprised, he made no effort to resist. Most likely, he expected to lie and charm his way out of jail within hours.

Kosta was pleasant and cooperative while the officers handcuffed him and searched him. As usual, he was carrying a gun, which the police confiscated.

On the same Tuesday night and Wednesday morning, while police were arresting Kosta Fotopoulos, Deidre Hunt was spilling her guts. She told the police about her affair with Kosta, his CIA connections, his terrorist exploits, his days of hiding underground like Rambo ("that's the kind of training that man went through," she said) the armed robberies he had planned to pull off with Kevin and other kids, the counterfeit bills he passed, the array of weapons he owned. She squealed about her attempt to recruit killers, the foiled plans to knock off Lisa, the Teja holdup, and the murder of Kevin Ramsey.

It was in this statement that Deidre began what would become her public relations strategy for months to come. She portrayed Kosta as a sadist and a Svengali who had a powerful hold over her; she painted herself as a victim of intimidation and torture who was forced to kill Kevin Ramsey or be killed herself. But her tone in that confession, which is punctuated by fits of crying, is one of admiration of the successful student for her sage teacher.

"I know how to rob a bank," she said, "because he told me. You go in with three people, and you have one driving. You go in with three people wearing ski masks, you have automatic weapons and you tell people to freeze. You go out, you get in the car, and you have thirty seconds to get away. You have two snipers in the building. When the police arrive they snipe at the police cars."

At another point she told police, "Kosta was receiving ten thousand dollars a week in real money from people he had laundering it."

"I think," she said, "that even if you catch him he's going to end up killing himself, he'll be able to do it."

At two-thirty on Wednesday morning Deidre Hunt agreed to show the police where she and Kosta had killed Kevin Ramsey.

"We drove out on Clyde Morris to Williamson, near the Strickland range," Officer Larry Lewis says. "When we got to Williamson she said, 'Now you have to go to the other side.' This was a mile away from where we had looked earlier [without Deidre]. We drove toward I-95 about half a mile and she said, 'Okay, stop here.' She was sitting in the backseat. I said, 'Is this the spot' and she said, 'Yes.' I got out of the car and could smell the foul odor in the air. We got out. I gave her a flashlight and said, 'You show me where it is.' She walked in the woods about thirty-five feet or so and she said, 'It's just over this little hill.' As we walked over she said, 'There should be a tree that is kind of horizontal, broken off at ground level,' and she flashed the light toward the east. As she brought the light around she said, 'There it is, right there.' I took her back to the car, then went back to the woods to make sure it was a human body because I couldn't tell for sure. When I got close I could tell. The skull was missing. The spinal cord was poking up. He had a black shirt with some gold writing on it and dark pants. His legs were under him kind of in a sitting position."

One note of interest: When Deidre Hunt was first questioned at her apartment, Detective Allison Ebel was present. Ebel noticed that there was a single book on Deidre's coffee table. It was a novel published in 1988 called *Frenzy*, written by Rex Miller. She turned the cover to the front sales page and the first words she read were, "Juan LaBellamonde came to with his hands wired behind him, bound to a tree. Frank Spain reached down on the grass for his bloody implement and held it in front of the screaming man."

Certainly the fact that Deidre was reading a book in which a man is bound to a tree and murdered could be a coincidence. But it does nurture some suspicions. For one thing, Kosta Fotopoulos was not a reader of novels, so if the idea of tying Kevin to the tree did come from the book, then it would probably have come from Deidre to Kosta, not the other way around. (On the other hand, Kosta did a lot of shooting in those woods, and if you are going to kill somebody in the woods, tying him to a tree is a fairly obvious thing to do.) However, this oddity, in combination with the fact that Deidre's ex-boyfriend in New Hampshire was allegedly hired to murder someone's wife, and then watched the murder, makes one wonder in whose nest the plot to murder Lisa was hatched.

David Damore says, "Where did the idea to kill Lisa come in? Was it that one night they were lying in bed and Kosta was thinking about how much money he would have with his wife dead, and did he say, I want to kill my wife? Or was it Deidre saying, 'Look, you love me and you want to be with me. Well, you need to kill your wife'? We'll never know for sure."

Once Deidre, Kosta, Lori, Teja, Mike Cox, and J. R. were locked up, the focus of the police investigation shifted to the search for physical evidence. Kosta was of no help. He proclaimed his innocence and refused to take a lie detector test. Specifically the police searched for the weapons that Kosta had used in the Ramsey murder, and the videotape, which Deidre claimed he had made of that murder.

Police searched Kosta's car. There they found ten thousand dollars in cash and several nude photos of Deidre. They searched Joyland. They found a small quantity of triacidtone triphosphate, an explosive. In a secret drawer they also found several copies of *Playboy* and *Penthouse.*

At Joyland they also looked into Kosta's private safe.

"Kosta liked his privacy," Dino says. "So we had given him an old safe that was in Joyland under the stairs. He had changed the combination. After he was arrested I hired a locksmith to meet me at Joyland with people from the state attorney's office. When the door to the safe was ready to be opened, they tied a rope to it and extended it all the way out of the building and told everybody to get out, because the safe could be booby trapped. I'm thinking, Oh, great, my sister's been shot, my father might have been murdered, my brother-in-law is a psycho, and now I'm going to have my business blown up."

The safe, as it turned out, contained nothing explosive, either literally or figuratively.

Both Peter Kouoracos and Vinnie Speziale cooperated with the police investigators. Each described going with Kosta while he buried something in the woods. Speziale remembered that Kosta's marker was a telephone pole with a notch carved in it. Using this information police were eventually able to dig up a cannister containing weapons, an ammunition box, a .38 revolver, 169 counterfeit one-hundred-dollar bills, and two hand grenades. They also found evidence of fresh digging nearby, suggesting that some Kosta cohort might have come along and dug up other weapons or money.

The police searched the house. They impounded Kosta's comic books and *Soldier of Fortune* magazines, thinking they might contain clues to his behavior. They took his guns, his ammunition, and his tools for making silencers and bullets.

One day while police and investigators from the state attorney's office were at the house, Kosta called Dino collect.

"I picked up the phone and put on the speakerphone so everybody could hear," Dino says. "Kosta kept saying, 'Dino, I'm innocent. Dino, I didn't do any of those things they say. The whole thing is a frame. I didn't kill Dad.' 'Well, why didn't you take a lie detector test?' I said. 'Oh, you know, those things aren't admissable in court,' he said. I said to him, 'Kosta, there is a little part of me that might have believed you right up until today.' Then there was a pause and Kosta got all nervous. He says, 'Why, did they find something today?' And you could tell from his voice that there was something he was afraid that they would find. After I hung up the phone I said to the police, 'That tape is in this house, I'm sure of it.' "

The search for the videotape and the weapons continued. It was late November when the police finally got a break.

"When I was in the hospital the police asked me if I knew any of the places where Kosta buried things," Lisa says. "I didn't know where he buried stuff, just that it was in the woods somewhere. Then one day after I got home from the hospital I was looking out at the river and I thought, 'Oh, my God.' It all flashed back to me, the night he was burying something out by the barbecue. I called the cops and told them I had seen Kosta burying something there."

On Wednesday, November 22, the police came to look for the weapons. As it turned out, they got a lot more than they had hoped for. David Damore recalls:

"I went to the Paspalakis house at nine in the morning. I was there to have a carpenter cut out a piece of the bedroom floor containing the bullet that Kosta had put through Bryan Chase's head. When I pulled into the driveway Dino came up to me and he had this big smile on his face.

'Dave,' he said, 'we found the guns.' As I looked up I saw that Bob Wheeler and Joe Gallagher were there and they both had Cheshire cat grins on their faces, so I thought, Okay, it's a joke. They sent Dino over to yank my chain, because they knew how desperate I was to find some physical evidence. We do this sort of thing. You need to have a little humor when you're dealing with such heavy stuff.

"We were in a race against time and our main concern was that some of the people we did not have in custody might dig up some of the evidence and get rid of it. So I was the doubting Thomas and I said, 'Yeah, yeah, yeah, sure you've found the guns.' These two guys were like a couple of kids, practically dancing, but I wasn't even going to talk to them because I knew they were joking. So they tugged at me and literally towed me around the house to the barbecue area and there were the cops inventorying the weapons they had found. They had the .22 Ruger with the silencer that Deidre had used to kill Kevin Ramsey, and they had the AK47 that Kosta had used for that final shot. It was unbelievable and I was very excited.

"After we dug out the piece of floor that we needed for evidence, I went down to the garage with Detective Bill Adamy. I wanted to show him a few things that I thought were evidence of the fact that Kosta was making silencers. And since we had missed the weapons on previous searches of the house I wanted to come back and look more thoroughly for the videotape. I was saying to Bill that we need to redraft the search warrant and come back and look into every box in the house, just turn the place upside down. While we were talking we were just kind of staring at the wall of the garage, and on one of the shelves against the wall there was a bag. I said to Bill, 'You know, I feel like there's evidence here and it's right in front of us and we just can't see it.'

"So we started to walk out of the garage and suddenly Bill spun around and pointed directly up at that bag on the shelf and he said, 'Dave, that bag stinks.' I said, 'What do you mean?' He said, 'I'm telling you, that bag stinks.' I looked at him and I said, 'Bill, you're having delusions. Look,' I said, 'we had a good day, we found the murder weapons, let's go, and we'll come back another day and really search this place.' He says, 'David, I'm telling you, there's something about that bag.' So I said, 'Okay, if you feel that strongly about it, let's take a look.' By this time I'm thinking, Okay, now they really are pulling my leg.

"So Bill gets on a ladder and he climbs up and looks in the bag without touching it. Then he looks down and smiles and he's grinning ear to ear. 'Dave,' he says, 'there's a videotape in this bag.' I was sure he was yanking my chain, so I called him a name, which has to do with a person's backside. But he brought the bag down and sure enough the videotape was in it. Incredible. I'll never forget the way his hand just went up suddenly and he said, 'That bag stinks.' "

Later that night Damore and several other officers and investigators viewed the videotape of Kevin Ramsey being murdered.

"Afterward," he says, "there was just silence."

Though there would be a trial and reams of publicity ahead, the discovery of the videotape was a kind of closure for Lisa and Dino. All along they had worried, justifiably, that if the videotape was not found, Kosta would not be convicted. Without that tape David Damore would have gone into court against a well-liked, well-dressed business-man with only a gang of lowlifes for witnesses, all of them admitted felons and accomplished liars. But now, with the irrefutable videotaped evidence in the hands of the police, Lisa and Dino could breathe easier. It was over. Kosta would never walk the streets again.

When the house was quiet again, after Damore and the others left with the videotape, Lisa and Dino stood in the living room talking about all that had happened.

"Now, it's really over," she said to Dino. Until this

moment she hadn't realized how scared she was that Kosta would be set free, that he would come into her life again.

"Yes, it's over," Dino said.

She stared at her brother for a long moment. They had always been close, but this crisis had brought them even closer. She thought she would just hug him and leave it at that. Instead, she said the words that had been on her mind all along, words that had been haunting her since her first night in the hospital.

"I should have known," she said.

"Huh?"

"I should have known. I should have known he was . . . nuts."

"How could you know?" Dino said. "I didn't know. Mom didn't know. Nobody knew. Kosta fooled everybody."

"Well, the guns," Lisa said. "All the crazy schemes."

"A lot of people collect guns," Dino told her. "A lot of people have dreams. God, Lisa, I'm the one who should have known. I should have known he would try something that night. You could have been killed. I was right there, two doors away when they were shooting you, and I wasn't there to protect you."

"Dino, you're being ridiculous," Lisa said. "There's no way you could have known what would happen. I don't want you ever to even think such a thing."

"You don't? What are you, my sister or something?"

Lisa smiled.

"Look," Dino said, "we can go on forever about who should have seen what. But it's crazy. Every day you read in the papers about somebody who was nuts and nobody in the world suspected it until he went out and slaughtered half a dozen people at a mall. We're intelligent people, all our friends are intelligent, all the businesspeople on the boardwalk are intelligent, and not one of them ever came to us and said, 'Hey guys, Kosta is a psychopath.' "

"And your point?" Lisa said.

"My point is that if we didn't see it, then it wasn't there

to be seen, so there's no sense beating ourselves up about it."

"Okay," Lisa said, "I won't if you won't," though she knew it was not that simple, and it would be months before she forgave herself for bringing this man into her family.

"It's a deal," Dino said. They shook hands.

"I thought he was such a perfect husband," Lisa said as her brother put his arms around her. "Do you think he ever loved me, Dino? I mean did he really love me at first, or did he plan this all along?"

Dino's answer was to say nothing, just hold her, and gently stroke her forehead. It was enough to make her cry. She felt comforted in her brother's arms. Soon she could feel that Dino was crying, too. Those Greek men, she thought, they know how to cry. They can show their feelings. He'll make a good husband some day, she thought. He'll make some girl very happy.

EPILOGUE

In April 1990, Kosta Fotopoulos was tried in federal court in Orlando, Florida, on counterfeiting charges. He pleaded guilty to six charges and was sentenced to thirty-three months in prison.

On May 30 Kosta was placed in solitary confinement at the Volusia County Branch Jail in Daytona when jail officials suspected that he planned to escape. A floor plan for the jail had been found on Kosta along with several mysterious messages. County Corrections Director Terry Moore told the Daytona *News Journal*, "There have been notes in the past, notes that have been coded that we could not decipher."

(Though it did not come out in the press, the search of Kosta also turned up a revealing letter. It was an unmailed letter to his illegitimate son, who had been born to Kosta's old girlfriend, Donna, the year Kosta married Lisa. The letter was an attempt to tell the boy about his heritage. Considering the circumstances, it was a cold and emotionless letter, little more than a catalog of which uncle came from which city and who was married to whom. The letter ended, however, poignantly, with Kosta writing to his boy,

"I'm sorry, this is my fault." It was an ending that might have been used against Kosta in trial, but David Damore, concluding that the letter was too personal and would bring unwanted attention to the boy and his mother, chose not to use it.)

On September 6, a sentencing hearing was begun for Deidre Hunt, who had pleaded guilty months earlier to the murder and attempted murder charges. For the first time the videotape of Kevin Ramsey's murder was shown publicly.

On September 14, Deidre Hunt was given two death sentences and six life sentences for the murders of Bryan Chase and Kevin Ramsey, and six life sentences for the various attempts on the life of Lisa Fotopoulos, conspiracy, and burglary. Deidre had portrayed herself as the helpless victim of a madman who would have killed her if she did not do what he said. The judge, apparently, did not believe her. At twenty-one, she became the youngest woman in the United States on death row.

In October 1990 Kosta was tried for the murders and attempted murders. Deidre Hunt, after changing her mind several times, had decided to testify against him. The trial was moved to Palatka, forty miles west of Daytona, because of publicity.

One bizarre revelation from the trial was the fact that State Attorney John Tanner, Damore's boss, and the man who was responsible for prosecuting Fotopoulos, along with Damore, had for ten months packed the very pistol that Kosta used to kill Bryan Chase.

Peter Kouracos had worked as John Tanner's campaign manager in the 1988 election. In January 1989 Tanner received death threats after trying to delay the execution of Ted Bundy, so Kouracos lent Tanner the 9-milimeter semiautomatic, which he had borrowed from Kosta. In October 1989, Kouracos says, he got the gun back from Tanner and returned it to Kosta, and passed along to Tanner a Walther PPK, a gift from Kosta.

Tanner, who has built a reputation as a smut fighter for his war on porno videos, figured in another strange story about the trial. During the jury selection phase Tanner told the court he was dismissing potential juror Elizabeth Roberts because she was so pretty that she might distract the lawyers from their tasks. The heat on Tanner for this blunder had hardly cooled when the incident took another twist. Miss Roberts received a letter from Kosta Fotopoulos, apologizing to her for her loss of two days' work and saying he was sorry she had not been selected.

"I felt because of your age and the special circumstances surrounding you that you could relate to the situation, and really understand how things were," Kosta wrote. At the end of his letter he added a P.S.: "Love your black outfit."

On October 23, Kosta took the stand in his own trial. He had an explanation for everything. He said he buried guns in cannisters in the woods because the guns were illegal and they were dangerous. That, he explained, is the same reason he buried guns in the backyard near the barbecue pit. "I did not want them in the house. You never know what happens."

Kosta admitted to having an affair with Deidre Hunt and laid the guilt for everything at her feet. He said she was trying to frame him for the murder of Kevin Ramsey and that it was she who was trying to kill Lisa. The way Kosta explained it, Deidre did all this without his knowledge. She had borrowed his videotape camera and promised to make him a film. Knowing that she was a bisexual, Kosta said he thought she would make him a sex film of her in bed with another woman. "I thought it would be interesting," he explained. Before he had time to look at the film his wife was shot. "The last thing on my mind was looking at naked women." This explained why his fingerprints were on the videotape of Kevin Ramsey being murdered. As for the fact that his voice was also on the tape, Kosta denied that it was his voice, even though an expert, as well as

Dino and Lisa, had testified that it was Kosta's voice on the tape.

"I might like weapons," Kosta told the courtroom, "but I'm not mentally disturbed."

He said that he was livid that Deidre had hurt his wife and his marriage. He said he wished he'd never gotten involved with Deidre. "I hit myself on the head now," he said. Kosta also told the courtroom that he still loved his wife. He said that he could understand her wanting a divorce, because of the publicity about his affair with Deidre.

On October 25, Kosta Fotopoulos was found guilty of the murders of Kevin Ramsey and Bryan Chase, as well as six attempts on the life of his wife, Lisa. Later that night, in his cell, Kosta somehow managed to cut his ankles and his left wrist. Thirty stitches were required and, according to jail officials, no sharp instruments were found in his cell. Jail and courthouse officials concluded that Kosta was not attempting suicide but was trying to injure himself so that he would not be shackled and handcuffed when he went before the jury for the sentencing phase of the trial. Another possibility: he wanted to be transferred to a prison hospital so that he could try to escape.

On October 29 the jury, by an eight-to-four vote, recommended the death sentence for Kosta Fotopoulos.

On November 1, three days less than a year after the shooting, Judge James Foxman gave Kosta two death sentences and six life sentences for the murders and attempted murders. Kosta's mother, who was at the trial, ran from the courtroom, shouting, "My son is innocent."

On November 14, 1990, Lori Henderson and Teja James, both of whom had testified for the state at Kosta's trial, were each sentenced to four years in prison for conspiring to commit first-degree murder and attempted first-degree murder.

Newman Taylor, J. R., testified at the Fotopoulos trial.

247

He later was released from jail, violated probation, was put in jail again, and released again.

Mike Cox was released and became a Christian. He later returned to his grandparents' home in Kentucky.

Of Peter Kouracos, David Damore says, "It is not unreasonable to say that eyebrows are certainly raised concerning Kouracos. He seems to be everywhere when events are about to happen. There are a lot of questions concerning his relationship with Kosta. Certainly the most vociferous defenders of Kosta Fotopoulos at his trial were Peter Kouracos and his mother, Lydia."

No charges relating to the murders or attempted murders have been filed against Peter Kouracos.

Vinnie Speziale works at an auto dealership in Daytona Beach.

Lisa Fotopoulos is fully recovered from her wound and suffers no ill effects from the bullet, which remains in her brain. She is well and happy and is today operating Joyland with her brother, Dino.

In January 1991 the body of Steno Paspalakis was exhumed at the request of the family. A medical examination of the body revealed no toxin, and no reason to believe that Mr. Paspalakis died from anything other than an aneurism. Examiners did note that, since it had been three years since Steno's death, no conclusion could be reached with certainty.